CW01084179

The State

Past, Present, Future

Bob Jessop

polity

First published in 2016 by Polity Press

Polity Press
65 Bridge Street
Cambridge CB2 1UR, UK

Polity Press
350 Main Street
Malden, MA 02148, USA

ISBN-13: 978-0-7456-3304-6
ISBN-13: 978-0-7456-3305-3(pb)

A catalogue record for this book is available from the British Library.

Library of Congress Cataloging-in-Publication Data

Jessop, Bob.
  The state: past, present, future / Bob Jessop.
      pages cm
  Includes bibliographical references and index.
  ISBN 978-0-7456-3304-6 (hardback) – ISBN 978-0-7456-3305-3
(paperback) 1. State, The. I. Title.
  JC11.J47 2015
  320.1–dc23
                                                2015013426

Typeset in 10.5 on 12 pt Sabon
by Toppan Best-set Premedia Limited
Printed and bound in the United Kingdom by Clays Ltd, St Ives PLC

The publisher has used its best endeavours to ensure that the URLs for external websites referred to in this book are correct and active at the time of going to press. However, the publisher has no responsibility for the websites and can make no guarantee that a site will remain live or that the content is or will remain appropriate.

Every effort has been made to trace all copyright holders, but if any have been inadvertently overlooked the publisher will be pleased to include any necessary credits in any subsequent reprint or edition.

For further information on Polity, visit our website: politybooks.com

In Memoriam, Josef Esser (1943–2010)

Contents

Preface

The present book is the latest in an unplanned series on state theory, states, and state power that reflects changing conjunctures and shifting interests. It differs in three main ways from its precursors. First, rather than focusing on postwar capitalist states or states in capitalist societies, it comments on the genealogy of the state, the periodization of state formation, contemporary states, and likely future trends discernible in the present (in other words, present futures). Second, reflecting this broader scope, it offers a conceptual framework for studying the state that can be used in more contexts, integrated with more theoretical approaches, and applied from several standpoints. Third, while it draws on diverse theoretical positions and occasionally provides brief critiques, it is concerned, not to draw sharp dividing lines between them, but to synthesize them – where this is both possible and productive. Thus, even where I focus on one particular approach, I also note possible links, intersections, or parallels with other approaches that are not developed here.

This book draws on many years of intermittent engagement with questions of state theory and critical investigation of actual states, above all in Europe. At other times I have been more preoccupied with the critique of political economy, especially postwar capitalism, the development of the world market, and their crisis tendencies. This explains why my analysis often adopts a capital- or class-theoretical entry point. But, as noted above, this is one of many options, none of which can be privileged on a priori grounds but only in terms of its explanatory power for particular problems in particular contexts (see chapter 3). Many scholars have influenced my understanding of the state through their reflections and historical analyses or through personal discussions with me – and, in several cases, through trenchant criticisms! My personal interlocutors know who they are and their influence is clear in the text and references.

I do want to mention eight sources of continuing inspiration: Nicos Poulantzas, whom I met only once, but to whose work I return regularly, for fresh insights and stimulation; Alex Demirović, who is a tireless and enthusiastic source of critical intelligence and theoretical wisdom; Joachim Hirsch, who has produced some of the best historical materialist analyses of the state and applied them critically to Germany; Jupp Esser, who emphasized the importance of rigorous empirical testing of state-theoretical claims; Martin Jones, who introduced me to economic and political geography, who has been a supportive co-author and interlocutor over many years, and whose influence is evident in chapter 5 and throughout; Ulrich Brand, who reminds me that theoretical engagement can be combined with social and political activism; Michael Brie, who welcomed me at the Rosa Luxemburg Foundation in Berlin and emphasized the importance of an emancipatory unity of theory and practice; and, last but not least, Ngai-Ling Sum, with whom I have been elaborating a cultural turn in political economy with implications for the state as well as for economic analysis.

Special thanks are also due to Louise Knight and Pascal Porcheron at Polity Press for gently nudging and steering this book through the final stages of writing to submission of the final version in 2015. The final version of the text benefited from comments by Colin Hay and three anonymous referees and the knowledgeable and highly professional copy-editing of Manuela Tecusan.

The writing of this book was undertaken in part during a Professorial Research Fellowship funded by the Economic and Social Science Research Council, 2011–2014, under grant RES-051-27-0303. Neither the ESRC nor the friends and colleagues named above are responsible, of course, for errors and omissions in this text. Indeed, the usual disclaimers apply with unusual force.

I dedicate this book to the memory of Jupp Esser, an inspiring colleague, critical interlocutor, and dear friend, who died too soon from cancer in 2010.

Den Haag
21 March 2015

Tables

Abbreviations

BC	before Christ
DHS	Department of Homeland Security
ECB	European Central Bank
ESM	European Stability Mechanism
EU	European Union
IMF	International Monetary Fund
KWNS	Keynesian welfare national state
MECW	*Marx/Engels Collected Works*, 50 vols (Progress Publishers: Moscow, Lawrence & Wishart: London, and International Publishers: New York, 1975–2005)
OECD	Organisation for Economic Co-operation and Development
Q	quaderno (notebook)
SRA	strategic–relational approach
STF	spatiotemporal fix
TPP	Trans-Pacific Partnership
TPSN	territory, place, scale, network

TTIP	Transatlantic Trade and Investment Partnership
UK	United Kingdom
UN	United Nations
USA PATRIOT Act	Uniting and Strengthening America by Providing Appropriate Tools Required to Intercept and Obstruct Terrorism (2001)

1

Introduction

The 'modern state' has been part of the political landscape for several centuries, if sometimes only faintly visible on its horizon. Yet social scientific interest has waxed and waned, its foci have shifted, and approaches vary with fad and fashion. Indeed, here as in other fields, it seems that social scientists do not so much solve problems as get bored with them. Interest revives when another generation of scholars or another epistemic community finds new potential in older theories, encounters new problems and research opportunities, or adopts insights, metaphors, or paradigms from other schools or disciplines. In this spirit, my analysis aims to show the continued relevance of theoretical work on states and state power and the need to renew state theory as its referents change. This is reflected in five related tasks that are pursued in part sequentially and in part iteratively, at different places in this book. Limitations of space meant that not all of these tasks are pursued to the same extent or with the same intensity, but I hope to have written enough about each of them to demonstrate their respective heuristic values and the benefits of combining them.

The first, initially question-begging, task is to outline six strategies for analysing states and state power that, if we combine them to exploit their respective strengths, might offer a powerful heuristic for addressing the complexities of these topics. This does not commit me to developing a general and transhistorical theory of the state – an ambition that I have long rejected for reasons given elsewhere (Jessop 1982: 211–13). It does imply support for (meta)theoretical, epistemological, and methodological pluralism in analysing the state and careful consideration of the most appropriate entry points and stand-points in particular theoretical and practical contexts.

The second, provisionally question-answering, task is to define the state in ways that capture its distinctiveness as a form of political organization and support analyses of its institutional and spatiotem-poral variability. Starting from the continental European tradition of state theory, which highlights three core elements of the modern state, I add a fourth one: the sources of its legitimation in state projects. These four elements can be extended and qualified for diverse theo-retical and practical purposes. The revised approach also provides a basis for exploring the multiple pasts and presents of the state and for speculating about possible futures.

The third, briefer, task is to consider the historical semantics of the modern state, that is, the emergence and consolidation of a spe-cialized vocabulary to describe the state – and indeed its role in constituting, consolidating, reproducing, and guiding the various institutions, modes of calculation, practices, and imaginaries, whether in high politics or in everyday life, referred to in this semantic frame-work. This task matters, even if one maintains that the state, regarded as a form of political organization, preceded its own explicit concep-tualization in terms of statehood. The task involves more than exam-ining the history of ideas, intellectual history, or the history of political thought: it extends to the links between semantic change and societal transformation and, in this context, to contestation over the nature and purposes of the state. It also invites critical reflection on the language used to describe state-like political authority before the semantics of the state emerged and on the societal changes that have prompted the semantics of governance and meta-governance to describe emergent political institutions and practices that are less territorially focused than their statal counterparts. The historical semantics of the state also poses questions about the Eurocentric nature of state theory and, on this basis, about the relevance of (Eurocentric) state theory to territorially organized forms of political authority beyond the centres of European state formation, especially before the rulers and subjects of these other political regimes encoun-tered the representatives of European states – as plunderers, traders, explorers, missionaries, diplomats, conquerors, or in some other guise. Such reflections can help reveal the historical specificity of different forms of political organization, political regime, and types of state.

The fourth task, building on the first three but influencing their pursuit, is to offer some theoretically informed reflections on key aspects of the state and state power, especially in advanced capitalist regimes in the world market. This focus reflects my interests and expertise and is not meant to prioritize such states ontologically or normatively – especially as they belong to a world of states marked by other forms of domination. This said, profit-oriented, market-mediated accumulation is the dominant principle of societal organization in world society, and this does warrant focusing on capitalist features of the modern state without implying that this is the only useful entry point (see Jessop 1990, 2002, 2011, 2015a). The results of the other tasks, together with the illustrative force of this exercise, should offer readers concepts and ideas for studying other kinds of state and state power from a strategic–relational perspective.

The fifth task, pursued in most chapters, is to indicate how to subject the state, state power, state semantics, claims to legitimacy, and indeed state theory itself to critiques of their imbrication in domination and ideology. Rejecting views of the state as a neutral instrument or benevolent agent, this task requires critical engagement with the asymmetries of authority and domination inscribed in the state – seen as a form of political organization – and in its instantiations in political regimes; with its structural and strategic role in reproducing wider patterns of exploitation, oppression, and domination at particular times and in particular places; and with the scope for challenging, modifying, or overturning these asymmetries and their effects. Critique should not be limited to rogue, pariah, predatory, violent, totalitarian, or authoritarian states but extend to those conventionally described as benevolent liberal democratic regimes. There is no domination in general and no general form of domination. Forms of domination vary across social fields (including nature–society relations) and intersect with each other (see chapter 4). So one should clarify which modes of domination are being critiqued.

The histories of states and state systems are closely connected to those of political philosophy, normative political theory, and accounts of geopolitics and geoeconomics, as well as to theoretical inquiries into actual (inter)state systems. Indeed, all five fields of intellection, with their different rationales and rationalities, have figured strongly in state formation and transformation. Conversely, the changing form and functions of (inter)state systems have prompted shifts, gradual or ruptural, in the leading forms and styles of philosophical, normative, and theoretical reflection on the state. So we should approach these five fields as contested terrains that both shape and reflect changes in the state apparatus and state power. Indeed state authorities are rarely, if ever, indifferent to political philosophies, political theories, and state theories. They tend to discriminate among them (and among their organic intellectuals, their other supporters, and

their institutional bases), promote those that conflict least with currently preferred state traditions and projects, and refute, marginalize,
or oppress the ones they fear. Monitoring and managing *dissent*
matters as much as shaping *consent*. Thus one approach to a history
of the state might study its coevolution with ideational change
(whether one or the other is leading or lagging). There are many
examples of this approach in the literature – whether idealist, institutionalist, or materialist in approach. The present work is not one
of them. But it will engage at times with philosophical positions,
normative political theories, and policy paradigms that have shaped
the state and state power.

Although this book does not focus on the *history* of state theory,
some brief remarks are in order. The origins of the 'modern state'
and state system were associated with many competing philosophical
reflections on this innovation (think of Jean Bodin, Emmerich de
Vattel, Hugo Grotius, Francesco Guicciardini, G. W. F. Hegel, Thomas
Hobbes, Immanuel Kant, John Locke, Niccolò Machiavelli, Samuel
Pufendorf, and Jean-Jacques Rousseau)[1] – reflections that were also
in part performative, that is, contributed to the shaping of the institution on which they were reflecting. Likewise, the consolidation of the
state in the nineteenth century was linked with influential work in
state theory, law, political science, policy science, and public administration. The 1920s and 1930s saw another round of intense engagement with the changing forms and functions, and indeed crisis, of the
liberal state – along with theories, justifications, and critiques of
authoritarian or totalitarian regimes. A similar revival in state and
regime theory occurred in the west in the immediate postwar period
(especially in relation to postwar reconstruction in Europe) and,
again, in the 1970s and 1980s, being prompted partly by crises in
the resulting postwar form of the state, partly by interest in state
building in the wake of decolonization, and partly by interest in
export-oriented developmental states in East Asia.

After a fallow period in the 1990s, the general form and functions
of states returned to the top of the theoretical and political agenda.
The crisis of the national state in so-called late modern societies (even
as it became more important in state- and nation-building efforts
after the Soviet bloc collapsed) led to new state-theoretical concerns
and efforts to develop alternative accounts of politics that looked
beyond the institutions of the sovereign state. Attention turned from
the contrast between capitalism and socialism and their respective
state forms to varieties of capitalism and political regimes; from the
national state and the nation-state to global–local dialectics and multilevel governance; and from the state's relative autonomy or class

character to the micro-physics of power and identity politics. More recently, the North Atlantic and Eurozone financial and economic crises, the state's role in crisis management, and serious fiscal and sovereign debt crises have revived interest in the limits of state power and in the challenges of global governance. Another stimulus has been state failure and so-called rogue states, notably in the Middle East and North Africa, together with interest in the distinctive features of Arab or Islamic states, including recently the Islamic caliphate.

The range of literature relevant to the state is immense and impossible for one scholar to survey, let alone master. This book touches on many issues and draws on many disciplines and interdisciplinary approaches. Conceptual history and historical semantics, which differ in terms of their respective concern with (1) the genealogy and pragmatic use of concepts or (2) the historical relation between new or changing concepts and societal transformation, are crucial sources for exploring the state idea or imaginary (e.g., Bartelson 1995; Koselleck 1985; Palonen 2006; Skinner 1989; on these two approaches, see Sum and Jessop 2013). I also draw on insights from critical discourse analysis, which has much to offer for an *Ideologiekritik*. My analyses of the core questions about statehood as a form of domination draw heavily on the continental European tradition of state theory and its revival in Marxist guise in the 1970s and 1980s. This is supplemented by juridico-political scholarship and work in public administration, political economy, and international relations. For issues of historical constitution, major reference points are archaeology, anthropology, historical institutionalism, and historiography. More recent changes in the state, especially when it is viewed as an ensemble of forms of government and governance, are illuminated by studies of the micro-physics of power, governmentality, and statecraft. The list could be continued; but the full range of sources will become evident in due course.

The range of sources needed to address the state illustrates three key claims advanced below. First, there can be no general, let alone transhistorical, theory of the state – especially if this is understood as a single theory that aspires to comprehend and explain the origins, development, and determinations of the state without reference to other kinds of inquiry. Second, as a complex political association, apparatus, *dispositif*, ensemble, or assemblage (language varies) linked to a wider set of social relations, the state system can be studied from many theoretical entry points and political standpoints (on standpoints, see Lukács 1971; Althusser 2006; Hartman 1979; Harding 1991, 2003; D. E. Smith 1990; Calhoun 1995). Indeed there is intellectual value in analysing the state idea, the state and interstate

Table 1.1 Six approaches to the analysis of the state

Approach	Focus	Key Themes	Some Disciplines
Historical Constitution	Primary state formation; later evolution of state; the genealogy of diverse elements of the state apparatus	Territorialization of political authority Core features of state apparatus State crisis, failure, revolution	Archaeology, anthropology, geopolitics, history, military science, organization studies, public administration
Formal Constitution	The state as a form of domination; types of state and regime; functional differentiation	Form follows function vs form complicates function 'Relative autonomy' Democracy and dictatorship	Historical materialism, international relations, law, policy science, political science, state theory
Institutional Analysis	Relation among branches of state The state (system) as institutional ensemble Institutional design	Institutional isomorphism or complementarity Path dependency and path shaping	Historical, organizational, network, and sociological institutionalism in various disciplines
Agent-Centred Institutional Analysis	State managers and other state agents, political actors and political behaviour, balance of forces	Leadership, decision making, political calculation, political recruitment, social bases, hegemony	Actor-network theory, historical institutionalism, policy studies, sociology
Figurational Analysis	'State and society' 'State and civilization' Social embeddedness	State in context, historical cleavages, base–superstructure, societalization	Comparative politics, geography, history, historical sociology, political economy
State Semantics, Political Discourse	Concept of the state, the 'state as idea', philosophies and theories of the state and of the state system	State projects, political imaginaries, policy narratives, the ethico-political, hegemonic visions, *Ideologiekritik*	Conceptual history, critical discourse analysis, cultural studies, political philosophy and theory, semiotics

Source: Original compilation

system, and state power from different, albeit commensurable, theoretical perspectives – as well as in studying the phenomenology of state power as experienced from different subject positions. Third, despite tendencies to reify the state system as standing outside and above society, this system must be related sooner or later to the world society in which states are embedded. This poses an interesting series of part–whole paradoxes (chapter 3).

In this context I suggest that state formation and the state system can be, and have been, analysed from at least six perspectives (see Table 1.1). Adopting one or more of these as appropriate for specific theoretical or practical purposes reveals the complexity of the state as a polymorphous institutional ensemble, insofar as different viewpoints reveal different facets of the state and state power. In addition, each perspective has its specific blind spot, which prevents us from seeing what we cannot see from it. So combining *commensurable* perspectives allows a more complex analysis, which may put apparently contradictory statements about the state into a more comprehensive analytical schema that reveals how the truth value of observations and statements depends on the contexts in which they are made (on the significance of the intersecting 'contextures' of such observations, see Günther 1973). These themes also bear on the polymorphic or polymorphous nature of the state (see chapter 2).

The first perspective is that of the 'historical constitution' of the state, studied in terms of path-dependent histories or genealogies of particular parts of the state. Chapter 5 adopts this approach in exploring the passage from simple and complex chiefdoms to early forms of state and empire. This perspective can also be deployed to study the development and integration of such key components of the modern state as a standing army, a modern tax system, a rational bureaucracy, the rule of law, parliament, universal suffrage, citizenship rights, and recognition by other states.[2] And, relatedly, it can be used when considering why the modern state, rather than other forms of political organization, was frequently selected and finally retained as the dominant political form, as feudalism decomposed or was overthrown (Tilly 1975; Spruyt 1993).

Second, another body of work addresses what is sometimes termed the state's 'formal constitution', that is, its character as a distinctive form of social relations. Whereas historical constitution requires a diachronic approach, a more synchronic one is needed to address the formal constitution of the state. At stake here is the complementarity – sometimes even isomorphism – among features of a given type of state (on the difference between isomorphism and complementarity, see Amable 2009; Crouch 2005). This approach is more suited to the modern state insofar as the latter is clearly demarcated from other institutional orders and can be studied on its own terms rather than as a socially embedded or intertwined part of a more complex, multifaceted societal order. Thus one might study how the modern state gets formally separated (disembedded) from other spheres of society, acquires its own political rationale (*raison d'état*) and modus operandi, and claims a distinctive constitutional legitimation that is based on adherence to its own political procedures rather than on values such as divine right or natural law. Chapters 3 and 4 adopt this approach; but all chapters emphasize that states are polymorphic, displaying different forms depending on changing principles of societal organization or on specific challenges and conjunctures – if not on both (for further discussion of polymorphy, see chapter 2).

Third, there are diverse institutionalist approaches to the state, all of which assume that somehow 'institutions matter'. These approaches are informed by a broad but underspecified view according to which institutions involve complexes of social practices that (1) are regularly repeated; (2) are linked to defined roles and social relations; (3) are associated with specific forms of discourse, symbolic media, or modes of communication; (4) are sanctioned and maintained by social norms; and (5) have major significance for social order. The term 'institution' is also used to denote organizations or social bodies that have major significance for the wider society and act in a quasi-corporate manner. In addition to the executive, legislative, and judicial branches of government, other examples are transnational firms, banks, peak organizations of capital and labour, and established religious faiths. While rational choice paradigms are ignored in what follows,[3] historical, network, organizational, sociological, and ideational (also known as constructivist or discursive) institutionalisms all provide useful insights into the state and politics. In addition to studying particular institutions or institutional assemblages, institutionalist work has extended to other topics. These include differences in individual institutional forms, interinstitutional configurations, institutional histories, orders or functional systems, institutional isomorphism or complementarity, and the design and governance of institutions and their relations (on types of institutionalism in politics, see Hall and Taylor 1996; for a critical review of institutionalisms, including ideational institutionalism, see Sum and Jessop 2013: 33–71).

Fourth, agent-centred institutionalism studies how social forces make history – their own and that of others – in specific institutional contexts. These studies pursue more detailed analysis of specific institutional arrangements and consider the scope they give for various kinds of individual and collective agent to make a difference. In dealing with actors, agent-centred institutional theorists focus on complex actors rather than on individuals; on actors' interests, identities, action orientations, and resources in specific actor constellations rather than in generic, context-free terms; and on different forms of interaction (e.g., negotiation, multilevel decision-making, or hierarchical command). This approach eschews the methodological individualism that starts from individual actors, their motives and behaviour; and rejects functionalist and structuralist accounts that privilege the alleged functions of institutions or the inevitable constraints imposed by specific structural configurations. It focuses instead on the emergent logics and dynamics of different institutional orders or functional subsystems and on the associated asymmetrical opportunities they grant different actors in specific interaction fields, including multilevel, multisite interactions or multispatial arenas. This approach is similar to the strategic–relational approach (chapter 3) and has influenced my accounts of governance, state failure, and normal and exceptional states (chapters 7 and 9). It differs from (neo) pluralist traditions, which are far more agent-centred and pay less attention to, even if recognizing, institutions as sources of constraints and opportunities. (For critiques of pluralism, see Connolly 1969; for a critical defence of this paradigm, see M. J. Smith 1990; for an account of neopluralism oriented to an emerging world politics rather than national states, see Cerny 2010.)[4]

Fifth, figurational analyses focus on 'state-civil society' relations, broadly interpreted, and aim to locate state formation within wider historical developments. Exemplary here are Shmuel Eisenstadt's (1963) work on the rise and fall of bureaucratic empires, Norbert Elias's (1982) studies on the very *longue durée* dynamics of state and civilization, including their disintegration and integration phases, Wim Blockmans's (1978) study of medieval systems of representation. Stein Rokkan's (1999) research on European state formation over the last 400–500 years, and Samuel Finer's (1997a, 1997b, 1997c) magisterial 3-volume study of the history of government. Michael Mann's massive and wide-ranging project on the history of social power also belongs here (1986, 1996, 2012a, and 2012b). This approach also has affinities with historical institutionalism. Certain versions of the figurational approach and historical institutionalism inform some of the arguments below.

Sixth, conceptual history and historical semantics have been used to analyse the emergence of the state idea, the consolidation of the state concept (and cognate terminology) in the early modern period, the spread of the state idea from Western Europe, and the diverse political imaginaries, state projects, and hegemonic visions that shape the contest for state power within and beyond the state. Relatedly, critical discourse analysis explores how discourse(s) shape the state and orient action towards it. Broad economic and political visions as well as specific policy paradigms are relevant here. Given the multiplicity of competing visions (at most we find a temporarily dominant or hegemonic discourse) that orient the actions of political forces, this reinforces the view of the state as a polyvalent, polycontextual ensemble. This is especially clear when we consider the many scales and sites on which *the* state is said to operate; and thereby it highlights once again problems of the institutional integration of the state and of the distribution of state functions and powers.

Following this short introduction, Part I addresses some basic theoretical and methodological issues. It contains three chapters. Chapter 2 explores the concept of the state and opts for a seemingly conventional 'three-element' approach oriented to the relationship between a state's territory, apparatus, and population, as this is modified by the introduction of a fourth element, namely the 'idea of the state' or the state project, which defines the nature and purposes of state action. Chapter 3 expands on the claim that the state is not a subject or a thing but a social relation. This elliptical statement refocuses attention from the elements of the state to state power. In strategic–relational terms, state power is an institutionally and discursively mediated condensation (a reflection and a refraction) of a changing balance of forces that seek to influence the forms, purposes, and content of polity, politics, and policy. The chapter then provides a heuristic schema for exploring the state and state power and for locating them both in their wider natural and social context. In terms of the four-element theory, this chapter is mainly concerned with the state apparatus and the idea of the state. Chapter 4 provides some general comments on power, interests, and domination and relates them to one important dimension of domination, namely the relation between class power and state power. It challenges the conventional interpretation of this question and offers an alternative, strategic–relational account that also supports a fruitful distinction between the capitalist type of state and the state in capitalist societies and re-emphasizes the polymorphic nature of the state.

Part II comprises three shorter chapters that expand upon and supplement earlier arguments about the four elements of statehood, its formal configuration, and its substantive nature. Chapter 5 examines the sociospatial organization of the state, going beyond the issue of territoriality, narrowly conceived. It addresses two issues. It first considers the genealogy of the state in terms of primary state formation, that is, those widely dispersed cases where a 'state' emerged for the first time through the territorialization of political power. Second, it comments, more briefly, on the complexities of secondary state formation. And, third, it looks beyond the obvious link between territoriality and statehood (one of its four elements) to consider statehood in terms of place, scale, and network and sociospatiality more generally. Chapter 6 turns from the territorial aspect to another element of statehood, namely the state's population. It distinguishes the national state and the nation-state, identifies types of nationhood as imagined communities, and explores the relevance of civil society to the state and to state power. Chapter 7 returns to the topic of the state apparatus and state power in the form of a relation between government and governance. This approach has two aims. On the one hand, it provides a less form-centred account of the state by exploring the modalities of the exercise of state power through the prism of its role in moderating and modulating different forms of governance. And, on the other hand, it considers the specific features of different modes of governance, their tendencies to fail, and the role of the state in dealing with problems of governance failure, either on its own initiative or as an addressee of the last resort that is called upon to act by other social forces.

Part III also comprises three chapters, concerned this time with the recent and current history of the state and with alternative (present) futures. Chapter 8 examines the changing relation between the world market and the world of states and considers whether globalization undermines the territorial and temporal sovereignty of states. It argues that this topic is poorly conceived and that, once reformulated, it could be explored with interesting results that would be based on the heuristic theoretical framework developed here. Chapter 9 examines the elective affinities between capitalism and liberal democracy, considers the rise of authoritarian statism, and asks whether the state of exception is becoming the 'new normal'. Chapter 10 closes the book with some comments on missing links and open questions; it also identifies some broad macro-trends that are likely to shape the future of the state in the next few decades.

Part I

The State as Concept, Relation, and Reality

2

The Concept of the State

It is hard – some claim impossible – to give a clear definition of the state when this form of political organization has so long a history, assumes so many forms, and changes so often. These issues call into question the descriptive validity and normative power of the state idea and, especially, invites questions as to whether it obfuscates, fetishizes, or mystifies political power. Even assuming there is an 'it' to which state theory refers is problematic. This challenge is not unique to the state and state power. It applies to other social phenomena, such as the family, law, money, capital as a social relation, and religion. Indeed the German nihilist philosopher Friedrich Nietzsche declared that '[a]ll concepts in which an entire process is semiotically concentrated defy definition; only something which has no history can be defined' (1994: 53). Nietzsche was discussing punishment (itself linked, of course, to the state), but his remark highlights the wider problem of defining a concept with no fixed referent. This certainly holds for the moving target comprised by states and the interstate system. The problem is compounded when the moving target or shifting referent is essentially contested, in other words raises important theoretical and normative questions. This calls for a comparative historical and dynamic analysis of the state and state power – an analysis that should be sensitive to the contested nature of its subject.

Without engaging directly with Nietzsche's observation, the Romanian existentialist writer Emil Cioran seems to offer another response to this definitional challenge. He remarked that 'we define only out of despair, we must have a formula...to give a façade to the void'

(Cioran 1975: 48). On this reading, it is our impotent and disempowering incomprehension of the state – even an alleged fundamental inability to establish whether 'the state' really exists or not – that forces us to give a definition in order to 'get on' with analysing so-called 'affairs of state' or, again, to 'go on' in a world where political practice is concerned with the exercise of state power.

A different response is indicated by the British historical sociologist Philip Abrams, who, without engaging directly or indirectly with Cioran, seems to turn his claim on its head. He suggests that, if the state is a façade (Abrams calls it a 'mask'), this does not disguise a void but prevents us from seeing the true and awful reality of political practice. A false belief in the existence of the state as the deep structure of political life masks the actual role of substantive political institutions and practices in securing domination (Abrams 1988; more detail below).

Of these contrasting views on the challenges that face state theory – namely that it would define the indefinable, hide a void, or unmask what actually exists – the last one comes closest to the position developed below. Once we recognize rather than ignore the messy, polymorphic, and polycontextual features of the state as a special kind of social relation, we need not despair about the apparent intractability of the state concept. Indeed, chapter 3 offers a perspective (the 'strategic–relational approach') that aims to meet the challenge of analysing the state, its restructuring, its strategic reorientation, and its nature as a stake in social conflicts.

Notes on the Difficulties of Studying the State[1]

The state has been studied from many entry points and standpoints. This gives its analysis the contested qualities for which it is renowned (or notorious, depending on one's perspective). It is a complex ensemble (or, as some scholars put it, assemblage) of institutions, organizations, and interactions involved in the exercise of political leadership and in the implementation of decisions that are, in principle, collectively binding on its political subjects. These institutions, organizations, and interactions have varying spatiotemporal extensions and horizons of action and mobilize a range of state capacities and other resources in pursuit of state objectives. These complexities have led some analysts to focus on particular cases and ignore general questions about statehood and state power. Indeed, many theorists have rejected the notion of the state as nebulous or vapid and have proposed to replace it by focusing on politics as a functional system, oriented to the authoritative allocation of values or to collective goal attainment (Almond 1960; Easton 1965; Parsons 1969). Others have focused on the micro-foundations of political relations, either in individual orientations and actions (e.g., Coleman 1990; Elster 1982) or in specific microcontexts (Foucault 1980), sidestepping the question of whether political behaviour has any systematic emergent properties that merit inquiry in their own right. Neither approach fully escapes the need to engage with the state. For a consistent interest in politics requires at least some attention to the polity, politics, and policy (see Heidenheimer 1986 and, for global politics, Lipschutz 2005). The 'polity' – a word formed on the Greek *politeia* – is the institutional matrix that establishes a distinctive terrain, realm, domain, field, or region of specifically political actions (Weber 1978, 1994; Palonen 2006). This is equivalent to statehood *in its inclusive sense*, as explored here and in chapters 3, 7 and 9. Further, while the polity offers a rather static, spatial referent, politics is inherently dynamic, open-ended, and heterogeneous. It refers to the forms, aims, and objects of political practices. It includes contention over the architecture of the state and wider political sphere, together with struggles occurring outside the state that modify political calculation or views on the purposes of state power (or both). Politics in turn constrains the set of feasible policies – that is, policymaking as an art of the possible. Thus, if politics concerns the overall strategic direction of the state and its division of 'policy labour', policy denotes specific fields of state intervention and abstention, decisions and nondecisions, and so on. This said, some policies transform politics (witness the depoliticizing role of neoliberal policies, or the repoliticizing effects of the feminist claim that the personal is political) and reshape political practices, for instance by changing the balance of forces and stimulating new political claims and movements (on depoliticization, see Jessop 2014b).

In addressing this conceptual morass, Philip Abrams (1988) argued for another approach. He identified three ways to thematize the state, indicating that one of these is doubly misleading and two are potentially useful in its analysis. These three ways can be summarized as follows:

1 a reified *account of the state*[2] as a substantial unitary entity, agent, function, or relation that is separated from the rest of society and operates as the essential but hidden structuring mechanism of political life;

2 the *state system*[3] as the real, palpable nexus of institutions, agencies, and practices that is more or less extensive, more or less

connected with economic and other social relations, and, at best, only ever relatively unified;

3   the *state idea* as an explicit ideological force (*idée-force*) rooted in the collective misrepresentation – masking – of political and economic domination in capitalist societies in ways that legitimate subjection thereto.

Abrams argues that the phantasmagorical[4] notion of the *state* as a unitary entity obscures the inevitable disunity of the actually existing *state system* as a fragmentary and fragile arrangement of institutionalized political power. It also blocks many, if not most, people from realizing their ideological captivity to the *state idea* – which, in quasi-Hegelian terms, presents the state as the disinterested servant of the common interest. So the challenge for social scientists is to demystify the state, to unmask it radically, to prove that *the state as a substantial, unitary entity does not 'always already' exist*. This opens space to study efforts by state personnel and others to impose some provisional, temporary, and unstable unity on the actually existing state system and to create relative coherence across official policies in diverse fields of action. It also opens space, and calls for, a critique of the *state idea* and its fetishistic hold over the protagonists on the political stage. Indeed, only when we abandon the reified notion of 'the state' can we begin serious study of the state system in all its messy complexity and undertake a serious critique of different state ideas (Abrams 1988: 82). Only then can we hope to transcend the misrecognition of the state in the 'state idea' and to examine the state as it actually exists and operates, on its own terms and in its wider political and social contexts.

This conclusion indicates the value of case studies that focus on the development of the notion of the state and specific state ideas – ideas not limited to that of the state as a disinterested servant – in specific historical contexts. Such exercises in *intellectual genealogy* are based on semantic history or, more loosely, the history of political thought. For example, why did one particular word or concept get selected from many, in a particular period, to describe (and perhaps to contribute to constituting) a particular historical apparatus, namely the modern state? Put differently, why did 'state' (and etymological equivalents such as *estado*, *état*, *Staat*, or *stato*) become the accepted term to describe a specific type of government in Western Europe and its subsequent diffusion – why 'state' rather than competing terms such as '*regnum*', 'body politic', '*res publica*', '*monarchia*', 'realm', 'nation', 'civil society', or 'commonwealth'? Conversely, why did the historically specific semantics of the 'state' lag so many centuries, indeed millennia, behind the historical process of state formation? Some social scientists argue that states or state-like assemblages did not exist before the modern concept or form of the state. For example, Richard Lachmann, a historical sociologist, places its origins about 500 years ago, linking it to the rise of capitalism in Europe (Lachmann 2010: viii). Martin van Creveld, a military historian, dates its rise to the period 1300–1648 and its decline to a period starting in 1975: in the intervening three centuries the state would have operated as a distinct sovereign, a territorial 'corporation' with a clear identity, separate from its personnel, and would have sought to protect its frontiers, national interests, and the citizens within its territory, achieving its apotheosis in two world wars and then declining as it ceded power to other organizations or simply collapsed (van Creveld 1999). Both scholars argue that, while tribes, chiefdoms, city-states, empires, and theocracies existed, few consolidated states existed before these scholars' preferred date. Such arguments remove much of human history from the purview of state theory and research, except as *pre*history. (For a critique of such claims, based on a 5,200-year perspective on government and state formation but conceding the late rise of modern states in 1776 and of national states with clear frontiers in 1815, see Finer 1997a: 1–15, 31, 99–103, and passim; also, with a wider geographical scope, Breuer 2014: 9–38.)

This problem is also reflected in state theory and political sociology in the common if ill-specified distinction between 'traditional' and 'modern' states. An alternative to this often Eurocentric approach is to focus on the modalities of the territorialization of political power and to explore alternative political imaginaries and descriptions of precursors to the modern state. More generally, I argue that what traverses these diverse institutional and organizational forms and reveals their shared state-like qualities are efforts to establish, exercise, and consolidate political power over the population of a specific territory – efforts that began well before the idea of the modern state emerged but that eventually led to the contingent triumph of this state form over others, which were at one time historically feasible (see also chapters 5 and 10).

The analytical approach described in the preceding paragraph is quite different from the study of the historical constitution, modification, and breakdown of states as well as from the study of their formal constitution, that is, of the development of relatively coherent, complementary, and reproducible state forms. The approach requires historical and comparative case studies from particular periods and particular spaces or places; and, insofar as this is empirically and theoretically possible, it requires placing these episodes and sequences in a world-historical perspective oriented to changing state and inter-state systems. Such an approach can also encompass a figurational analysis that combines historical constitution, formal constitution, and associated state ideas. In turn, this analysis can provide the basis for well-grounded critiques of ideology and domination.

With these issues in mind, the present chapter introduces some definitions of the state (or its core features) taken from different theoretical traditions. It also argues that the state and the political system are parts of broader sets of social relations and cannot be adequately understood and explained without reference to their embedding in these wider arrangements. Sovereign states do not exist in majestic isolation, overseeing the rest of society, but are closely linked to other institutional orders (notably the economic and the legal systems) and to their respective 'civil societies' (the scare quotes signal the analogous difficulties of defining civil society, its equally contested nature, and the utopian expectations often invested in it). This relation varies greatly in and across states. Indeed, whatever the degree of the state's autonomy from other orders, the exercise and impact of state power (or, better, state powers) are activated through changing sets of politicians and state officials located in specific parts of the state apparatus, in specific conjunctures, and reflect the prevailing balance of forces, as it obtains beyond as well as within the state (chapter 3). It follows that the state's structural powers and capacities cannot be fully grasped by focusing on the state alone and, unsurprisingly, different social theories are associated with different accounts of the state and state power.

So What Is the State?

As hinted above, this innocuous-sounding question hides a serious challenge to students of the state. Some theorists deny the state's very existence (or, at least, the possibility and value of studying it), but most still accept that states (or, following Abrams, state systems and, a fortiori, interstate systems) are real and provide a feasible and valid research focus. Beyond this broad agreement, however, we find conceptual anarchy. Key questions include: Is the state best defined by its legal form, coercive capacities, institutional composition and boundaries, internal operations and modes of calculation, declared aims, functions for the broader society, or sovereign place in the international system? Is it a thing, a subject, a social relation, or a construct that helps to orient political action? Is stateness a variable and, if so, what are its central dimensions? What is the relation between the state and law, the state and politics, the state and civil society, the public and the private, state power and micropower relations? Is the state best studied in isolation; as part of the political system; or as one element in a broader social formation, or even in world society? Do states have territorial and temporal sovereignty or institutional, decisional, or operational autonomy and, if so, what are the sources and limits of this sovereignty or autonomy?

Everyday language is of little help here. It sometimes depicts the state as a subject – not in a specific juridical sense, for example as a *persona ficta* (artificial person), *personne morale*, enduring 'corporation sole', and so forth – but in an interpellative sense, that is, in terms of how the state is 'hailed': addressed or discussed as if it were an individual person or a collective subject endowed with consciousness, will, and agency (on interpellation, see Althusser 1971). Thus it is said that the state does, or should do, this or that – or should stop doing it. In similar vein, albeit at great remove from common sense, realist international relations theory treats the state as a unitary actor in world politics, as if it had a mind and interests of its own (e.g., Morgenthau 1954; Waltz 1979). Equally, the state is sometimes discussed as a thing-like instrument, machine, engine, ship (of state), cybernetic or regulatory device – to be used, driven, activated, steered, monitored, or modulated by a given economic class, social stratum, political party, official caste, or other agents, with a view to advancing its own projects, interests, or values. Yet how, if at all, could the state act *as if* it were a unified subject, and what could constitute its unity as a 'thing'? Coherent answers are hard to find because the state's referents vary so widely across times, places, and contexts as well as with the forces acting towards the state, the situations in which 'it' acts, and so on.

First, insofar as the state is treated as a subject, in what does its subjectivity reside? In premodern states, this could be answered, perhaps too easily, in terms of the person of the ruler. This is reflected in the early modern statement attributed, perhaps apocryphally, to Louis XIV of France: *L'État c'est moi* ('I am the state'). Opinions differ as to whether he said this on his deathbed or when deputies in the French parliament challenged the authority of his edicts. But, in the former case, it is also reported that he said: *Je m'en vais, mais l'État demeurera toujours* ('I am leaving but the state shall remain forever'). Interestingly, whereas the first statement, if made, signifies the embodiment of the state in the person of the king, the second denotes its impersonal character, separate from any single individual.

This separation was reflected in the growing use of the concept of the state to describe an enduring, impersonal apparatus responsible for producing a good 'state of affairs' in the territory controlled by that apparatus (Boldt et al. 1992; Luhmann 1989; Skinner 2009). The state concept signified the historical contrast between (1) the identification of the polity with a specific personage, agency, or institution (*polis*, *civitas*, *regnum*, *imperium*, etc.) and (2) the more abstract character of political rule in modern, functionally differentiated societies. In such societies the political system, with the state at its centre, is institutionally and operationally disembedded from the wider society and the state takes the form of an impersonal power that is separate from those who exercise power in the name of the state and, at a later stage, separate from the parties or political alliances that form the government from time to time. In the fifteenth century the European 'mirror of princes' literature revealed a semantic slippage between status, estate, and state. Such treatises advised rulers how to maintain their own *status*, maintain a *peaceful state of affairs* in their dominium, and maintain a functioning *state apparatus* (Skinner 1989; Viroli 1992). In turn, the natural law tradition that justified absolutism in the sixteenth and seventeenth centuries made a sharper distinction between the newly emerging single, supreme sovereign authority, those who held office in that state and exercised power on its behalf, and the people over whom sovereign authority was exercised, whether in their own name or not. In addition, since a state of peace occurs in a given territorial realm, the state apparatus that secures peace comes to signify dominance over the territory itself. In short, in contrast to the different connotations of the earlier plurality of competing terms, the semantics of the state highlighted the distinctive features of this new form of territorialization of political power. Further, as the political system itself grew more complex internally, juridico-political discourse also became more complex within the framework of constitutional, administrative, and public law (Luhmann 1989: 107–8; Nettl 1968; Loughlin 2014). And, finally, once this new state lexicon emerged it started to play a key role in the institutional integration and strategic orientation of the state (see Jessop 1990: 347–9).

The process of political institutionalization is reflected in the contrast between Louis XIV's remark in the seventeenth century that he embodied the state, *L'État, c'est moi*, and the claim to be 'the first servant of the state' made in the eighteenth century by the Prussian Emperor Frederick II, who thereby sought to justify his position through deeds rather than divine right (Brubaker 1992: 58). An associated theme is that of *lèse majesté*: a slight or injury to the person of the sovereign and his/her immediate family, or even to the heads of other states. This idea survives in some constitutions (e.g., of

Denmark, Jordan, Malaysia, Morocco, Saudi Arabia, Spain, and Thailand) and such slights or injuries (real or imagined) have met with punishment in dictatorships identified with a leading personality (e.g., Joseph Stalin, Adolf Hitler, Moammar Qaddafi, Kim Il-jun) or with a tight-knit high command (e.g., Myanmar's military junta). It can also extend to attacks on state symbols, for instance by burning a national flag or by counterfeiting coins. With the rise of the modern state, however, authority becomes more impersonal and its 'personality' is seen as a legal fiction. In turn, *lèse majesté* is absorbed into the crime of *sedition* against the government (as opposed to *treason* against the state and its people). This impersonal character underpins the continuity of the contracts and obligations of the state as well as the authority of individuals to act in its name, especially when they hold a defined office in a (quasi-)constitutional document.

While idealist and speculative philosophers such as Hegel may posit that the state is a knowing subject, endowed with supraindividual and supernatural intelligence, one might well ask, with Badiou (2005: 87): Does the state think? Or is it mindless – not only literally, but also metaphorically (Marx 1975)? In what do *raison d'état* and the intelligence of the state consist? More generally, how can we consider the role of the state in the mental–manual division of labour and the role of its intellectuals in constituting the state and state idea? (On these last points, see Balasopoulos, 2012.)

Turning from the state viewed as a real or fictitious juridico-political *Subject*, we can ask about the plurality of *subjects* who act as the state's agents. This poses interesting questions in terms of principal agent theory. On the one hand, who is authorized to make decisions on behalf of the state, as its agent, and to exercise a political authority that is backed, where appropriate, by physical violence? And, on the other hand and more intriguingly, who or what constitutes the principal in this principal–agent relationship? On behalf of whom (or what) do the agents act? The answer depends on the list of institutions deemed to belong to the state. It is relatively easy to identify the state's core apparatuses as its agents; but it becomes progressively harder to do so as the list of state apparatuses is extended. At the margins, for example, do they include the trade union leaders who policed income policies in the 'national economic interest' during the stagflationary 1960s and 1970s in advanced capitalist societies? Do they include media owners and compliant journalists who relay false justifications for the state's launching of wars of aggression, or who accept its rewording of torture as no more than 'enhanced interrogation'? Do they include mercenaries hired from private firms to fight wars, and private militias backed by states to further their politico-military aims? Do they include outsiders' interests that coproduce regulation or capture regulatory agencies ideologically, politically, or economically? Further problems arise when we study the internal stratification, parallel power networks, and external policy linkages that animate the state. Here we might refer to agents outside the state, who have high-level security clearance and contribute to strategy elaboration, policy formulation, and implementation (on this kind of 'deep state', see chapters 3 and 9).

Second, regarding the 'thingness' of the state, a common response is to list its component institutions, identifying a core set with increasingly vague outer limits. The political theorist Ralph Miliband adopted this approach in a cathartic modern classic: *The State in Capitalist Society*. He began with an ostensive definition of key governmental institutions as 'the government, the administration, the military and the police, the judicial branch, sub-central government and parliamentary assemblies' (Miliband 1969: 54). But he then included antisocialist parties, the mass media, educational institutions, trade union leaders, and other forces in civil society as parts of the wider state system (Miliband 1969: 180–211, 220–7; cf. Miliband 1977: 47–50). Also writing in the late 1960s, the French Marxist philosopher Louis Althusser proceeded similarly in a famous essay on 'Ideology and Ideological State Apparatuses'. He distinguished a relatively unified 'repressive state apparatus' from diverse, relatively autonomous 'ideological state apparatuses' (Althusser 1971). The former comprise the core of the state (the executive, the legislature, the judiciary, and the police-military apparatus); the latter include the family apparatus, education, organized religion, and the media. This said, while the repressive state apparatus relies more on coercion, it has a crucial ideological moment; and, while ideological state apparatuses rely more on ideology, coercion remains in reserve. Inclusive lists like Miliband's and Althusser's – and there are others, for example those given by Antonio Gramsci and Nicos Poulantzas – often recognize that state institutions exist on both sides of the legal boundary between 'public' and 'private' (see below on constituting the state). However, this boundary is sometimes dismissed as a juridical mystification with legitimating effects, at the risk of minimizing the distinction between democratic and totalitarian regimes (chapter 9).

These two accounts, with their expansive lists of institutions and apparatuses, suggest, correctly, that being in charge of one institution, even if that is the executive branch, does not ensure control over the entire state system. In addition, since the state is 'a peopled organization' (Jones 2007: 17–20 and passim), personnel of the state may not follow authorized procedures or exercise its members' discretion to promote the prevailing state project (see also Finer 1997a, 1997b, 1997c). The challenges of overall control are especially evident where the state is integrated into inter- or transnational arrangements or subordinated to another state, formally or informally. Such lists also invite us to ask what exactly justifies treating these institutions and apparatuses as being inside rather than outside the state. In both cases, the answer is functionalist. Miliband (1969: 3) argued that the state's essential function is to defend the interests of the dominant class; and Althusser (1971), that it is to secure social cohesion in class-divided societies. But if the quality of statehood is defined in terms of such broad functions, especially where these are equated with alleged effects rather than declared purposes, why not extend the list of relevant institutions to the entire field of social relations? Such lists may seem more plausible when they are more restricted and correspond to everyday understandings of the state. Yet even then they usually fail to clarify what lends the institutions in question the specific quality of *statehood*. This is hard because, as the renowned German social scientist Max Weber noted, there is hardly an activity that modern states (or their historical precursors) have never undertaken and none that they always undertake, let alone exclusively (Weber 1994: 310). Thus definitions that rely on a predefined set of state tasks are imprecise; and this indicates, he argued, the need for another approach.

The Three-Element Approach

Weber's alternative was to define the state initially in terms of *means* rather than *ends*, that is, in terms of the distinctive organizational form and capacities of the state apparatus rather than its alleged functions or purposes. Thus he defined the *modern* state (not, be it noted, all states) as the 'human community which (successfully) lays claim to the *monopoly of legitimate physical violence* within a certain territory, this "territory" being another of the characteristics of the state' (Weber 1994: 310–11). In this context 'human community' refers, restrictively, to the administrative staff of the 'compulsory political organization' that exercises continuous domination within a territory (Weber 1978: 53–4; cf. Weber 1994: 313). This definition assumes that the territory is 'peopled' – an aspect he explored elsewhere.

Weber argues that this monopoly of violence can be legitimated in several ways. The most significant modes comprise: traditional authority, including divine right and dynastic succession; charismatic domination; and a formal constitution that governs the transfer and exercise of the authority to make collectively binding decisions. Weber qualifies his reference to coercion by noting that states usually resort to nonviolent means to secure their existence and maintain general political order in their respective territories. The tasks and activities that states perform in this regard are highly variable and the state, *qua* political community, must seek to justify them in terms of general values (Weber 1978: 54–6, 902, 905–6). Lastly, what he initially treated as a defining feature of the modern state (its right to define the legitimate use of violence) soon disappears from Weber's account, as he turns to bureaucracy and its crucial role in effectuating the unity of state administration (1968: 56, 212–26, 956–1003). In short, even this most famous of definitions, once introduced, was amended to allow for the complexities of real states. (For good reviews of Weber's state theory, see Anter and Breuer 2007; on Weber and two other leading German theorists discussed later, Carl Schmitt and Franz Neumann, see Kelly 2003.)

Weber's definition is related to the 'three-element' approach of continental European constitutional, juridical, and state theory traditions (see, for example, Jellinek 1905; Heller 1983; Kelsen 1945; Schmitt 1985). This approach is also common in international law, which is concerned with issues of the mutual recognition of states. The three elements that it identifies are: (1) a politically organized coercive, administrative, and symbolic apparatus endowed with both general and specific powers (variously described as *Staatsgewalt*, *Staatsapparat*, or *Staatshoheit*: respectively, state power, state apparatus, or state sovereignty) – reflected in Weber's interpretation of 'human community' as the administrative staff of the state; (2) a clearly demarcated core territory under more or less uncontested and continuous control of the state apparatus (*Staatsgebiet*: state territory); and (3) a permanent or stable population, on which the state's political authority and decisions are binding (*Staatsvolk*). Similar ideas, without the use of explicit juridico-political language, are found in anthropological studies of state formation (chapter 5).

I now consider each element in terms of general state theory, constitutional law, and international law. General state theory is mostly concerned with the domestic relations among these elements and emphasizes their institutional features, which makes this approach compatible with questions of historical or formal constitution and institutionalist approaches (see chapter 1). A focus on constitutional law is both a strength and weakness. On the one hand, the constitutionalization as well as the territorialization of political power are key features of the modern state, especially if one wants to distinguish legitimate authority based on the rule of law from domination by warlords and mafia-style organizations with different codes of right and wrong. On the other hand, constitutional legitimacy is quite recent in world-historical terms by comparison with traditional or charismatic authority or the brute and often brutal reality of 'might makes right'. In addition, the world of states includes failing, failed, collapsed, or shadow states where there is no rule of law and, often, no effective internal sovereignty. Third, while some political scientists may accept a practical or a legalistic focus on the 'internal state', international law also examines the external dimension of statehood. At stake here is the principle that no state should be formally subordinate to external authority: it should be sovereign in its own territory and over its own population. Yet, as much recent work on the world market and on global governance indicates, state sovereignty is being challenged in various ways, externally as well as internally (see chapter 8). A related issue is the extraterritorial reach of 'superpowers' (most notably, the post-Cold War United States), which overrides in various ways the internal and external rights of other sovereign states. This issue has implications for empire and imperialism in different periods (see chapters 5, 8, and 9). For now, however, I return to the three elements (for a summary representation, see Table 2.2).

State apparatus

This phrase designates a politically organized coercive, administrative, and *symbolic* apparatus with sovereign authority vis-à-vis its own population and other states. This does not limit state power to direct and immediate coercion, whether deployed for internal purposes or for external defence. Indeed, if most of its subjects deem state power legitimate, compliance normally follows without recourse to physical as opposed to symbolic violence and is often mediated through micro-techniques that seem to have little (if anything) to do with the state (cf. Foucault 1980; Bourdieu 1994, 2014; Bratsis 2006; Miller and Rose 2008; Neocleous 2000). We can also distinguish coercion that is normally exercised intermittently through the legal system from the open, often unconstrained use of force in emergencies. Massive reliance on violence would signify weak legitimacy, even where the violence is effective. It is often a sign of state crisis, or even of state failure. The importance of basing authority on something more than violence is evident even in the earliest states, where bureaucratic forms (or at least a hierarchy of offices and associated personnel) emerged and were linked to ritual or charismatic authority as well as to military power (Service 1975: 10; Breuer 2014). In short, a relative monopoly of organized coercion is just one state capacity among several forms of 'hard power' and generally coexists with forms of 'soft power' rooted in sociocultural relations. Indeed Joseph Nye, a US American political scientist, international relations theorist, and influential foreign affairs policy advisor, advocates 'smart power' based on a judicious mix of hard and soft power (Nye 2004).

This said, many states routinely infringe their own legality – whether openly or beneath the cloak of official secrecy, whether at home or abroad – by relying on a mix of terror, force, fraud, and corruption to exercise power. (On different forms of state criminality, see Maran 1989; Barak 1991; Giraldo 1996; Reno 1998; Campbell and Brenner 2000; Green and Ward 2004; Bayart, Ellis, and Hibou 2009; Rothe 2009; Wilson 2009; on grand and petty corruption, see Dobel 1978; Kang 2002; Bratsis 2003; Satter 2003; Tsoukalas 2003; Kofele-Kala 2006.) Individual state agents may also abuse state power for fraudulent enrichment on a petty or grand scale. Furthermore, all states, considered as legal subjects, reserve the right – or claim the need – to suspend the constitution or specific legal provisions in exceptional conditions. Carl Schmitt, the famous – or notorious – German legal and political theorist writing in the 1920s–1950s, even proposed that 'sovereign is he who decides on the exception' (Schmitt 1985: 5;[5] cf. Scheuerman 1994; Agamben 2005; Boukalas 2014a; and chapter 9 here). The resulting 'states of emergency' are, in principle at least, temporary and tied to specific threats or challenges – initially around security issues, more recently extending to economic emergencies (Scheuerman 2000). In some cases, however, the state of emergency may be declared permanent, and this is used to justify an enduring rather than temporary dictatorship.

In short, even for Schmittian scholars, sovereignty is not equated solely with state violence – whether in the form of police powers or further resort to military force. A simple typology of state resources has been proposed by the German sociologist Helmut Willke (1992). He distinguished four general means that can be deployed, alone or in admixture, in exercising power: force, law, money, and knowledge. While the first three are intuitively plausible, the fourth merits explanation. Knowledge has been a major aspect of state power for millennia and involves many forms of information gathering, political calculation, and surveillance (e.g., Scott 1998 on 'seeing like a state'; and Bourdieu 2014 on the state's 'informational capital'). Indeed 'statistics' initially referred to the state's collection of demographic and economic data for its own purposes. The more general nexus of power–knowledge has often been explored – including, famously, by Michel Foucault (1980, 2007, 2008). And, with the rise of the security state, information becomes critical to state capacities of pursuing national, social, economic, and environmental security.

On this basis Willke identified four stages in the development of the *modern state*, each stage being characterized by the relative predominance of one medium of power. His analysis has also been elaborated by Stefan Lange, a German political scientist, whose version is summarized in Table 2.1.

The first stage was that of the territorial security state (*Sicherheitsstaat*), which mobilized and deployed force to defend its boundaries and to impose order within them. Next was the constitutional state, based on the rule of law (*Rechtsstaat*), which relied on law to secure domestic order and to promote international peace. Third came the social state (*Sozialstaat*), which used taxes and state credit to promote the social security associated with different forms and degrees of citizenship. The most recent stage, according to Willke, is the *Supervisionsstaat*. This concept is hard to translate. It connotes both a state that exercises super-vision as a result of its relative monopoly over collective intelligence *and* a state that exercises control through its supervisory or disciplinary capacities (Willke 1997; also Lange 2003). As the scope of state intervention expands and state capacities depend more on soft and reflexive law, targeted spending, and knowledge, traditional political leaders and state managers increasingly find themselves forced to adjudicate on broad *political* grounds on the solutions proposed by experts (cf. Gramsci 1971: 28 = Q 12, §1).[6] This is reflected in the shift from government to (meta)governance (on this, see chapters 3, 7, and 9).

State territory

While the legitimate monopoly of violence offers one entry point into the analysis of the state, another is the territorial organization of political authority. Some theorists regard this as the essential feature of the state, *pre*modern as well as modern (e.g. Luhmann 1989). Such territorialization of political authority certainly gives a common form to all effective states in the modern interstate system and thereby provides an important criterion for the destatization of authority and, in other contexts, for state failure. It also provides a basis for distinguishing politics in general (e.g., office politics) from politics that is oriented to the exercise of state power (cf. Weber 1994).

Territorialization denotes the division of the earth into more or less clearly demarcated areas that are governed by a political authority empowered to make decisions binding on the residents of these areas (Delaney 2005). Territory in this sense should not be confused

Table 2.1 Cumulative genesis of the modern state

Time Axis	Historical Caesura	Social Discourse	Leading Science	Power Basis	Political Steering Medium	State Form
xv–xvii centuries	Secularization	Power question	Military science	Army, police	Force	Absolute or security state
xviii–xix centuries	Constitution	Legality question	Legal science	Sanction system	Law	Constitutional state
xix–xx centuries	Industrialization	Poverty question	Political economy	Fiscal capacity	Money	Social or welfare states
xx–xxi centuries	Technologization	Risk question	Informatics	Communication networks	Information	Supervision state

Source: Translated and adapted from Lange 2003: 57

with the more generic notion of *terra* – 'the terrestrial' (which encompasses 'land' in its broadest sense, i.e., land and the subterranean, the sea, its depths and seabed, the air above, and outer space) – which provides a variable, technologically conditioned, and relational 'raw material' of territorialization as a specific political process. Land without centralized political authority is sometimes declared to be *terra nullius*, 'no one's land' – that is, land without a sovereign (the Antarctic land mass is a rare current example); its maritime parallel is 'the high seas'. An important moment in the rise of the modern Westphalian state was the papal declaration that Europe would be governed by independent, sovereign, and Christian national states, that war would only be conducted between states (which thereby prohibited civil wars), and that the New World, regarded as *terra nullius*, would be divided between Portugal and Spain, to be colonized as their rulers saw fit, according to European natural law traditions – admittedly a commitment to good governance that was more often honoured in the breach than in practice (see Schmitt 2003).

Clearly the nature of this raw material shapes claims to sovereignty (contrast, for example, continental and archipelagic states) and prompts different kinds of territorial dispute (e.g. rights of navigation through straits). This is the stuff of geopolitics, customary law, and international law. Different principles are at play when it comes to sea and air, and this leads to oscillations in the principles and practices applied in territorialization. One example is the changing priority that individual states give at different times to 'freedom of the high seas' and to 'sovereignty over territorial waters' and interstate disputes that follow from this. Further, as maritime technologies have changed and aviation technologies evolve, so does the scope of territorialization (e.g., as it comprises, successively, 'territorial waters', exclusive maritime economic zones, continental shelves, and high seas).[7] While one might think of territory as fixed, ships and aircraft not only have *national* identities but also can have *sovereign territorial* status, and hence gain immunity from uninvited intervention (Bernhardt 1989).

The scope for territorial conflict also alters with technologies and strategic interests, as seen in the new struggle for 'full spectrum dominance': a struggle to control outer space and cyberspace as well as land, sea and air (cf. Bernhardt 1989; Haanappel 2003: 1–27; and Engdahl 2009). Finally the terrestrial, the territorial, and, most recently, the telematic (or, more broadly, cyberspace) are objects of cartographic representation. States engage in mapping them as part of state projects and for wider purposes (Escolar 1997; Biggs 1999; Hannah 2000; Elden 2007, 2010; Barkan 2011).

Territorialization takes different forms, beginning with groups of hunter-gatherers or herders that tend to roam within a space with porous borders but also crucial nodes (such as oases, ritual sites) that they seek to defend and developing through simple and complex chiefdoms to early forms of state and empire (van der Pijl 2007; see also chapter 5).[8] Nomadic empires have also developed, sometimes in the shadow of, and partly parasitic upon, sedentary empires, as in the coevolution of successive Mongolian federations vis-à-vis early imperial China (Finer 1997a, 1997b; Barfield 2001; van der Pijl 2007). Such empires later formed the basis of the Eurasian Mongol Empire and its vassal states founded by Chinggis Khan (see Amitai-Preiss and Morgan 2000). Control over territory was also a defining feature of the feudal mode of production and distinguished it from its capitalist successor, which has the world market as its ultimate spatiotemporal horizon of expansion and reproduction. In sum, it would be wrong to identify territorialization or its results solely with the 'Westphalian' state system allegedly established by the Treaty of Westphalia in 1648 but realized only stepwise and incompletely during the nineteenth and twentieth centuries.

There are solid historical grounds for questioning the powerful originary (founding) myth of the Westphalian system, especially regarding its ruptural character. Indeed, rather than establishing independent states or polities, the treaty was actually expected to contribute to the survival of the Holy Roman Empire (Schmitt 2003). The latter was eventually ended through intervention by the newly hegemonic continental power, Napoleonic France, rather than being displaced by multiple Westphalian states or withering away (Beaulac 2004). Nonetheless, in its mythical character, this system is normally said to involve the systematic division of a potentially global political system into a series of exclusive territories controlled by mutually recognizing, mutually legitimating states that are not *legally* subject to the authority of another state. In contrast, feudalism is frequently alleged to involve a tangled patchwork of partly overlapping or superimposed territories, 'in which different juridical instances were geographically interwoven and stratified, and plural allegiances, asymmetrical suzerainties and anomalous enclaves abounded' (Beaulac 2004: 189). This patchwork of political regimes is sometimes said to have been revived in the guise of neo-medievalism or neo-feudalism (see chapter 5).

Westphalian territorial principles are, rightly or wrongly, the main reference point in modern political struggles; and they also provide the basis for the division of political matters into domestic and international affairs. This reference point can be negative, as when some scholars suggest that it is dissolving into, or reverting towards, earlier forms of territorial organization. It can also serve to highlight the variable coincidence or disjunction between different boundaries, borders, or frontiers of action and emphasize the changing primacy of different tiers or scales of political action. The latter involves multilevel or multispatial government and governance arrangements (see chapters 5 and 7). More generally, these principles – or at least their repetition as founding myths – also provide the symbolic, institutional, and organizational basis for geopolitical interaction on a global scale – an interaction that would be inherently anarchic if indeed there were no enforceable rules governing the nature of these interactions. (On the Westphalian state, see, inter alia, Kratochwil 1986; Osiander 2001; Ruggie 1993; Spruyt 1993; and Teschke 2003.)

State population

Originally 'to populate' and 'population' denoted the populating of a place or space (McNicoll 2003; Petit 2013). Regardless of nomenclature, efforts to promote this process predate the formation of chiefdoms, let alone city-states and territorial states, because people plus land were crucial economic and military resources in pre-industrial societies. More recently this is reflected in struggles over *Großraum* – a large land mass – or *Lebensraum* – the additional territory and resources needed to support a state with a large population (still a major concern, though the term has been discredited as a result of its association with Nazi geopolitics) – as well as in population policies concerned with birth rates, marriage, migration, ageing, and so on and with broader questions about the family as apparatus and organization and daily, lifecourse, and intergenerational reproduction. A related aspect is that of deliberate efforts at population displacement or depopulation (which can lead to genocide in the second case) – whether for economic and political advantage, as a form of punishment, or due to 'racism' or ethnic antagonisms (Levene 2005a, 2005b). Population was also related to interest in 'populousness', that is, the number, age, composition, quality, and capacities of the populace (Biller 2000; Curtis 2002; Petit 2013). Only later did population signify an object to be enumerated, categorized and governed: the households, families, or persons who populated a place or space.[9] The first recorded censuses (including possessions, property, and resources as well as population numbers) date back to Mesopotamian states, almost 6,000 years ago. Censuses have been organized by states and other authorities ever since, for diverse fiscal, productive, religious, policing, military, eugenic, and pastoral purposes. Census taking generates categorizations and classifications oriented to the social division of labour and to social divisions; it is also a contested process, especially when associated with taxation, tribute, military service, policing, and other governmental practices (Ojakangas 2012).

As Michel Foucault emphasized, population is an object of both anatomo-politics and biopolitics – of disciplining individual bodies and governing populations, respectively. In other words, the population of the state is not just the aggregate of individuals residing in or passing through a state's territory, but is construed, constituted, and governed as a more or less complex object of state policy that varies across types of state, historical periods, and political regimes. In 'modern' states, for example, population is

> understood not as the crude number of people but instead in terms of such features as variable levels of health, birth and death rates, age, sex, [nuptiality, fecundity], dependency ratios, and so on – as an object with a distinct rationality and intrinsic dynamics that can be made the target of a specific kind of direct intervention. (Thompson 2012: 42)

Thus the rise of population as an object of governance involves 'the creation of new orders of knowledge, new objects of intervention, new forms of subjectivity and...new state forms' (Curtis 2002: 507; cf. Dean 1990; Petit 2013; also note how this relates to Willke's account of knowledge as a state resource and to the more general importance of 'statistics', on which see Woolf 1989; Kalpagam 2000; and Petit 2013). Further, in governing population, policymakers in modern states consider issues such as migration, taxation, family policy, education and vocational training, health care, housing policy, and spatial planning. Finally, interest in population and in biopolitical practices extends beyond city-states and territorial states to colonial rule and, from the 1930s onwards (if not earlier), also emerged at the level of global policy, for example in health issues (see Bashford 2006; Kaasch and Martens 2015).

The population element of the threefold state doctrine is sometimes interpreted to connote a community of feeling (*Gemeinschaft*) as opposed to a shared sense of belonging to the same political association (*Gesellschaft*), a shared sense of nationhood, and common citizenship based on shared duties, rights, and benefits. These connotations are anachronistic in terms of the history of state formation – the ancient Egyptian and Hebrew states were rare exceptions for shared identity (see Finer 1997a: 3) – and citizenship is far from universal even in contemporary states. It is more appropriate to regard the population as comprising those who are subject to state authority and to consider how these subjects are constituted in different forms of state and political regime. Citizenship, with its obligations and its rights (including rights against the state), is only one such modality. The organization of the population associated with a state territory and apparatus typically institutionalizes *exclusion* as well as inclusion, within or beyond the boundaries of a given state. An interesting example concerns the 'third space of sovereignty', that is, the relations between a colonial or settler state's plenary power and the rights of indigenous peoples to (partial) sovereignty within (or indeed cross-cutting) the frontiers of the state (Bruyneel 2007). This creates the paradox that indigenous peoples must often use the laws and related juridico-political discourses of a state whose legality and legitimacy they contest in order to gain recognition for their rights to 'national' sovereignty, when their own folkways, mores, and traditions lack a concept of nation (Purvis 1998). The paradox raises further issues in constitutional, international, and human rights law concerning whether states alone should be able to determine nationality and citizenship and thereby be able to render some people stateless or deprive them of recently instituted (and still contested) human rights.

I should add that the population governed by states is subject to nationalizing, gendering, 'racializing', and other identity-based divisions; and that it is differentiated in terms of class composition and relations, as well as in terms of patterns of uneven local, regional, and national territorial development. National identity is one basis for inclusion and exclusion, either permanently or at particular stages of state development or in specific conjunctures. In this sense, the 'nation-state' is one particular form of territorialization of state power – one based on socially constructed national identities, whether already consolidated, potentially realizable, or merely aspirational (chapter 6). Indeed, 'territorial delimitation antedated the policy of nation-formation, and the latter, as a blanket principle, has as yet not been fully realized, whereas the principle of territorial statehood has established itself world-wide' (Albert and Brock 1996). A final issue concerns how the state exercises binding authority over various kinds of association or organization based in or operating on its territory, and indeed whether they are accorded the same rights as individual citizens.

Five issues related to population in the modern era are: (1) the recognition of states by other states; (2) the right to national self-determination; (3) the relation between population and 'nation' (however understood); (4) the relation between population and citizenship (including issues of social inclusion and exclusion and legal

Table 2.2 Aspects of the traditional three-element theory

	State Apparatus	State Territory	State People
Defining Features	Special staff with division of labour and specific state capacities	Bordered territory subject to control by state authority	Population of state
Similar Concepts	*Appareil* Dispositive State sovereignty	Border, frontier, *limes,* domain, realm, region	Residents, denizens Sojourners Constituent power, *pouvoir constitué*
External Dimension	Recognition of state sovereignty by other sovereign states	Exclaves, colonies, protectorates, dependencies Claims to extraterritoriality	Aliens, refugees, stateless persons
State Crisis	Failure of state capacity, crisis of legitimacy Government-in-exile	Insecure borders, occupation	Demographic decline
State Failure	Administrative failure, loss of legitimacy	Military defeat Loss of territorial sovereignty	Forcible removal, genocide, civil war, dual power, divided loyalties
One-sided Analysis	Failure to distinguish the state from mafia-like organizations	Neglect of space of flows, articulation of place, scale, network	Methodological nationalism
Remarks	Not reducible to organized force Can be multilevel or multitiered May be undemocratic or illegitimate There may be no constitution to govern state organization	Not to be confused with terrain, terrestrial, telematic Does not need to be contiguous (e.g., the cases of enclaves or exclaves) Does not need to be national in scope	Not the same as a community of feeling, a nation, or citizenship Subject to both anatomo- and biopolitics Subjects may be 'corporate' agents as well as individuals

Source: Original compilation

and political rights); (5) the international legal question of formal rights to belong to, and receive protection from, a state – and, relatedly, the rights of stateless persons. I address the first issue briefly here and the others in chapter 6.

There are three forms of state recognition: *de facto*, diplomatic, and *de iure*. These distinctions date back to the secession of the Spanish provinces in South America in the early nineteenth century. The forms of recognition depend on the intentions of the recognizing government; and these are as much political as legal in nature. In general, following the three-element doctrine, recognition of a state depends on whether a *population*, inhabiting a certain *territory*, is organized under an effective *public authority* that has internal sovereignty or constituent power – in other words can define the constitution – and, in addition, enjoys formal external sovereignty – in other words is not formally subordinate to another state.[10] International law also distinguishes (1) *recognition of a state*, in line with relevant legal criteria of statehood, from (2) *recognition of a government*, which is linked to its legitimacy and the expedient calculation of other states. Options range from hostile intervention through nonrecognition and conditional recognition to positive embrace. Some states formally recognize only states, others recognize – formally or *de facto* – governments, including those 'in exile' or 'in waiting'.[11] This is tricky, diplomatically and politically, if there are attempts at secession or rival governments that lay claim to control over the same territory – or, again, if foreign powers favour different governments in exile or governments in waiting (Talmon 1998). This does not exclude subordination to international law – although some states (e.g., the United States) also claim exemption from some or all of the obligations inscribed in (or emerging in) international law.

Revisiting the three elements

Accepting for now the three-element approach as a useful analytical starting point (later on I add a fourth element), we should consider all three elements *and their interrelations*. These can be articulated in different ways, discursively and institutionally. For example, whereas the contested Jacobin formula for the state, after the French Revolution, was *un peuple, une terre, un état* ('one people, one territory, one state'), it was *Ein Volk, ein Reich, ein Führer* ('one people, one empire, one leader') in Nazi Germany. Likewise, institutionally, there is wide variation in the sequencing of and in the political priority attached to territorialization, apparatus making, and population or nation building. Two contrasting historical examples (among many) are the challenge following Italian unification – *Italia fatta, bisogna fare gli Italiani* ('now that Italy's made, we must make the Italians') – and the Zionist project to create a Jewish state. The consequences of neglecting these conceptual and practical issues can be seen in the distortions introduced by different kinds of one-sidedness.

- A one-sided concern with the state apparatus and its capacities would highlight the emergence of a division of labour between state leaders and the population that they lead or govern. An extreme form of this concern is the reduction of the state to 'special bodies of armed men, prisons, etc.' (Lenin 1972), which makes it hard to distinguish the state from warlordism, protection rackets and mafia-like organizations (Tilly 1975; Volkov 2000; Breuer 2014; but see Blok 1975 on the mafia's role in Sicilian state formation). This is why a defining feature of the modern state is the *legitimacy* of coercion and of *other modes* of exercising state power. One-sided concern with the distinctive properties of the state as an administrative or repressive organ also informs so-called state-centred research on the state as an independent variable. Such research highlights how the state's distinctive political resources enable it to penetrate, control, supervise, police, and discipline modern societies even against resistance from nonstate forces – especially where a pluralistic universe of social forces creates significant scope for manoeuvre; and how they enable state managers to pursue their own bureaucratic, career, and political interests against other agents and interests (the modern classic text is Evans, Rueschemeyer, and Skocpol 1985; see also Skocpol 1979; Nordlinger 1981; Mann 1984; Giddens 1985; Bourdieu 2014).
- A focus on state territory rests on a contrast with 'gentile' societies organized around segmentary differentiation between tribes, clans, or *gentes* (singular *gens*) orders (cf. Engels 1972; Service 1975; Wright 1977; Finer 1997a; see also chapter 5) or, in more recent terminology, nomadic societies (cf. Deleuze and Guattari 1983). It can also be used to contrast the premodern tendency to develop state power by extending the territorial reach of the state with the modern state tendency to intensify control within a given territory. However, such views forget that stateless societies, too, had their own ways of appropriating territory; for example, nomadic groups generally occupy a recognized but porous home territory that lacks clear boundaries. These views may also produce a one-sided focus on the de- and reterritorialization of

political power, to the neglect of other forms of organizing political cal space. A related issue is the existence of enclaves and exclaves that disrupt the continuity of state territories. Extraterritoriality is also relevant; and it has taken at least two forms. One form is that of parallel legal systems for expatriates in other territories (e.g., nineteenth-century courts for Europeans living in China, Japan, and the Ottoman Empire); the other form is that of post-World War II legal imperialism based on the maxim that might is right and on claims about the superiority of US legal norms, US exceptionalism, and the Unites States' unique global role (on these examples, see Kayaoğlu 2010).

- Finally, a one-sided concern with state subjects can lead to a demographic preoccupation with population issues, a focus on the nature (primordial, imagined, or constructed) of the *Staatsvolk* as a 'nation', or an interest in citizenship regimes to the neglect of other forms of domination, subjection, or exclusion. It may also encourage 'methodological nationalism', namely the assumption that an economic, political, or social order is defined by subjection to the authority of a given *nation-state* or a given *national territorial state*. We must nonetheless ask how a population is constituted as an aggregate of objects of rule, whether as subjects, citizens, denizens, aliens, and so forth; how these are organized as a basis for governing (e.g., as individuals, households, communities, populations); and how associations, corporations, and other collective bodies are constituted as legal subjects, with rights and obligations separate from those of their individual members. And it is certainly worth inquiring into nation building, types of nation, issues of inclusion, exclusion, and inequality, debates on diasporas and migration, and so on (chapter 6). Lastly, from the viewpoint of radical democratic theory, we can ask about the conditions in which the population or any of its representatives becomes a 'constituent power', that is, someone empowered to write a constitution and to exercise popular sovereignty.

A further question when developing a theoretically informed general account of the state is whether one needs a separate and parallel account of state decline, crisis, or failure. The answer proposed here is that, just as there can be no general theory of the state, there can be no general theory of its decline, crisis, or failure. Nonetheless, the strategic–relational approach to state power developed below does indicate the abstract possibility of such events or processes. Explaining this is prior to, and independent of, any particular account of the actual causes of a given instance of decline, crisis, or failure (cf.

Kenway 1980). In other words, we can reflect on the general conditions in which crises might develop and, in another step or steps, consider the specific causes of specific crises. If it is also possible to identify crisis tendencies and countertendencies inherent in specific forms or sets of social relations, this will facilitate explanations for periods of instability, decline, crisis, or failure as well as for periods of relative stability. These conditions and tendencies can be examined at different levels of abstraction, just as one examines the state and its particular instantiations in different historical and comparative contexts. Given that I reject an essentialist account of the state that takes its territorial control, operational unity, and political authority for granted, it follows that, insofar as these features exist, this is a practical, contingent achievement that must be continually reproduced and reinforced. By the same token, we can identify in equally abstract terms the main sites and likely forms of crises (see Tables 2.2, 3.1, 6.1, and 7.1 for various more or less abstract examples; and chapters 3, 4, 7, 8 and 9 for further textual indications and cases).

Thus state decline, state failure, or the rolling back of the state can take the form of:

1   the failure of state capacity, whether through administrative failure, legitimacy crisis, or loss of legitimacy, so that the collective goals specified in state projects about the nature and purposes of government are not attained;
2   the loss of control over state territory through catastrophe, conquest, fusion, or secession, the rise of multilevel government, the development of dual power within one territory as incumbent and revolutionary forces contest sovereignty, or the emergence of claims to extraterritorial authority or immunity (or both);
3   the dissolution of the *Staatsvolk*, whether through processes such as genocide, forcible removal, or demographic decline or by other routes such as civil war, dual power, or divided loyalties.

More on the Territorialization of Political Power

The great majority of states today – and all of the most powerful states – enjoy mutually recognized formal sovereignty over their respective (large) territories and have established mutual, if sometimes frosty, diplomatic relations. In addition, these states' subjects are subordinate in principle to common laws and should, ideally, recognize their state (and perhaps its subnational tiers) as exercising legitimate authority within its territory. In this sense, all states are equal. Nonetheless, with rare exceptions, sovereign city-states and small island states lack significant geoeconomic and geopolitical power. Indeed, when the League of Nations was formed in 1919, some microstates were denied membership on the grounds that they could not fulfil the obligations entailed by membership because they had tiny territories and small populations and no army (e.g., Andorra, Liechtenstein, Monaco, and San Marino; see Ferguson and Mansbach 1989: 26). Many such states belong nonetheless to the United Nations; but they have minimal influence and are often pawns in strategic games played among major powers. This indicates certain limits to the alleged statization of the world (Reinhard et al., 1999; Schuppert 2010: 2; Albert 2005).

Three qualifications are required immediately; and they are elaborated upon in chapters 3 and 5. First, the territorialization of political power and the creation of the population over which such power is exercised are historical accomplishments grounded in struggles. They are also reproduced (or transformed) through constitutional, institutional, and organizational struggles that seek to maintain, transform, or overthrow states. Relatedly, political power can be exercised in ways that are only loosely related to tightly demarcated territory (e.g., nomadic or other stateless societies, network governance, governance without government, charismatic rule, transnational religious authority like that of the Vatican or the Islamic *ummah*, informal empires, or consociational confederations of communities governed by representatives).[12]

Second, there are many and varied forms of territorialization. The national territorial, Westphalian state is only one among several historically possible (and, indeed, compossible) modes of organizing political power on territorial lines. Other modes include chiefdoms, feudalism, principalities, city-states, absolutism, empires, suzerainty, tributary relations, vassal or client states, modern imperial–colonial blocs, and colonies (Braudel 1975; Dodgshon 1987, 1998; Anderson 1996).

Third, some other forms of territorialization still coexist with the Westphalian system (e.g., city-states, client states, enclave states, warlordism, despotic rule, and informal empires) and new expressions of statehood are emerging (e.g., the European Union). Emerging modes that have been identified, rightly or wrongly, include the reemergence of empire as an organizing principle, the prospects for a global state, networks of world cities as a new form of Hanseatic League, the revival of subnational regions as key economic and political players, cross-border regional cooperation, a new medievalism, supranational blocs, a western conglomerate state (Shaw 2000), and an embryonic world state – or even global governance – oriented to securing perpetual peace. The complications are further illustrated by the competing interpretations of the EU as a rescaled 'national' state, a neo-medieval revival of the medieval political patchwork, a postsovereign form of authority, a Westphalian superstate, a consociation, or a new type of empire (see Beck and Grande 2007; Brenner 2004; Costa and Magnette 2003; Anderson 1996, Friedrichs 2001; Segesvary 2004; Shaw 2000; Taylor 2004; Ohmae 1995; Voigt 2000; Wendt 2003; Zielonka 2001, 2006; Ziltener 2001). In addition, for Hardt and Negri (2000), the world of sovereign territorial states is being replaced by a singular, nonterritorial, networked Empire that operates globally (on emerging forms, see chapter 8).

The Polymorphic Character of the State

An important comparative–historical approach to these complexities is the view that the state is polymorphous. In the natural sciences, polymorphy signifies that a species passes through different forms in its life cycle or can assume several forms without having its capacity for interbreeding disrupted; or, turning to chemistry, a physical compound can crystallize into two or more durable forms. Analogously, critiquing the view that states in capitalist societies are necessarily capitalist, Michael Mann (1986) argued that the state's organization and capacities may be primarily capitalist, military, theocratic, or democratic according to the balance of forces, especially as these affect the state ensemble and its exercise of power. Its dominant crystallization is open to challenge and will vary conjuncturally. We can add to this list, on the basis of other scholars' work, bureaucratic despotism (Wittfogel 1957), technocratic rule (Bentham 1970), an ethnic or racial state (Goldberg 2002), an apartheid state (based on ethnic separation, Price 1991), a patriarchal state (the patriarch general, MacKinnon 1989; Brown 1992), or an ethico-political state (Gramsci 1971).

Similarly, as the political geographer Peter Taylor (1994) notes, since the origins of the modern interstate system during the long sixteenth century, the state's role as a territorial 'power-container' has expanded in several directions. These include: (1) war making and military defence; (2) the mercantilist containment and development of national economic wealth; (3) the promotion of nationalized politico-cultural identities; (4) the institutionalization of democratic forms of political legitimation; and (5) the provision of various forms of social welfare. Thus, from the war machines of early modern Europe and the wealth containers of the mercantile era to the national developmental–imperialist states of the second industrial revolution and the national welfare states of the Fordist–Keynesian period, states have deployed a great variety of politico-regulatory strategies and have attempted to use the principle of territoriality to 'contain' very different types of socioeconomic activities within their borders. Territorial borders are best viewed as a medium and outcome of historically specific strategies and ceaselessly renewed attempts to shape the geographies of political–economic activities within and between states (Newman and Paasi 1998).

One way to make sense of these different crystallizations is in terms of the dominant principle of societal organization, if any, and of its role in state (trans)formation. Among the competing principles are marketization, internal or external security, environmental stewardship, inclusive citizenship, the rule of law, nationalism, ethnicity, and theocracy. Any of these (or others) could – and have – become dominant, at least temporarily, and would tend to be reflected in the leading crystallization of state power. It follows that capital accumulation is not always the best entry point for studying the complexities of the social world, even though one might later ask whether states that seem to prioritize, say, national security and nation building actually pursue policies that favour capital (e.g., East Asian developmental states).

The scope for alternative crystallizations highlights the importance of the historical semantics of state formation and the variability of political imaginaries and state projects. Indeed, whatever the precise origins of the components of the modern state (such as the army, bureaucracy, taxation, legal system, legislative assemblies), their organization as a relatively coherent institutional ensemble depends crucially on the emergence of the state idea. Thus state discourses have played a key role in the separation of the political sphere from other institutional orders and, whether as mystification, self-motivation, or self-description, still shape the state as a complex ensemble of political relations linked to their respective social formations. The discursive as well as material constitution of the state–civil society boundary enables state managers to deploy that movable boundary in the exercise of state power – and may in turn provoke counterproposals or resistance from social forces. This line of demarcation also shapes how other actors on the political scene orient their actions towards the 'state', acting *as if* it existed. And struggles over dominant or hegemonic political and state imaginaries can be decisive in shaping the nature, purposes, and stakes of government (Gramsci 1971; Mitchell 1991; Bartelson 1995, 2001; Neocleous 2003).

In short, the fact of competing state and societalization projects rules out that the modern state will always (or could ever) be essentially capitalist. Moreover, even when accumulation is deeply embedded in its organizational matrix, state managers (politicians and officials) in modern states usually consider other functional imperatives and other pressures from civil society as they try to secure the institutional integration of the state and social cohesion in their respective territories.

This approach views actually existing state formations or assemblages as polyvalent, polymorphous crystallizations of one or another dominant principle of societal organization that varies according to the most pressing issues in a conjuncture, general crystallizations defining long periods, and specific crystallizations emerging in particular situations. The approach raises provocative questions regarding the range of axes or projects around which, and the spatiotemporal matrices within which, crystallizations can occur. This poses intriguing problems about the integration of different institutional orders and their potential disjunctions in time–space. It suggests that the state may be unable to function effectively because of competing state or societalization projects (or both). It is precisely this incompletion that led Abrams to recommend abandoning the *reified* notion of the state in favour of the state idea (which can be linked to competing state projects) or of the state system (which reflects different, incomplete crystallizations of state power). In this context, the state system would involve 'state effects' achieved by the institutionalization and legitimation of some projects, with all their additional interstitial, residual, marginal, irrelevant, recalcitrant, and contradictory elements. The same idea can be extended to social formations more generally, such that the nature of a given society would vary with its collective identity and with how it was reflected in the prevailing social institutions and practices (cf. Jessop 1990, 2007b).

A related idea is that the state is polycontextual (Willke 1992). Whereas polymorphous crystallization refers to state effects derived from competing state and societalization projects, polycontextuality refers to the complexities of these effects in multiple contexts. These contexts may be embedded within each other or may exist in tangled hierarchies – or both. So states and state power are both polymorphous *and* polycontextual – and the term polycontextural is also used. States exist at many sites and scales and undertake different (sets of) tasks in each context. They will appear differently according to context – sometimes appearing mainly in one guise, sometimes in another. This explains the many alternative definitions in which the state is qualified by different adjectival descriptors: administrative state, constitutional state, cooperative state, democratic state, national state, nation-state, network state, patriarchal state, security state, tax state, transnational state, welfare state, and so on. It is also why context-sensitive research methods are needed even for the same 'kind' of state, and why efforts are required to render different approaches commensurable.

Stateness as a Variable

Given the preceding remarks, especially the three-element approach, it is clear that the existence of 'the state' cannot be judged in simple yes/no terms. This explains the long-established and regularly revived interest in the historical and comparative variability of actually exist-ing states as compared to one or another abstract or ideal type. Thus some theorists focus on the state as a conceptual variable and examine the varied presence of the idea, institutions, or capacities that define the state (e.g., Nettl 1968, Badie and Birnbaum 1983, Schmitter 1996; Evans 1997, Fukuyama 2003, Axtmann 2004). Others examine the state's differential presence as a distinctive political form. Such approaches historicize the state idea and stress its great institutional variety. These issues have been studied on all territorial levels or scales, from the local to the international, with considerable concern for meso-level variation.

A related issue concerns the factors that make for state strength. Internally this refers to a state's capacities to exercise authority over social forces within its territory; and externally it refers to the state's power in the interstate system (on the latter, see Handel 1990). This concern is often linked with interest in the state's capacity to pene-trate and organize the rest of society. It is especially marked in recent theoretical and empirical work on predatory states and on develop-mental states. The former are essentially parasitic upon their economy and civil society, exercise largely the despotic power of command, and may eventually undermine the economy, society, and the state itself. In contrast, developmental states also have infrastructural and network power and deploy it in allegedly market-conforming ways (e.g., Castells 1992; Evans 1989, 1995; Johnson 1987; Weiss 1998; Weiss and Hobson 1995). One problem with much of this literature is that it uses a blanket contrast between strong and weak states rather than a polycontextu(r)al approach. The wide variety of inter-pretations of strength (and weakness) further threatens coherent analysis. States have been described as strong because they have a large public sector, authoritarian rule, strong societal support, a weak and gelatinous civil society, cohesive bureaucracies, an interventionist policy, or the power to limit external interference. Most seriously, some studies run the risk of tautology insofar as they define strength purely in terms of outcomes (for reviews, see Clark and Lemco 1988; Migdal 1988; Önis 1991; Waldner 1999). A possible theoretical solution is to investigate the scope for variability in state capacities by policy area, over time, and in specific conjunctures. In this way one could test those particular state capacities with respect to which policy fields and economic sectors are effective in promoting economic performance and over what spatiotemporal horizons of action and in what circumstances they can do so. For example, state capacities that promote catch-up export-led growth in low-tech sectors may not be equally appropriate for consolidating innovation-led competitiveness in knowledge-intensive sectors once catch-up is achieved.

Constituting the State

State theory cannot take the state for granted as an analytical object; but it can, and should, explore the practices that produce highly variable *state effects*. This invites concern with the changing institutional architectures and the changing activities.

For example, in this regard, Badie and Birnbaum write:

> It is still possible even today to distinguish between political systems in which there is both a center and a state (France), a state but no center (Italy), a center but no true state (Great Britain and the United States), and neither a center nor a true state (Switzerland). In the first two cases, the state dominates civil society and is responsible for its organization albeit in different degrees. In the last two cases civil society organizes itself. It is therefore possible to distinguish between societies in which the state attempts to run the social system through a powerful bureaucracy (of which France is the ideal type, with Prussia, Spain, and Italy exhibiting similar trajectories) and societies in which there is no need for a strong state and governing bureaucracy because civil society is capable of organizing itself (of which Great Britain is the ideal type, with the United States and 'consociational democracies'…such as Switzerland exhibiting similar trajectories). (1983: 103–4)[13]

Michel Foucault provides an even more radical gloss on the idea of 'state effects':

> it is likely that if the state is what it is today, it is precisely thanks to this governmentality that is at the same time both external and internal

to the state, since it is the tactics of government that allow the continual definition of what should or should not fall within the state's domain, what is public and what private, what is and what is not within the state's competence, and so on. So, if you like, the survival and limits of the state should be understood on the basis of the general tactics of governmentality. (2007: 144–5)

Statecraft is not confined, then, to the exercise of sovereign power. It extends to the practices that distinguish the political from various nonpolitical spheres and, on this basis, to the complex art of governing activities that straddle these divides. Tim Mitchell (1991) makes a very similar point:

The state should be addressed as an effect of detailed processes of spatial organization, temporal arrangement, functional specification, and supervision and surveillance, which create the appearance of a world fundamentally divided into state and society. The essence of modern politics is not policies formed on one side of this division being applied to or shaped by the other, but the producing and reproducing of this line of difference. (1991: 95)

In both cases, a key aspect of statecraft and governmentality is how they (re)define some issues as private, technical, or managerial, removing them from overtly political decision making and contentious politics (Miller and Rose 2008; see also chapter 7 here). Further, as indicated above, similar material and discursive borders divide the globe into *different* states and societies, creating a more or less complex segmented and stratified interstate system in an emerging world society. The state's frontiers and temporal horizons are not fixed once and for all and, as they change, they influence political processes and state capacities (see chapters 5 and 8).

Lastly, from his distinctive Marxist perspective, Antonio Gramsci remarked:

the general notion of the State includes elements which need to be referred back to the notion of civil society (in the sense that one might say that the State = 'political society + civil society', in other words, hegemony armoured with coercion'). (Gramsci 1971: 263 = Q 6, §88: 763–4)

Gramsci studied the state as a complex social relation that articulates state *and nonstate* institutions and practices around particular economic, political, and societal projects and strategies. He emphasized the centrality of private institutions, organizations, and movements in state power, the formation of political alliances, and the disorganization of subaltern forces. 'Civil society', a domain of ostensibly 'private' associations, was an integral part of the state and, a fortiori, of politics and policy. This insight has since been extended to 'global civil society'.

Building on these arguments, the 'three-element' approach can be supplemented by noting the role of discursive and material practices in delimiting territorial boundaries *and* in redefining the division between the state *qua* institutional ensemble and other institutional orders and everyday life in a given society. This also has implications for definitions of the nature and purposes of the state and state power. I have already discussed territorial frontiers in this regard (and see also Chapter 8); here I offer some further comments on the other line of demarcation indicated above – namely the demarcation of the political from one or more ostensibly nonpolitical spheres, which also involves locating social relations or sets of social issues on one or the other side of this divide. The nonpolitical can comprise an unmarked residuum situated *outside* the political sphere (e.g., state vs society, public vs private) or marked spheres with their own institutional order, operational logics, subjects, and practices (e.g., religious, economic, legal, educational, or scientific fields). Such dividing lines are not natural, even if they are sometimes taken for granted: they must be policed and can be repoliticized or reactivated. Likewise, attempts to redefine the dividing line between the political and the nonpolitical spheres can provoke controversies and contention about what properly belongs on the unmarked side or, more specifically, about what belongs within a given, positively demarcated, nonpolitical sphere.

This creates the space for politicization (here one might even speak of politization) by extending the frontiers of the polity into nonpolitical spheres and subordinating them to political factors, interests, values, and forces. Conversely, depolitization would roll these frontiers back – for example through sacralization, marketization, juridification, scientization (expertise), or, in Foucauldian terms, governmentalization and self-responsibilization through disciplinary or governmental practices. This process may backfire if it provokes controversies and contention about the demarcation of political and nonpolitical spheres and what properly belongs on the unmarked side or a given, positively demarcated, nonpolitical sphere (cf. Jessop 2014b).

Noting that the state is discursively, structurally, technically, and agentially related to other institutional orders such as economy, family, religion, sport, art, or 'civil society' does not exclude (indeed it assumes) specifically state-generated and state-mediated processes.

Typically political struggles are relatively autonomous from these other sites and their associated forms of struggle and, because the state has distinctive resources and capacities, the state can facilitate their operation and reproduction (and, of course, vice versa) but can also hinder, undermine, or destroy them. The manner in which this occurs varies with forms of societalization, differing across segmented, centre–periphery, and functionally differentiated societies, and is in line with the degree of integration of different orders or systems in an emerging world society. This same autonomy also motivates diverse social forces to conduct struggles addressed to the state or to seek to transform some or all of its features in these forces' own material and ideal interests (see later chapters).

A Four-Element Definition of the State

Some readers may reject this line of argument or, if not that, at least worry that it casts doubt on the validity of attempts to develop 'state theory'. There is some justification in such worries, insofar as a theoretically sound account of the state must address far more than the state as an institutional ensemble. But this is not an insuperable problem. Thus, rather than turn immediately to other issues, I offer a general definition of the state and then explore some of its many ramifications. Given my remarks on the state system and state idea, any general definition should refer to state discourse or political imaginaries as a fourth element, alongside the conventionally identified three core components of the state. This is my suggestion:

> The core of the state apparatus comprises a relatively unified ensemble of socially embedded, socially regularized, and strategically selective institutions and organizations [*Staatsgewalt*] whose socially accepted function is to define and enforce collectively binding decisions on the members of a society [*Staatsvolk*] in a given territorial area [*Staatsgebiet*] in the name of the common interest or general will of an imagined political community identified with that territory [*Staatsidee*]. (Adapted from Jessop 1990: 341)

This definition identifies the state in terms of its generic features as a specific form of macropolitical organization with a specific type of political orientation; it also indicates its links to the political sphere, and indeed to the wider society. It can guide research on specific states and political regimes as well as on the conditions in which states emerge, evolve, enter into crisis, and are transformed. It also puts the contradictions and dilemmas involved in political discourse at the heart of work on the state. This is because claims about the general will or common interest are a key feature of the state system and distinguish it from straightforward political domination or violent oppression. This said, the definition requires six qualifications:

1 Above, around, and below the core of the state ensemble are institutions and organizations whose relation to the core ensemble is uncertain. State systems never achieve complete separation from society and their institutional boundaries are often contested. This means that they never achieve full closure; and this, in turn, complicates any efforts at institutional integration. In addition, their operations depend on diverse micropolitical practices dispersed throughout society but coordinated, more often in intent or aspiration than in reality, in the 'core' of the state. They also enter into links with emergent state-like institutions in the interstate field.

2 The nature of these institutions and organizations, their articulation to form the ensemble, and their links with the wider society all depend on the nature and history of the social formation. A capitalist type of state differs from the feudal type, for example; and, in addition, regime forms vary across capitalist societies. Questions about state polymorphy are also crucial here. Such distinctions are the stuff of historical sociology and comparative government.

3 Although the socially acknowledged nature of a state's political functions for society is a defining feature of normal states, the forms in which this is institutionalized and expressed vary. I call these functions 'socially acknowledged' because their content is constituted in part through politically relevant discourses, imaginaries, and projects. Even in single states there are, typically, several competing political imaginaries bearing on the tasks of the state and on its contributions to the wider society, which may well be mutually contradictory. This is one area where the threefold distinction between polity, politics, and policy is especially resonant. Moreover, as one might expect, these issues bear directly on critiques of domination and ideology.

4 While coercion is the state's *ultimate* sanction, a state also has other means of intervention at its disposal, both material and symbolic. Their articulation and deployment involves various contradictions and dilemmas and poses important strategic issues (chapter 3).

5 The society whose common interest and general will are administered in line with the state idea is no more an empirical given

than the state is – although the two are sometimes conflated in everyday discourse and theoretical work.[14] Its boundaries and identity are often constituted through the same processes by which states are built, reproduced, and transformed. This is a key aspect in defining and forming the *Staatsvolk* (chapter 6). As an aside, the state idea or state project in this context does not refer to the general legitimation of state authority (for example, in Weberian terms, traditional, rational–legal, or bureaucratic) but to political imaginaries that present the nature and purposes of the state for the wider society in particular periods.

6   Whatever the political rhetoric of the common interest or general will might suggest, these are always 'illusory' insofar as attempts at definition occur on a strategically biased structural and discursive terrain and involve the differential articulation and aggregation of interests, opinions, and values. The common interest or the general will is always asymmetrical, marginalizing or defining some interests at the same time as it privileges others. There is never a general interest that embraces all possible particular interests (see also chapter 4). This is reflected in Abram's notion of the 'state idea' and is an important area for the development of *Ideologiekritik*.

Interim Conclusions

Four provisional lessons can now be drawn. First, let me endorse Abrams' recommendation that we focus on the complexities of the actually existing state system and acknowledge the obfuscating role of the state idea regarding the state as a system of domination. Seen in these terms, the aim of state theory should be to demystify the state or, in Michel Foucault's phrase, to 'cut off the King's head' (1980: 121) by removing the sovereign state from its privileged position in political analysis. This conclusion prepares the ground, second, for a critical engagement with the state that combines historical semantics, a critique of domination, and a critique of ideology. A third preliminary lesson is that the state is a complex and polymorphous reality that is best analysed from several entry points and standpoints rather than by focusing one-sidedly on just one of its elements and possible crystallizations. Nonetheless (and this is the fourth lesson), in order to move the analysis forward rather than remain mired in a conceptual morass, we need a preliminary definition of the state. The fourfold definition given above can provide a starting point for analysis but should not constitute its endpoint.

To make this analysis more specific, a hierarchy of concepts can be developed: this would move from the abstract, formal concept of statehood down to ever more highly specified types of political regime. The most abstract level requires an account that establishes the generic elements of the state as a form of political organization (see above). This can inform both the history of state formation and comparative analyses. Beneath the concept of statehood come different types of state, associated with different types of social formation – the latter being distinguished, for example, in terms of their dominant modes of production or their main axial principle of societal organization. Next we could delineate typical variant historical forms and, at the next level, distinguish between normal and exceptional types of state[15] and their variant forms (chapter 9). A further step might be to differentiate types of regime in terms of the specific articulation of their modes of representation, internal architecture, forms of intervention, social bases, state projects, and hegemonic visions (chapter 3).

Such a conceptual hierarchy also enables critique of the state, state idea, and state power to be conducted at different levels of generality, which can range from a transhistorical anarchist critique of the state as a machine of domination rather than embodiment of a society's general will down to, say, a specific critique of the policies pursued in an 'economic emergency' that rescues large financial institutions and imposes austerity on the population in the name of the state's responsibility for maintaining sound finance, in the national interest. A conceptual hierarchy such as this also gives a far better basis for analysing the state than a single definition would and provides a heuristic for examining stateness as a variable. This approach will be explored in several chapters below.

3

The State as a Social Relation

The present chapter elaborates a strategic–relational approach to the state. This approach shifts focus from the state to the topic of state power and rests on the enigmatic claim that the state is a social relation. This claim can be translated into an apparently concept-begging, six-part proposition that 'the state' may be fruitfully analysed in the following terms: (1) the exercise of state power (2) as an institutionally and discursively mediated condensation (a reflection and refraction) (3) of a changing balance of forces, (4) which seek to influence the forms, purposes, and content of the polity, politics, and policy (5) in specific conjunctures, marked by a variable mix of opportunities and constraints, (6) themselves linked to the wider natural and social environment. The chapter unpacks this overly condensed proposition and seeks to show its heuristic value. In terms of the four-element approach, the chapter is mainly concerned with the state apparatus and the idea of the state. Later chapters consider other elements in greater detail.

The Strategic–Relational Approach

Building on the work of Karl Marx and Antonio Gramsci among others, Nicos Poulantzas, a postwar Greek political theorist whose most intellectually productive years were spent in Paris, proposed a better response to the difficulties of studying the state than the prevailing mainstream alternatives. His solution derived from his historical reinterpretation of Italian fascism and German national socialism in the interwar years and from his broadly contemporaneous analyses of the fall of the military dictatorships in Greece, Portugal, and Spain in the mid-1970s. He argued that the state is best studied as a social relation. This implies that, whether regarded as a thing (or, better, as an institutional ensemble) or as a subject (or, better, as the repository of specific political capacities and resources), the state is far from a passive tool or neutral actor. Instead, 'like "capital", *it is...a relationship of forces, or more precisely the material condensation of such a relationship among classes and class fractions, such as this is expressed within the State in a necessarily specific form'* (Poulantzas 1978: 128–9). This elaboration reflects Poulantzas's concern with the class character of the state but also has a more general force. It postulates that the state has inbuilt biases that privilege some agents and interests over others; but whether, how, and how far these biases are actualized depends on the changing balance of forces and their strategies and tactics. Poulantzas added that social conflicts and contradictions are reproduced inside the state, albeit in ways that reflect its specific forms of organization and operation (Poulantzas 1978; for comment, see Jessop 1985; Wissel 2007; Bretthauer et al. 2011).

The present author elaborated this distinctive perspective as the strategic–relational approach (hereafter SRA), initially in the field of state theory and then for issues of structure and agency more generally (Jessop 2007b). Others, especially the British political scientist Colin Hay, have also elaborated, operationalized, and applied the SRA (Hay 1995, 2002; Brenner 2004; Heigl 2011; Clark and Jones 2012; Valler, Tait, and Marshall 2013; Boukalas 2014a). Those who use the SRA reject attempts to capture the 'essence' of the state and aim instead to elaborate useful theoretical and methodological tools to study its changing forms, functions, and effects. Instead of looking at the state as a substantial, unified thing or unitary subject, the SRA widens its focus, so as to capture not just the state apparatus but the exercise and effects of *state power* as a contingent expression of a changing balance of forces that seek to advance their respective interests inside, through, and against the state system. Political and politically relevant struggles can take many forms, ranging from consensus-oriented debates over the (always illusory) common interest to open, systematic, and bloody civil wars or acts of genocide. The changing balance of forces is mediated institutionally, discursively, and through governmental technologies. It is conditioned by the specific institutional structures and procedures of the state apparatus as embedded in the wider political system and environing societal relations. The effectiveness of state capacities depends in turn on links to forces that operate beyond the state's formal boundaries and act as 'force multipliers' or, conversely, divert, subvert, or block its interventions.

The interaction of the structurally inscribed strategic selectivity of the state system and competing forces with diverse strategies generates a 'state effect' (Jessop 1990: 9; cf. Mitchell 1999; Foucault 2007; Bourdieu 2014). Developing this approach can help to interpret and elaborate upon Abrams's arguments about the state system and to link it to different types of misrepresentation or misrecognition of the state as a system of domination. It also offers one way to create a structure–agency dialectics in state theory around issues of path dependency and path shaping.

The SRA derives its self-designation from its respecification of structure and agency in relational terms. It highlights the importance of the strategic context of action and the transformative power of actions. In these terms, structure consists in differential constraints and opportunities that vary by agent; agency in turn depends on strategic capacities that vary by structure as well as according to the actors involved. This complementary pair of statements can be contrasted with the more usual mainstream approach that regards structure as equally constraining or facilitating for all agents. In particular, the SRA emphasizes that the biased composition of constraints and opportunities can only be understood in relation to specific strategies pursued by specific forces in order to advance specific interests over a given time horizon in terms of a specific set of other forces, each advancing its interests through specific strategies. This invites consideration of whether – and, if so, how – politically relevant actors (individual or collective) take account of this differential privileging by engaging in 'strategic context' analysis when choosing a course of action. In other words, to what extent do they act routinely or habitually, as opposed to evaluating the current situation in terms of the changing 'art of the possible' over different spatiotemporal horizons of action?

Because structures are only *strategically selective* rather than *absolutely constraining*, scope exists for actions to overwhelm, circumvent, or subvert structural constraints. Likewise, because subjects are never unitary, never fully aware of the conditions that affect (their) strategic action, never fully equipped to engage in strategic reflection and learning, there are no guarantees that they will largely realize their strategic goals. Indeed, for most subjects, this is unlikely. In addition, changes in the identities, interests, resources, goals, strategies, and tactics of particular forces also modify the emergent constraints and opportunities associated with particular structures. In turn the calculating subjects that operate on the strategic terrain constituted by the state are in part constituted by the current strategic selectivity of the state system (its forms of representation, its internal structure, and its forms of intervention) as well as by past state interventions. I will relate this shortly to the six dimensions of the state system and its embedding in the wider social order. Current statal biases are in part the result of interactions between past patterns of strategic selectivity and the strategies (successful or not) adopted for its transformation.

A spiral of path dependency and path shaping operates here. Opportunities for reorganizing specific structures and for strategic reorientation are themselves subject to structurally inscribed strategic selectivities. For example, it may be necessary to pursue strategies over several spatial and temporal horizons of action and to mobilize different sets of social forces in different contexts to eliminate or modify specific constraints and opportunities inscribed in particular state structures. Over time, reflexively reorganized structures and recursively selected strategies and tactics coevolve to generate a relatively stable order; but this may well depend on an ensemble of institutional and spatiotemporal fixes that secures stability at the cost of displacing problems elsewhere or deferring them to the future (chapters 4 and 7).

The balance of forces also changes with shifts in the strategic terrains of the economy, state, and wider social formation as well as with changes in the organization, strategy, and tactics of specific forces. A given type of state, state form, or regime will be more accessible to some forces than to others, according to the strategies that such forces adopt to win state power. This indicates the need for historical analyses of changing forms of statehood, for example, to be made in terms of types of state (e.g., feudal vs capitalist), state forms (e.g., absolutist, liberal, interventionist), modes of political representation (e.g., democratic vs despotic), political regimes (e.g., military, fascist, or bureaucratic authoritarian exceptional regimes or parliamentary, presidential, mass plebiscitary democratic regimes), particular policy paradigms (e.g., Keynesian demand management vs neoliberal supply-side policies), and so on (Jessop 1982, 1990, 2007b). The historical and formal constitution of states always results from past struggles and is reproduced (or transformed) in and through struggle.

As an ensemble of power centres and capacities that offer unequal chances to different forces within and outside the state, the state cannot exercise power. In other words, it is not the state as such that exercises power. Instead its powers (plural) are activated by changing sets of politicians and state officials located in specific parts of the state, in specific conjunctures. Although these 'insiders' are key players in the exercise of state powers, they always act in relation to a wider balance of forces within and beyond a given state. To talk of state managers, let alone of the state itself, exercising power masks a complex set of social relations that extend well beyond the state system and its distinctive capacities. The constitutionalization and centralization of state power in the modern state, which enables responsibility to be formally attributed to named officials and bodies, may be useful for holding political actors accountable, in elections or other forums; but it also misrepresents the complex and mediated ways in which power circulates within and beyond the state. The ambivalence of power is often voiced by state managers themselves. Sometimes they proudly claim credit for having initiated and carried through a general strategic line or a specific policy; at other times they happily seek to offload responsibility for state actions or outcomes to other social forces (or to *force majeure*) in the struggle over power.

How and how far state powers (and any associated liabilities, vulnerabilities, and incapacities) are actualized depends on the action, reaction, and interaction of specific social forces located in and beyond the state. These in turn depend on the structural ties between the state and its encompassing political system, on strategic links among state managers and other political forces, and on the complex web of interdependencies and social networks linking the state and the political system to its broader environment.

Exploring these themes highlights the role of strategic concepts in analysing state apparatuses and state power. Given the existence of social contradictions and political struggles as well as the internal conflicts and rivalries among the state's diverse tiers and branches, the state's capacity to act as a unified political force – insofar as it does so – depends on widespread acceptance, within the state apparatus, of a relatively coherent (and unifying) state project. If an overall strategic line is discernible in the exercise of state powers, it is due, as Michel Foucault and Nicos Poulantzas emphasized, to strategic coordination enabled through the selectivity of the state system – and, for Poulantzas, also through parallel power networks that cross-cut and unify the state's formal structures and connect them to civil society (Foucault 1980, 2007; Poulantzas 1978; compare the remarks on the 'deep state' in the next section and in chapter 9).

Relevant strategic concepts for states in capitalist societies include state-sponsored *economic strategies* – which may originate elsewhere – oriented to economic development and, in a specifically capitalist context, to differential accumulation (i.e., above-average competitiveness and profits, however derived); *state projects* oriented to creating and reproducing the institutional unity of states; and *hegemonic visions* about the nature and purposes of the state for the wider society. These concepts involve specific articulations of elements drawn from wider technological, economic, juridico-political, and

Table 3.1 Six dimensions of the state and their crisis tendencies

Dimension	Definition	Significance for SRA	Crisis Aspects
Three formal dimensions			
Modes of representation	These give social forces access to the state apparatus and to its capacities	Unequal access to state Unequal ability to resist at distance from state	Crisis of representation
Modes of articulation	Institutional architecture the levels and branches of the state	Unequal capacity to shape, make, and implement decisions	Crisis of institutional integration
Modes of intervention	Modes of intervention inside the state and beyond it	Different sites and mechanisms of intervention	Rationality crisis
Three substantive dimensions			
Social basis of state	Institutionalized social compromise	Uneven distribution of material and symbolic concessions to the 'population' in order to secure support for the state, state projects, specific policy sets, and hegemonic visions	Crisis of the power bloc Disaffection with parties and the state Civil unrest, civil war, revolution
State project	Secures operational unity of the state and its capacity to act	Overcomes improbability of unified state system by orienting state agencies and agents	Legitimacy crisis
Hegemonic vision	Defines nature and purposes of the state for the wider social formation	Provides legitimacy for the state, defined in terms of promoting common good, etc.	Crisis of hegemony

Source: Original compilation based on arguments in this chapter

social imaginaries, and their success depends on complementarities with the deeper structure and logics of a given social formation and its insertion into the world market, interstate system, and world society. Such strategies, projects, and visions are most likely to succeed where they address the major structural constraints associated with the dominant institutional orders and with the prevailing balance of forces, as well as with the conjunctural opportunities that could be opened by new alliances, strategies, spatiotemporal horizons of action, and so on. There are, of course, many other kinds of imaginary and strategy, which might be explored in relation to other principles of societalization or sets of social forces, identities, and ideal and material interests.

Indeed, although this approach was first developed in relation to political class domination mediated through the state and the balance of political forces, it can be extended fruitfully to other forms of social domination. These include (but are far from being exhausted by) gender, ethnicity, 'race', generation, religion, political alignment, or regional location. Indeed a concern with other points of reference and principles of explanation is needed in order to theorize and explain concrete, complex phenomena adequately. Exploring states in this way does not exclude specific state-engendered and state-mediated structures and processes: it actually presupposes them.

To translate this account into detailed analyses of specific political periods, stages, or conjunctures requires work on three interrelated moments: (1) the state's historical and formal constitution as a complex institutional ensemble, with a spatiotemporally specific pattern of 'strategic selectivity' that reflects and modifies the balance of forces; (2) the historical and substantive organization and configuration of political forces in specific conjunctures and their strategies, including their capacity to reflect on and respond to the strategic selectivities inscribed in the state apparatus as a whole; and (3) the interaction of these forces, on this strategically selective terrain or at a distance from it, as they pursue immediate goals or seek to alter the balance of forces or to transform the state and its basic strategic selectivities. I address state building in chapter 5 and turn now to the state's historical and substantive organization.

Dimensions of the State

To develop the SRA, it is useful to explore six dimensions of the state that can be studied from the most basic state forms through to specific regimes in particular conjunctures (see Table 3.1). Three of these dimensions concern mainly formal institutional aspects. They are modes of political representation and their articulation; the vertical, horizontal, and transversal articulation of the state as an institutional ensemble and its demarcation from, and relation to, other states; and mechanisms and modes of state intervention and their overall articulation. Each dimension has its own strategic selectivities and, while each one is analytically distinct, they all overlap empirically. The other three dimensions concern the discursive and action-oriented aspects of the state and give content and strategic meaning to its more formal features. They are the social bases that provide a stable core of support for the state and comprise its principal material or symbolic beneficiaries – or both; the 'state projects' that shape its internal unity and modus operandi (modes of policymaking, etc.); and the 'hegemonic visions' that define the nature and purposes of the state for the wider society or world. The last two dimensions relate to the 'part–whole' paradox that the state is just one institutional order (with its own problematic unity) among many in a given society, yet is also charged with responsibility for securing the integration and cohesion of that society.

The seemingly one-to-one correspondence between the three formal and the three substantive dimensions – representation–social base, architecture–state project, and intervention–hegemonic vision – is unintended. While they are distinguished analytically for presentational purposes, there are linkages and potential disjunctions *within* each set and cross-cutting connections between them. As a final caution for now, these dimensions should not be studied solely at the national level. For, even in the heyday of the national territorial state, politics was also articulated on other forms of areal organization and on other scalar grids of political practice. In other times and places, the complexities of spatial organization have been even more important in the period when the national state was the main form of the territorialization of political power (see chapter 5).

While not exhaustive, these six dimensions, taken together, provide an initial framework for analysing major aspects of the state, for comparing 'normal' and 'exceptional' forms (chapter 9), and for describing the hybrid character of particular states and their strategic selectivities. Indeed the internal organization of the state system has a key role in maintaining the hierarchies among forms of representation and intervention. Incongruence among these forms can lead to crisis within the state. A well-known example, studied in the 1920s and 1930s, is the crisis of liberal parliamentarism that followed the rise of mass politics and the expansion of the state's economic intervention (Schmitt 1988; Scheuerman 1996). More generally, this matrix helps to identify aspects of state crisis that take us beyond the three elements approach presented in chapter 2. Thus one could include representational, institutional, rationality, legitimacy, authority, and hegemonic crises of the state.[1]

Modes of political representation and their articulation

Although these may be formally defined in a constitution, constitutionally designated institutions may not be the most important mechanisms of political representation. Some may be more symbolic or 'dignified', some more 'efficient' even if informal. Using this distinction, which he himself introduced, Walter Bagehot contrasted the respective roles of Crown and Cabinet in the English constitution (Bagehot 1963). A key question for the critique of domination today is to separate the 'efficient' parts of the state from the 'dignified' parts (see chapter 9). A similar observation leads to the use of feudal metaphors to describe important *de facto* branches of government. Well-known examples are the 'fourth estate' (usually the press, occasionally the mob, the popular masses, or the proletariat)[2] and the 'fifth estate' (variously the trade unions, social media networks, or the new precariat).[3] Another useful concept is 'parallel power network' (mentioned above, but explored in more detail below). One must identify the actual modes of political representation at various sites and scales of action and how they operate, both formally and informally, to enable political forces to voice and promote their contingent material interests and their unconditional ideal interests (or values) by virtue of their differential access to centres of political formation, decision making, and implementation.[4]

Although access to the state apparatus in its narrow sense matters most for politics and policy, political representation also occurs away from the state insofar as official decisions take account of (potential) support or resistance. While formal channels of representation are important, they must be related to the roles played by political parties, various types of corporatist body, lobbies and pressure groups, old and new social movements, and state managers. (On the influence of electoral systems, see, for example, Grofman and Lijphart 2003; on political parties, see below.) These agents all provide links to the social bases of the state and help to organize them. The mediatization of politics has also become increasingly important – both as a relay of political interests and demands and as a distinct but internally differentiated force in its own right. (On the mediatization of politics, see Cook 2005; Esser and Strömback 2014; Luhmann 2000; Meyer

2002; Kriesi et al., 2013.) Groups without access to hegemonic media therefore tend to become marginalized in 'normal' conditions, but sub- and counter-hegemonic media channels can facilitate political mobilization in less institutionalized forms of mass politics. This explains the recent use of 'fifth estate' to denote decentralized social media and the so-called blogosphere.

It is useful to list five ideal–typical modes of representation, without claiming them to be exhaustive. They comprise clientelism, corporatism, parliamentarism, pluralism, and *raison d'état*. *Clientelism* is based on the exchange of political support in return for a favourable allocation of politically mediated resources. It involves a hierarchical relationship between dependent client(s) and superordinate patron(s). It is associated with cadre parties run by notables, with patronage parties, and with classical party machine politics.

Corporatism involves political representation on the basis of a socially designated function, role, or task within the division of labour in a given economic space and is characterized by the formal equivalence of 'corporations' whose members perform substantively different functions. It may be associated with multiple functional corporations (e.g., classically, Italian fascism) or with tripartism (e.g., classically, big business, big labour, and big government in the era of Atlantic Fordism). As Max Weber noted almost one hundred years ago, corporatist organizations are prone to factionalism (Weber 1994: 351–2), which limits their representative role. More generally, considered in abstract terms, corporatism as defined here is also found in patterns of governance based on networks that link groups with different roles in the wider social division of labour (see chapter 7).

Parliamentarism is based on the indirect participation in policy-making of *formally* equal individual 'citizens', through their exercise of voting and accompanying rights, in relation to an elected legislature or political executive (including here direct elections for a president with 'efficient' rather than 'dignified' powers). The extent of substantive equality can be quite different, depending on the role and sources of money in campaigning (see, notoriously, the effects of the 2010 Citizens United *v.* Federal Election Commission decision in the US). Parliamentarism is associated with a territorial basis of political organization (local constituencies) and is typically mediated through the organization of political parties. (On changing party forms and party dynamics, see the excursus on parties below.)

Pluralism is based on institutionalized channels of access to state apparatuses for political forces with voluntary membership, which represent interests or causes rooted in civil society (as opposed to function in the division of labour) and are recognized as legitimate by relevant branches of the state. This access is far from even: it does not occur on the proverbial 'level playing field'. Moreover, pluralist bodies face pressures to adapt to the structures and operational logic of the state. And, conversely, there is an ever-present possibility of 'disruptive' actions at a distance from the state that nonetheless enter into political calculation.

Pluralism in this context must be distinguished from pluralism and neopluralism as theoretical and methodological approaches in political science. Three key differences are the following. First, (neo)pluralism is an approach developed in opposition to constitutional and institutionalist approaches; as such, it emphasizes the importance of conflict, competition, and coalition building as the driving force in political stability and change. Second, such strategies and tactics can occur on different kinds of political terrain (including clientelism, parliamentarism, and corporatism) and are not, therefore, distinct modes of representation. Third, (neo)pluralism includes a wide range of individual and group actors with equally diverse power resources, interests, and values rather than being limited, as proposed in my own definition of pluralism presented above, to interests and causes rooted in 'civil society' (cf. Bentley 1908; McFarland 2004; Cerny 2010). The SRA advanced in this chapter presents some similarities with (neo)pluralism in its concern with the changing balance of diverse forces, its sensitivity to cross-cutting and intersecting groups and social forces, and its concern with conflict, competition, and coalition building. It differs in that it gives equal weight, analytically, to the structurally inscribed, strategic, selective asymmetries involved in institutions, institutional orders, and societal configurations. (For a recent statement that concedes these points in general terms, claiming – to my mind unconvincingly – that they have been integrated into neopluralism, see Cerny 2010: 10–11 and passim.) Furthermore, compared with the specific version of the SRA developed here and in my other work, (neo)pluralism is less attuned to the specificities of the capital relation – especially its inherent structural contradictions, strategic dilemmas, and social antagonisms; to the relative primacy of profit-oriented, market-mediated accumulation as a principle of societal organization; and to the ways in which these shape the overall pattern of constraints and opportunities in contemporary societies.

Raison d'état – the fifth mode of representation considered here – is a limit case of intervention without formal channels of representation. It involves attempts to legitimate such intervention by appeal to threats to the security of the state itself, to the security of society, or to some significant national or public interest.[5] The sovereign power may then engage in any act it deems necessary for preserving 'security', even if this act would normally be *ultra vires* ('beyond powers', i.e. it would exceed legal authority) or plain illegal. In many cases the interests of the state and those of the people are conflated and one or both are invoked in declaring a state of emergency and, more generally, in legitimating the practices of exceptional states. (On states of emergency, commissarial and constitutional dictatorships, the 'deep state', and exceptional regimes, see chapter 9.)

Raison d'état may be linked to informal channels of representation, such as parallel power networks that extend beyond the formal boundaries of the state to establish cross-cutting networks and complexes of power. These form the hard kernel of the state, which operates in a grey area between legality and illegality and shapes key political processes and policy issues. Other terms used to denote this phenomenon in particular contexts are 'dual state' (Morgenthau 1962, Fraenkel 1941), 'state within the state' (sometimes denoting the church, more often the police, the army, and the security apparatus), 'security state' (Tunander 2009), 'deep state' (Park 2008, Scott 2014a), and 'fourth branch' (Engelhardt 2014).

The principle of *raison d'état* has become more significant in recent decades. It is invoked in wars on terrorism, itself a term of growing elasticity, which covers many acts of political protest and civil disobedience, and even whistleblowing and investigative journalism. In states based on the rule of law, invoking *raison d'état* is usually subject to judicial intercession (real-time veto), subsequent inquiry, and possible post hoc sanction – or, after a return to political 'business as usual', legislative or electoral sanction. But, with the increasing consolidation of authoritarian statism, this principle is now more often honoured in the breach than in the observance (see chapter 9).

These forms of representation have definite (but not fully determinate) effects on how political forces are constituted, as well as on their ability to access the state system. Thus parliamentarism encourages the political fragmentation and disorganization of economic categories in favour of conceptions of individual citizenship, competing fisco-financial and client group interests, noneconomic identities, and territorial divisions. In contrast, corporatism promotes the organization of economic classes into distinct, formally equivalent, and interdependent functional groupings that are all expected to gain from collaboration and concerted action. Thus it discourages the organization of producer groups as polarized, antagonistic, contradictory classes and may also serve to depoliticize issues. For example, corporatist forms of organization were often introduced to address long-term economic and social issues where complex, reciprocal interdependence requires long-term cooperation – thereby placing the relevant policy areas outside the short-term time horizons of electoral cycles and parliamentary infighting, in the expectation (whether cognitive or normative) that the organizations involved – or at least their leaders – would act in 'nonpolitical' ways to implement policies in the national interest (e.g., wage restraint in tripartite bodies).

Clientelism and pluralism promote the particularistic reproduction of specific 'economic–corporate' and 'civil–corporate' interests and can lead to deadlock, stalemate, or centrist coalitions based on self-interested tactical alliances. In contrast, parliamentarism provides a medium through which political parties *may* seek to mobilize political support behind more encompassing state and hegemonic projects and thereby may help to consolidate an inclusive political, intellectual, and moral leadership. Nonetheless there are mixed forms, as in political parties that rely on patronage or spoils to secure support, or on programmes that appeal to sectional interests rather than to a national popular project (see the excursus on parties). A final example of such political effects is how corporatism benefits producer groups at the expense of consumers as well as forces seeking representation via electoral channels. Formal aspects apart, the selectivities of modes of representation also depend on the forces in contention and the links between representation and intervention. Channels of representation also exist in exceptional regimes, with major differences between authoritarian and totalitarian states in terms of the scope for advancing specific ideal and material interests (see Linz 2000; see also chapter 9).

The forms of representation also influence the identity and organization of the forces seeking representation; and this in turn leads to efforts to reorganize the forms, with a view to changing these forces or the balance of power between them. For this reason, classes should not be seen as pre-constituted political forces that exist outside and independently of the state and can manipulate it as a simple, passive instrument. For, although classes as objective categories of economic agents are defined primarily in terms of their place within the social relations of production, their political weight depends on the forms of organization and means of intervention through which their economic (and other) class interests are expressed. In this sense one can say that political class struggle is, first of all, a struggle to constitute classes as political forces – even before it is a struggle among classes (Przeworski 1977: 371–3). Similar reflections apply to other political forces, whether primarily class-based or not. This reinforces the view that the state can be studied as a system of political [class] domination whose structure has a definite effect on social struggle through its role in determining the balance of forces and the forms of political action. *Prima facie* support for this conclusion is provided by the strategic and tactical calculations behind efforts to reorganize specific modes and to modify their weight in the system of representation. In extreme cases, of course, this can lead to the suspension of the electoral principle or to the banning of certain political organizations, if not to both (see chapter 9).

The institutional architecture of the state

This dimension concerns the internal vertical, horizontal, and transversal organization of the state system as expressed through the distribution of powers among its parts, considered territorially and functionally. Obvious issues here are the relative weight of the legislative and executive branches of government, whether formally specified or simply reproduced in routine interaction(s), and the extent to which there is at least formal scope for oversight and veto of executive actions by an external authority or power (judiciary, church, or mob). Attention should also be paid to the weight of various parts of the administrative apparatus, the role of law, money, and knowledge in its internal organization, mechanisms of recruitment of state officials and to what extent they own their offices and means of administration, and the form and extent of its administrative unity. Too rigid a prescription of these arrangements and rules can limit institutional innovation and adaptability to unexpected shocks (see also the discussion of states of emergency below). Increasingly important here are the relations between national territorial states and emergent trans- and supranational state forms, as well as among central, local, regional, and parastatal forms of rule. According to Finer's (1997a, 1997b, 1997c) research on 5,200 years of state history, how well this institutional structure is designed and what its capacity for relatively unified action is are matters that constitute the secret of durable governments.

The concept of institutional architecture might imply a static view of the state apparatus. But attempts are regularly made to reorganize the division of political labour within the state and the wider political system. This can occur through institutional differentiation, through dedifferentiation, by adding new tiers or scales, or by moving particular topics across the state's branches and departments. The 'normal' forms of politics vary across branches of government: for example, there can be partisan and adversarial politics in legislatures, concern with the 'national interest' – if only as a legitimation – in the political executive, rational–legal administration in bureaucracies, formal legal reasoning in courts, and constitutional interpretation in supreme courts. The resulting checks and balances and countervailing powers may restrict politics as the art of the possible, and they may introduce frictions and delays into the political process when major changes are sought. This can occur when administrative or judicial offices or key positions in quangos (quasi-autonomous nongovernmental organizations) are allocated through a spoils system or, again, when bureaucrats do not act as good, Weberian officials, *sine ira et studio* ('without anger or enthusiasm'), but have their own personal, partisan, or sectional political agendas (Peters and Pierre 2004). Likewise, for regulators, the co-production of regulatory practices and the objects and subjects of regulation can create regulatory capture or willing submission to sectors that might offer lucrative future employment.

Ignoring this dimension would lead to the state being seen as a 'black box' inside which external demands and support somehow get translated in unknowable ways into specific policies that are then directed outwards. A 'black box' view assumes a rigid distinction between 'inputs' and 'outputs', neglecting what systems theorists call 'withinputs'. More importantly, it ignores the wide range of *sui generis* forms of organization and statecraft concerned with maintaining the state system itself as a mode of political domination. This requires not only the mobilization of resources for the state's continued operations – for instance finance, personnel, information, means of administration – but also the formal and substantive coordination of its different branches and activities. Balancing competing forces and interests is crucial here (compare Finer 1997a on the challenge that ancient states faced in controlling the military and in moderating the demands of temple priests). It is not easy to secure the unity of the state apparatus as an institutional ensemble and as an organ of societal domination. It has its own specialized fields and guidance in areas such as statecraft, state science, mercantilism, cameralistics (that is, the science of public finance, including raising revenue and controlling expenditure),[6] public administration, new public management, and so on.

The state's formal–institutional unity is typically related to bureaucratization. This involves (1) the formation of a special category of career officials, separated from the ownership of the means of administration, and (2) their subordination to formal rules of legal and financial accountability within a hierarchical chain of command that links different levels and branches of the state. The growth of bureaucracy involves an increasingly specialized division of tasks and more layers of command and execution (the role of bureaucratization in the transition from chiefdom to primary state formation is discussed in chapter 5). However, the extent to which this formal unity is also substantive depends on the extent of unity of the political executive at the top of the command chain; and, because the state is a 'peopled organization' (Jones 2007), it and can be circumscribed or undermined through the resistance or noncompliance of officials at other levels or in other branches of the state system. Moreover, although bureaucratic forms are appropriate to the execution of general laws or policies in accordance with the rule of law, they are less suited to ad hoc, discretionary forms of intervention, big one-off projects, or responsiveness to participatory forms of decision making and implementation (cf. Offe 1975). Indeed, the bureaucratic preconditions for the formal unity of the state system may limit the substantive efficacy of policies oriented to accumulation, legitimacy, and social cohesion. This is reflected in the coexistence of formal bureaucracy governed by clear procedures and more informal, flexible, or ad hoc modes of intervention. Corporatism, public–private partnerships, contracting out, regulated self-regulation, and so forth are different examples of these hybrid mechanisms that straddle the public–private divide. These generate interesting problems in the process of defining the formal boundaries of the state *qua* institutional ensemble; they also threaten the substantive unity of the state through their potential for clientelistic degeneration and through the pursuit of particular 'economic–corporate' demands. This suggests the need for bureaucratic mechanisms to be controlled by an overarching political executive authority or by cross-cutting networks that can secure the relative unity of state action.

The articulation of the branches and departments of the state system (including quasi-nongovernmental organizations and similar bodies) helps to structure power relations. The relative dominance of departments or ministries can underwrite the hegemony of specific material and ideal interests. For example, the dominant role of the Treasury–Bank of England nexus in Britain is an important element in the structural determination of the hegemony of national and international commercial and banking capital (cf. Ingham 1984; on the analogous 'dollar–Wall Street regime', see Gowan 2000). It continues to the present period, as successive UK governments have promoted the interests of the City of London as a financial centre for international capital and, in the last thirty years, a neoliberal, finance-dominated accumulation regime that favours London and the rest of the south-east of England. Likewise, for some thirty years, the

Ministry of International Trade and Industry in Japan actively promoted the interests of Japanese industrial capital through its industrial policies (cf. Johnson 1982). The National Security Agency has played a powerful, ever expanding, and largely hidden role in foreign security issues in the United States since 1949 (Stuart 2008; Glennon 2014) and it is also an important part, along with the Pentagon, of the American political–economic policy apparatus (Weiss 2013). A more recent example, marking a radical shift in the structure of domestic power in the United States, is the establishment and expansion of the Department of Homeland Security as a key transformational moment in the rise of a permanent state of exception (Boukalas 2014a; cf. Hodai 2013).

This structural dominance must be combined with a widely accepted 'hegemonic project' if the structurally privileged fraction is to become truly hegemonic; but, in the absence of this condition, state structures can undermine the pursuit of a project favourable to a class or class fraction other than the structurally privileged. This can be seen in the British Labour government's failure to pursue its project of industrial modernization and economic planning during its 1964–70 tenure of office. For, although it established a new planning ministry favourable to industrial capital in the Department of Economic Affairs and undertook other initiatives to promote industrial reorganization, the Treasury and the Bank of England remained dominant and were able to use their fiscal, expenditure, and monetary powers to turn the crisis of Britain's flawed Fordism to the advantage of banking capital. More recent examples of this tension are the opposition between 'Main Street' and 'Wall Street', in which systematic investment in infrastructure favourable to profit-generating capital is marginalized thanks to the structural dominance inside national, transnational, and international state apparatuses of interest-bearing capital (Ingham 1984; Gowan 2000; Harvey 2005; Peet 2011; Lapavitsas 2013). This indicates that a long-term shift in hegemony requires not only a new 'hegemonic project' but also the reorganization of the state system towards underwriting a more durable shift in the balance of forces.

The internal structure of the state is also crucial when considering 'normal' and 'exceptional' regimes. For, whereas normal states can be categorized in the first instance in terms of the relative dominance of different channels of 'democratic' representation (clientelist, corporatist, parliamentary, and pluralist), exceptional states can be differentiated in the first instance in terms of the relative dominance of different state apparatuses (such as the military, bureaucracy, political police, the security branch, the fascist party, religious police, or economic ministries). In the case of normal states, the hierarchy of state apparatuses provides a further means of distinguishing political regimes and their various selectivities; and, for exceptional regimes, it is important to examine the relative primacy of different channels of representation, especially to the dominant state apparatus. Combining forms of representation and the internal architecture of the state provides an initial perspective on the forms and extent of 'despotic power' – that is, following Michael Mann (1984: 187–8), the state's ability to act freely without the need for routine institutionalized negotiations with civil society groups. This said, the distinctions introduced above provide a more nuanced way of assessing the *potential* for despotic power, but its actual extent will also depend on the social bases of the state, the character of state projects and political imaginaries, and the extent to which state power involves hegemony as well as coercion.

The mechanisms and modes of state intervention and their overall articulation

This dimension concerns various forms of intervention beyond the boundaries of the state system in its narrow sense. It involves not only the state's role in demarcating the changing boundaries between public and private (cf. Mitchell 1991), but also the institutional and organizational mechanisms and resources available for intervention. These shape the art of the possible, whether the state appears to act despotically (or alone) or in more or less open alliance or coordination with other political forces. In consequence, this dimension also concerns what Michael Mann calls the state's infrastructural power: its capacities to penetrate society and organize social relations throughout its territory, on the basis of its political decisions (Mann 1984: 189; cf. Mann 2008).[7] These capacities are relational. For, even when they meet no resistance, states are not omnicompetent – because every mode of intervention has its strengths and weaknesses. An initial classification of general means of intervention includes: organized coercion; law, whether conforming to the general standards of the rule of law or a more contingent or reflexive kind; money, including credit and taxation; and knowledge (Willke 1992).

But this macroscopic classification, partial as it is, must be supplemented with more detailed studies of the microphysics of state power. The analysis of the latter is particularly associated nowadays with Foucault, actor–network theory, and other practice-oriented accounts of disciplinarity and normalization (e.g., Foucault 1980, 2007, 2008; Latour 2005, 2010; Law 2009; MacKay 2006; Scott 1998;

Miller and Rose 2008). It nonetheless has a longer history in the study of statecraft. These micro-concerns raise issues about the outer boundaries of the state apparatus and their overlap with other institutional orders, civil society, and the everyday world. This explains the growing interest in governance and governmentality as distinctive sets of practices connecting the state and other institutional orders (chapter 7).

As an aside, there is at least one aspect of state intervention that also concerns the other two formal features of the state: its character as a tax state. The state's need for revenues, especially through taxation (and, at first, often in connection with war) has been the basis for extending representation on the basis of the principle 'no taxation without representation'. Money is a key resource for the state, especially as it moves from despotic to infrastructural power. And its direct dependence on tax revenues designed to fund its activities or to act as security for government loans and bonds is a source of mercantile or capitalist power vis-à-vis the state (see chapter 4).

In addition, combined with demands for state expenditure – whether electorally driven, policy-driven, or based on alleged military or economic imperatives – this dependence can lead to fisco-financial crises. The latter may originate externally or derive from pressures generated inside the state system. They include crises over the right to taxation (with or without representation) and over tax resistance or avoidance; crises of institutional integration and coordination within the state apparatus; crises affecting the state's capacities for intervention (such that, for example, intervention undermines the tax base); legitimacy crises, as the social basis of the state mobilized behind a particular tax regime fails to consolidate or breaks up; administrative demoralization or disorientation, as political *esprit de corps* is undermined by a failed state project; or a hegemonic crisis around the nature and purposes of government for society (cf. Habermas 1976; Poulantzas 1979). Conversely, as Schumpeter (1954) noted, a fisco-financial crisis could trigger or intensify existing crises in or of the state. This could lead to demands to redesign political representation, reform the state's internal structures and operations, alter the amount and modalities of state intervention, recompose the social bases of the state, redefine state strategies, and alter the balance between consent and coercion to address hegemonic and wider organic crisis (cf. Gramsci 1971; see also O'Connor 1973).

The social bases of state power

This dimension matters because the state is much more than a mechanism to count and weigh 'votes', 'voices', and threats of violence in an instantaneous parallelogram of forces. 'Social basis' refers to the specific configuration of social forces, however identified as subjects and however (dis-)organized as political actors, that support the basic structure of the state system, its mode of operation, and its objectives. In the early stages of state formation and through to the contemporary period, military organization, its social stratification, and its social bases were important factors in the overall configuration of power (cf. Andreski 1968; Finer 1975; Finer 1997a: 15–23, 59–63). In more general terms, the configuration of social bases involves an unstable equilibrium of compromise, which is refracted in the state system. This equilibrium reflects (as well as being constituted through) the projects and demands advanced by different social forces that are represented within and beyond the state system and seek such representation or contest its current forms, functions, and activities. This representation of popular forces matters, especially once the masses formally enter politics (generally through enfranchisement, from the 1870s on in leading western states); but it has always been significant, albeit in different ways according to the form of state. For example, ancient city-states, feudal systems, classical empires, and societies organized along centre–periphery lines, with palace court systems, will not only have different social bases but also different modalities of organizing these bases. In modern states such political support is not reducible to 'consensus' but depends on specific modes of mass integration (or indeed exclusion) that channel, transform, and prioritize demands and manage the flow of material concessions necessary to maintain the underlying 'unstable equilibrium of compromise'. Nor does it exclude conflict over specific policies, as long as this occurs within an agreed institutional framework and an accepted 'policy paradigm', which establishes the parameters of political choice. Social bases are heterogeneous and different social forces vary in their commitment to the state in different conjunctures. There is also much variation in the mix of material concessions, symbolic rewards, and repression directed through the state to different social forces. These variations are typically related to prevailing state projects and hegemonic visions (if any) and to their implications for the form and content of politics.

Two useful concepts for analysing the institutionalized social compromises that define the social bases of the modern state are the power bloc and the hegemonic bloc (Gramsci 1971). A power bloc comprises a durable alliance among dominant classes and class fractions that structures the politics of power and defines the 'art of the possible' on the political scene. It can be represented electorally in one or more natural governing parties, but its durability is grounded in a viable mode of growth and in a solid presence in the wider state system – a presence that includes significant influence over the state project (see below). A hegemonic bloc is a broader ensemble of national popular forces mobilized behind a specific hegemonic project. To the extent that it exists, it reflects the historical unity of ruling classes, supporting classes, mass movements, and intellectuals. It depends on a durable alliance organized by a class (or class fraction) that has proved itself capable of exercising political, intellectual, and moral leadership over the dominant classes and popular forces alike. In different ways, the power bloc and the hegemonic bloc depend on the ability to manage inherently unstable equilibria of compromise through appropriate offensive and defensive strategies and tactics. This helps to create – and is in turn reinforced by – a historical bloc, in other words a mutually supportive relation among the economic base, juridico-political organizations, and the moral and intellectual field (see chapter 4).

Although sometimes criticized for failing to demarcate the state's boundaries, Gramsci was less concerned with the state apparatus than with the modalities of the exercise of state power. For him, state power was shaped by the relation between the state and the institutions and forces in the broader political system and in society as a whole. This is why he highlighted the roles of the party system and of intellectuals in articulating and mediating the relations between political and civil society. It is in the party that the leaders and the state officials are educated (Gramsci 1971; cf. Migliaro and Misuraca 1982: 81; Sassoon 1980: 134–50 and passim). These relations are crucial to the state's own strategic capacities and to the chances of compliance from forces beyond the state. This explains why so many of Gramsci's concepts deal with subjective elements in political life (common sense, identity, will formation, leadership, education, and so on; Jäger 1979). In particular, Gramsci attributed a key organizational role to 'organic intellectuals' who work within and across ethico-juridical and cultural institutions, as well as to political parties and other representative organizations. Intellectuals play different roles according to their social origins, place in the intellectual division of labour, spatiotemporal location, organizational responsibilities (if any), and relations with classes, other social forces, and parties (Portelli 1972). They actively participate in producing state forms and refine the spontaneous philosophy of the sociology of the state (Bourdieu 2014). And they may also be involved in producing and reproducing hegemony, sub-hegemonies, or counter-hegemonies.

Excursus on political parties

Parties have key roles in organizing political power across all six dimensions of the state. Parties and party systems vary across state forms and political regimes; such variations include the 'black parliamentarism'[8] that emerges when normal party politics is banned. Parties change with changing forms of political competition (especially the introduction of the mass franchise), changing forms of state intervention (coercion, law, money, and knowledge), the professionalization of politics, and the external political and extrapolitical environment. A party system, albeit not specific individual parties, is a crucial, indeed nonsubstitutable, element of liberal democratic regimes. This implies that, as formal organizations, parties are tied to the territorialization of political power, which is the prior condition of a representation based on territorially defined constituencies. This relationship stands in contrast, as Max Weber (1994) noted, with the one observed in economic associations, which shape policy on the basis of their economic power rather than on the basis of the individual votes they can muster in elections. It also means that, whereas economic associations can be international or cosmopolitan in character (although sometimes they have a strategic or tactical national 'face'), parties tend to be local, regional, or national, operating on the terrain of territorial constituencies within national states. This also holds for federal systems like the European Union, where European 'parties' are based on shifting alliances or are conglomerates of national parties.

Parties have a key role in reducing the complexity of political issues by packaging policies into programmes; they also mediate the part–whole paradox in the political system by representing particular interests and integrating them into an illusory national popular interest oriented to the political process in a fixed territory. In performing this role, natural governing parties and other programmatic parties have to mediate between many interests – old and new social movements, pressure groups and protest movements, and so on – and the agencies and institutions of the state, corporatist networks, and the media. The part–whole paradox is reflected in the strategic choice between (1) seeking to become a 'natural governing party' and (2) focusing on the representation of particular interests or on single issues (Gamble 1973). Likewise, Müller and Strøm (1999) have discussed trilemmas for party leaders around potentially hard choices among maximizing the votes, shaping the policy, and gaining office; and they show how these trade-offs are shaped in what we could call strategic–relational terms by prevailing electoral systems, membership profiles, party funding, the strategic configuration of competitive party systems, the visibility of party impact on policy, the balance between legislature and executive, and so on.

In all cases, as electioneering machines, parties must win votes in order to influence government through the electoral process – even protest votes have effects in this regard. This is because party politics in parliamentary and presidential regimes always revolves around the calculation of votes, real or potential, and their influence on the balance of forces – and hence on decision making. Thus, given the nature of party competition in well-ordered party systems, compromise *tends* to prevail in interparty relations and in parliamentary politics, in the form of electoral compromise or compromises on legislative proposals (which does not rule out dysfunctional party systems, which contribute to state failure). Indeed, the possibility of such legislative compromise is one of the chief merits of the parliamentary system, where the *ultima ratio* of the voting slip remains in the background. In other words, when compromises are reached, they are prompted by a recognition that, without compromise, the subsequent election or ballot could produce a result that is more or less undesirable for all concerned. In sum, the real or virtual counting of votes is an integral element of modern electoral contests and of the conduct of parliamentary business.

While parties are obviously means of political representation, they also shape other aspects of the state and linked practices – especially in political systems that are at least nominally democratic. In such systems, parties are still formally responsible in parliament for legislation and general rules and cannot be replaced by extraparliamentary organizations or movements even if the latter are influential at a distance from the state. This holds even when legislators consent to abandon their normal functions for the duration of a state of emergency (see chapter 9). Likewise, it is the parties represented in the legislature that determine the formal rules governing party competition. At best, the media and the courts have a corrective role in this regard. And, through fair means and foul, parties also influence rules about party finance and constituency boundaries, including through gerrymandering (Greven 2010).[9]

Parties can also comprise key elements in the state's institutional architecture (witness the notions of *Parteienstaat*, *partitocrazia*, or rule by political parties) insofar as they colonize key parts of the state apparatus *in both its narrow and its inclusive senses* (e.g., bureaucracies, the courts, public enterprise, state-owned media, universities, and foundations) and use their position for particularistic purposes.[10] They may be directly involved in forms of intervention, for example, through their role in clientelism, patronage, facilitating unusual deals with political authorities, exploiting opportunities for petty and grand corruption (Tsoukalas 2003). On top of the general role of parties and the party system in organizing and securing the social bases of the state (sometimes by disorganizing and fragmenting the opposition), parties may also be crucial organs in elaborating state projects (especially when they are 'ideological' or programmatic rather than patronage parties) and, likewise, in helping to articulate and relay hegemonic visions, both in periods of stability and at critical junctures.

In sum, a serious analysis of the party form (or forms) and of the role of parties in political power would encompass all aspects of the state. This would require another book. So here I focus on parties in advanced capitalist states with liberal democratic forms of representation, on the form of parties and party systems, on their role in organizing representation and developing government programmes and policies, and on the implications of these roles for social bases and state projects.

The modern political party system emerged in the period when *polities* (states) were acquiring the form of national territorial states with national parliaments. Parties had certainly emerged before, around key questions of *politics* and *policies*, but they tended to operate as political currents or loose factions manoeuvring to advance, modify, or block particular policies and to secure personal advantage. Such activities are more akin to court and palace intrigue than to mass politics. The rise of the latter in normal states, especially as the franchise was extended and more of the population lived in cities rather than in towns or rural areas, decisively shaped the modern party system. Parties became crucial in organizing the competition for votes in popular elections, in mobilizing voters, and in seeking mandates to participate in government decision making. They have different functions in exceptional states, where parliament has lost its key role in representation (see above and chapter 9).

This said, it is important to distinguish between parties oriented primarily to the politics of representation (which can be narrowly particularistic, especially in multiparty systems) and parties oriented to the acquisition and exercise of power. 'Governing parties' are those that combine sensitivity to the politics of representation and the 'imperatives'[11] of state power (see Gamble 1973). They can be understood in a narrow organizational sense and in terms of broader political functions. Governing parties are important forces in producing hegemony (Gramsci 1971; Portelli 1972; Elfferding 1985) and in managing differences within and between dominant class fractions or classes in order to elaborate a consensus that goes beyond a purely short-term tactical alliance. They must continually reorganize themselves in order to maintain their governing capacity to secure a state project and hegemonic vision, to reproduce and reorganize their class base, and simultaneously to move beyond that base so as to become hegemonic in terms of national popular will (Gramsci 1971; Elffferding 1983, 1985). Moreover, as Gramsci notes, there is another side to the governing parties' role in generalizing interests, forming alliances, and normalizing bourgeois rule. This is seen in efforts to marginalize, delegitimate, or disorganize opponents (Gramsci 1971: 102 = Q 1, §44). Gramsci described the 'most elegant form' of this role as the (metaphorical) decapitation of opposing forces through the absorption of their leaders and intellectuals into the bourgeoisie and bourgeois parties. Other forms are defamation, exclusion from the debate (often with the support of mass media aligned with the dominant party or parties or ruling forces), and, with the help of the executive and military-police powers, imprisonment, banishment, or 'disappearance'.

Modern parties in normal states have three main roles, which may be combined in different, often path-dependent ways to generate different party systems. First, there are established parties, which were already represented in government when a popular franchise was established and which could exploit old and new opportunities for patronage. Such parties focus on organizing support for local notables and politicians, who would in turn back political leaders able and willing to channel the 'spoils' of office (Weber 1994; Duverger 1954: 63–71; Shefter 1994: 29). These are often called notable or cadre parties. Examples are the Democratic–Republican Party and the Federalist Party in the US and the Liberal Party and the Conservative Party in the UK (Weber 1994).

Second, newer parties started to organize and coordinate large numbers of activists, both within a given geographic area and across space, to agitate for a (further) extension of the franchise and other political and economic rights and to campaign in mass elections in order to win votes on the basis of programmatic platforms. In such parties candidates, deputies, and party leaders were accountable to party members through mechanisms such as regular or extraordinary conferences and through an elected party executive. There is a Caesarist or charismatic aspect to party leadership once the masses enter the political arena. For the same reason, this party form typically depended on 'a network of mass organizations – labor unions, peasant leagues, churches, party sections – that did not need to be fueled by patronage' (Shefter 1994: 29). Such parties were the organizational basis for the development of 'mass integration parties' (Neumann 1956). Examples include working-class, Catholic, conservative, or nationalist mass-based parties before and after the Great War (Weber 1994) and, later, nationalist parties in the so-called 'third world' (Shefter 1994). The development of the former coincided with the rise of organized capitalism, the interventionist rather than liberal state, the concentration of political authority in the executive rather than legislative branch, and the rise of significant, organized producer groups and corporatist representation. These mass integration parties connect different spheres of society and different social forces, appeal to wider collective interests, and make principled programmatic promises that may derive from their class basis, confessional groups, a distinctive social and moral milieu, a particular worldview, or some other cleavage (Häusler and Hirsch 1987; Lepsius 1993; Rokkan 1999; Shefter 1994; Gunther and Diamond 2003; Puhle 2002). Whatever their specific form, mass integration parties had a key role in the transition from the liberal to the interventionist state in bourgeois democratic political regimes.

A third form began to emerge in the interwar United States; later on it spread to Western Europe in the aftermath of the Second World War and was consolidated in the heyday of Atlantic Fordism. This is the 'catchall party' or *Volkspartei* (Kirchheimer 1966, 1969). It is a vote-maximizing machine that resorts to commercial and professional marketing and plebiscitary public relations campaigns with a view to capturing the electoral centre ground by appealing to swing or floating voters. Abandoning the appeal to specific class bases and mobilizing party and campaign funds from sources beyond grassroots party membership (namely from the public purse, from major donors rather than individual party subscriptions, and from donors with foreign or transnational interests, open or hidden), catchall party leaders were less concerned to maintain the support of their traditional core electoral base of loyal voters and more interested in capturing key swing voters in swing constituencies (Crouch 2004; Blyth and Katz 2005; Rohrschneider and Whitefield 2012). Moreover, organizations that could provide volunteer labour (e.g., unions, churches) became less valuable than public relations expertise and 'big money' to the funding of campaigns.[12] As the postwar social compromise and its consensus get consolidated, parties may include in their programmes demands to maximize electoral support and may even give them an ideological left–right gloss – but such demands are really adopted for electioneering purposes.

Catchall parties became even more disciplined and centralized than mass integration parties, in order to maintain party unity, which was increasingly a condition of electoral success; and, correspondingly, their leaders and officials became more autonomous. Assisted by the development of national mass media and the spread of television, especially commercial television, these parties also became more 'national' in orientation, without fully losing their traditional regional electoral bases (Rohrschneider and Whitefield 2012). This marked another step towards oligarchy in party organization (Michels 1962). It also encouraged party elites to identify more with the state, as they began to live 'off' rather than 'for' politics (Weber 1994). This party form was, in effect, the Fordist mass party. In the heyday of Atlantic Fordism and of its Keynesian welfare national state (KWNS), from the 1950s to the 1970s, catchall parties won 90 per cent or more of the vote. Over time, however, the competition for the swing voter produced class dealignment and, later, detachment from specific parties (sometimes called partisan dealignment), as electoral support became more volatile. And this planted the seeds for a crisis in the catchall party form (see below and chapter 9).

Some commentators argue that there has been a further development in the party form since the 1960s to 1970s. New categories used to describe this new form include the cartel party (Katz and Mair 1995), the revamped decision-making cadre party (Koole 1994), the professional–electoral party (Panebianco 1988), and the authoritarian mass party (Poulantzas 1978). Cartelization is said to be discernible in the convergence of policies advocated by the 'natural' governing parties ('there is no alternative') and in the depoliticization of some issues as they are removed from campaign agendas. But this phenomenon also creates a space for protest parties, antisystem parties, and social movements to emerge in response to *Partei-* and *Staatsverdrossenheit* – a widespread condition of being fed up and disillusioned with political parties or the state respectively. Others have observed a trend towards the 'presidentialization of politics' in which attention and authority gravitate towards party leaders (Poulantzas 1978; Poguntke and Webb 2007) and a trend for parties to start to represent the state – including the parallel power networks that animate its actions – to society rather than vice versa. Concerning the latter, for example, Katz and Mair argue that decline in the mass electoral basis of parties is compensated for by growing links between parties and the state. Parties no longer act as intermediaries between the state and civil society – intermediaries sustained by a party press and broadcasting media. On the contrary, the state is now the intermediary between civil society and the parties. For access to state funds, patronage, public media and independent media regulated by the state, and other state resources is crucial for the survival of parties and their ability to reward party members. State-funded parliamentary party staff becomes more important than staff in central party offices, which now also depends on state subsidies to supplement other incomes. In addition, states also regulate intraparty democracy and other aspects of party organization (Katz and Mair 1994: 8–10; see also chapter 9).

A parallel trend is the growth of direct communication between politicians and voters: this communication bypasses mass parties, with the result that party members become redundant as campaigning is contracted out and the mass media acquire a bigger role. This is linked to an atrophy of the public sphere, as the 'fourth estate' becomes more influential and public opinion is manipulated via 'populist ventrilo-quism' (Hall 1983: 29, 35, 37) – a phenomenon whereby the press and the parties speak in the name of the people and may thereby remake public opinion. This has prompted the rise of the 'fifth estate', enabled by the Internet, the blogosphere, and other social media. Finally, for the moment parties tend to lose their previously important role in recruiting the political class, including decision-making elites: they lose it to business and governance schools and to consultancy firms. This process is reinforced as internationalization proceeds and suprana-tional governance becomes more important (Rüb 2005: 406ff). Parties are becoming cartel parties that neglect their social base in party mem-bership and comprise a complex organization of leaders, activist pro-fessionals, sympathetic experts who work for money, pure professionals (who may not be supporters), and groups of lobbyists who move between party, lobbying, and business organizations or between national and international politics and other institutional spheres (Crouch 2004: 72–3; Wedel 2009). So Crouch predicts that

> the classic party of the twenty-first century would be…a self-reproducing inner elite, remote from its mass movement base, but nested squarely within a number of corporations, which will in turn fund the sub-contracting of opinion-polling, policy-advice and vote-gathering services in exchange for firms that seek political influence being well regarded by the party when in government (Crouch 2004: 74).

The preceding analysis illustrates the importance of locating indi-vidual parties in the overall party system and of considering how their position relates to the state's institutional structure. The relations among parties are crucial for their role in (dis)organizing political forces and developing a collective will. It is the interaction of parties within the party system that defines the cleavages around which political life revolves and that influences the framework in which a national popular will might emerge. The institutional matrix of the state influences in turn the form assumed by party systems. Here again we are faced with a complex dialectic. For example, as the executive branch gains power at the expense of parliament, the role of political parties changes and becomes more marginal, while other channels for political representation and for articulating the political imaginary become more important. Policy networks and functional representation often play a crucial role in political organization (chapter 7).

To illustrate the importance of the institutional context for the operation of party systems, there are some basic differences between parties in parliamentary and presidential systems. Following Juan Linz (1994), we can say that presidential systems in which the president is directly elected and has real (efficient rather than dignified) powers tend to reduce the role of parties in producing and sustaining governments, programmes, and broad public policies. This is particularly likely where the president can rely on support from parties or rotating majorities in the legislature. Where they oppose the president, however, s/he may campaign on a non-, above- or antiparty platform. In addition, where presidents have a more or less direct popular mandate, legislators can focus on representing constituency interests – albeit at the risk of particularism, serving special interests rather than a broader collective will. This can lead – as in the United States, with its single-member, majoritarian electoral system – to a lack of party cohesion, discipline, and ideological or programmatic commitment and, one might add, particular vulnerability to bribery and corruption. (For an excellent recent typology of forms of corruption in United States politics, see Strether 2015.) Conversely, parliamentary systems tend to strengthen the ties between the legislature and the executive and to produce greater discipline within parties as a condition of electoral success and of delivering stable support to the political executive. These are stylized facts, of course, and the extent to which such descriptions apply to particular situations depends on the broader balance of forces (see also Linz 1990a, 1990b; and, for a critique, Mainwaring and Shugart 1997).

A further illustration of the structural selectivities of political regimes comes from Arend Lijphart's work on 'consociational democracies'. These are oriented to societal consensus (often because of a common perception of the risk of fragmentation and division); and examples are drawn from Lijphart's native country, the Netherlands. Without engaging issues of causation or coevolution, Lijphart noted key differences between regimes where consociational (or consensual) party systems existed and majoritarian systems, where a single party with a simple majority or plurality of votes tends to govern. He identified five contrasts, majoritarian rule being more common where (1) executive power was concentrated rather than shared; (2) executive dominance prevailed over an executive–legislative balance; (3) a two- rather than multiparty system existed; (4) the party system was organized around one major cleavage rather than around several cross-cutting cleavages; and (5) legislators were elected on a plurality rather than proportional representation basis. The United Kingdom would be majoritarian, Austria and Germany would came close to the ideal type of majoritarianism, and most other European states were found to be at the consensual end of the continuum (Lijphart 1999; more generally on the strategic selectivities of electoral and representative systems, see Lijphart 2008).

Crisis of the party system?

Representative democratic institutions facilitate the flexible, organic regulation of social forces and the smooth circulation and reorganization of hegemony, because they offer a structured space with rules of the game for framing and pursuing rival visions of the national popular interest (cf. Poulantzas 1978). This adaptability is reflected in the survival of many of the parties that emerged between the early nineteenth century and the 1920s on the basis of four critical cleavages that Seymour Martin Lipset and Stein Rokkan identified across some 400 years of state and nation building and economic development (Lipset and Rokkan 1967; Rokkan 1999; Linz 2002). These cleavages were: (1) a centralizing secular state versus corporate church privileges (or, more broadly, secular vs religious identities and values); (2) centre versus periphery in the process of nation-state formation (a cleavage reflected in oppositional regional, separatist, and other minority parties); (3) landed versus industrial interests (a cleavage partly reflected in disputes around protection vs free trade, although infant industries and industries that serve mostly domestic markets have also demanded tariff protection); and (4) proprietors versus tenants, labourers, and employees (a cleavage linked to right–left divisions). The fourth cleavage was the last to be reflected in party systems. On this basis, Lipset and Rokkan suggested a path-dependent sequencing of party development, linked, in addition, to institutional thresholds affecting the ability to mobilize popular support for new parties. The historical sequence was Reformation and Counter-Reformation, French Revolution and Counter-Revolution, and the Industrial Revolution. The party systems that had emerged in Europe during the 1920s remained significant into the 1960s, despite disruptions due to fascism, authoritarian rule, and national coalitions.

Yet there are recurrent crises in parties and party systems that reflect changes in the wider political and state systems. A crisis in the party system is often associated with a crisis in the state – especially if it affects the natural governing party or parties. For the relative operational unity, if any, of the state's powers cannot be derived from constitutional guarantees or explained simply in terms of the parallelogram of forces inside the state. State unity results from the exercise of a political leadership concerned to promote and manage a 'party spirit' that gives shape and coherence to the state and links it to a national popular consciousness that transcends both egoism and group particularism. Parties are nonetheless highly adaptable, if not nonsubstitutable, forms of political organization, especially in formal democratic systems.

A crisis in the party system can be illustrated with the help of the 1970s and 1980s crisis of Atlantic Fordism and its associated state form, the KWNS. Both parliamentary and presidential systems experienced a representational crisis due to class and partisan dealignment, declining turnout and electoral volatility, crises in party funding and membership, and the disorientation of parties and their programmes in the face of economic and political crisis. Economic and fiscal crises limited the room for material concessions. The development of neocorporatist crisis management had already diminished the role of parties and legislatures in economic and social policy and left less space for party programmatic differences. Further, internationalization weakened the effectiveness, already questionable, of KWNS policies (Jessop 2002) and increased the weight of supra- and transnational politics, where parties had less influence by comparison with executive authorities, producer groups, and corporate lobbies. This mix of representational, rationality, and legitimacy crises was associated for a time with the rediscovery and increased importance of civil society (reflected in the explosive growth of a multiplicity of new social movements and calls for more participatory or direct forms of democracy) and with the rise of minority, protest, populist and anti-system parties (Blyth and Katz 2005).

Nonetheless, social movements do not and cannot replace political parties. They are generally focused on single issues and less willing and less pressured to compromise for the sake of effective government or governance. In this sense, they tend to fragment the political agenda rather than develop coherent programmes and state projects. They mobilize strongly committed minorities, at least temporarily, but their long-term support is harder to sustain because of weak movement organization (Kornhauser 1959; Dalton and Kuechler 1990; Giugni 1998; Cox and Nilsen 2014). They also rise and fall with issues or must reinvent themselves to survive. While new social movements are more flexible in the aggregate, they are more vulnerable individually. Likewise, the survival of minority, protest, and antisystem parties depends on these organizations' ability and willingness to adapt to the pressures of electoral competition, where money talks, and to the pressures of 'acting responsibly' if they are included in governing coalitions – let alone if they form the government. In this context, minority parties are torn between remaining 'parties of representation' that serve as marginal irritants and may be able to exact minor concessions and becoming 'natural' governing parties with a need to compromise and to respect the art of the possible in the face of the limited powers of government to challenge the wider system of economic and political domination (Puhle 2002; Offe 1975).

Still other challenges to the party system originate in technological developments. Mass media have opened up new channels for direct access between citizens and their political leaders, so that their communications need not pass through traditional partisan channels. The rapid spread of access to the Internet has created massive and complex networks of direct horizontal communications among citizens, while at the same time establishing a potential basis for 'narrowcasting' messages between politicians and specific – if not highly specialized – sectors of society. The downside of these communications advances is the enormous cost of establishing such networks, which involve paying consultants for the purpose of crafting messages and attractive images of politicians, and in some countries (especially the United States) purchasing TV or radio time for commercial advertisements. Dramatic increases in the cost of campaigning have compelled parties to seek large sums from public and private sources, and this sometimes leads to corrupt practices or arouses suspicion.

State project

This concept presupposes the improbability of a unified state system. A state project denotes the political imaginaries, projects, and practices that (1) define and regulate the boundaries of the state system vis-à-vis the wider society and (2) seek to provide the state apparatus thus demarcated with sufficient substantive internal operational unity for it to be able to perform its inherited or redefined 'socially accepted' tasks (see chapter 2). The state apparatus, considered as an assemblage, does not exist as a fully constituted, internally coherent, organizationally pure, and operationally closed system. It is an emergent, contradictory, hybrid, and relatively open system. This characterization applies to the hard core of the state (e.g., the different branches of the armed forces, the central bank–treasury nexus and principal spending departments, the political executive) as well as to the wider ensemble of state apparatuses. In short, the state has no inherent substantive unity *qua* institutional ensemble, even where there is formal isomorphism or complementarity. State projects may originate outside a given state (e.g., through intellectuals allied to different social forces), may be elaborated within (parts of) the state apparatus, or may be copied from elsewhere or imposed by external forces. Enduring projects are usually embedded in a constitutional settlement or institutionalized compromise. In all cases, the (always relative) unity of the state must be created in substantial part within the state system itself, through specific operational procedures, means of coordination, and guiding purposes. In sum, state projects have a critical role in the process of state or *polity* building. A state project is associated with a distinctive *raison d'état* – which denotes here a specific *governmental rationality* rather than a form of representation, as above – and with statecraft that seeks to unify the activities of different branches and departments across its different sites, scales, and fields of action. The challenges involved in securing such unity explain why state crises often manifest themselves as crises of institutional integration and coherence of state action.

Unity can be understood narrowly, as the capacity of state functionaries to use constitutionalized violence and other means to the purpose of reproducing the state apparatus as an institutional ensemble and of securing compliance with its policies in the face of resistance. The challenges involved here are the theme of cameralistics, police science, and public administration. Unity can also be understood more broadly, in terms of the capacity of the state apparatus to maintain general political order and social cohesion within an associated territory. Thus conceived of, state projects aim to provide a coherent template or framework within which individual agents and organs of the state can coordinate and judiciously combine (collibrate)[13] policy and practices, and also connect diverse policies to pursue a (more or less illusory) national interest, public good, and social welfare. In this sense, state projects are also typically articulated with various *policy paradigms* that frame policy orientations and decisions in specific policy fields. The state projects of colonial, imperial, or great powers may well seek to extend this domain of control and the relative unity of political authority beyond these powers' respective national territorial boundaries.

Competition over state projects leads to struggles to impose contradictory 'apparatus unities' on (actual or potential) state organs. Thus the always tendential institutional logic and distinctive interests of the state must be related to the state projects, if any, that happen to be politically hegemonic or dominant at a given moment. There is never a point when *the* state is finally built in a given territory and after which it operates, so to speak, on automatic pilot, according to its own, definite, fixed, and inevitable laws. Nor, to be less demanding, does a moment arrive when a single state project becomes so hegemonic that all state managers simply apply an algorithmic model of their duties and interests as members of a distinct governing class. Whether, how, and to what extent one can talk with certainty about the state depends on the contingent and provisional outcome of struggles to realize more or less specific 'state projects'. For, whatever constitutions might decree or declare about the unity and sovereignty of the modern state as a juridical subject, there are often several rival 'states' competing for a temporary and local hegemony within a given national territory. (For a relevant case study of China, using the conceptual scheme presented above, see Mulvad 2015.)

National boundaries do not constitute a fixed horizon for emergent state projects: there is no more reason to rule out strategies aiming to build multi- and transnational networks and circuits of state power than there is to exclude local or regional state projects. This raises intriguing questions about the source of supra- or transnational state-building projects, as seen, for example, in the European Union. (For an analysis of three competing state projects aiming to rebuild an EU in crisis, see Georgi and Kannankulam 2012; Kannankulam and Georgi 2012.) Thus state actions should not be ascribed to *the* state as an originating subject but should be seen as the emergent, unintended, and complex resultant of what rival 'states within the state' or competing social forces have done and are doing on a complex strategic terrain.

Hegemonic visions

While 'state project' corresponds to the 'part' moment of the 'part–whole' paradox of the state, 'hegemonic vision' reflects its 'whole' moment. As noted above, this paradox arises because the state is just one part of a complex social order, has limited capacities to intervene in other parts of the whole, and is at the same time held responsible for the whole and expected to intervene in the last instance to maintain institutional integration and social cohesion. In this context, hegemonic visions elaborate the nature and purposes of the state for the wider social formation (in earlier work I called these visions 'hegemonic projects': see, e.g., Jessop 1990). They offer general guidelines for conducting state policy. These visions seek to reconcile the particular and the universal by linking the nature and the purposes of the state to a broader – but always selective – political, intellectual, and moral vision of the public interest, the good society, the commonweal, or an analogous principle of societal organization. This 'illusory' public interest privileges some material and ideal interests, identities, spaces, temporalities, and so on over others and may take an avowedly inclusionary form (e.g., liberal democracies) or one that is explicitly exclusionary (e.g., the apartheid state). These visions can be related initially to specific economic, political, and social imaginaries and then to the deeper structure and logics of a given social formation and its insertion into the world market, interstate system, and world society. They are most likely to succeed when they address the major structural constraints imposed by existing forms of domination as well as by the prevailing balance of forces and by the prospects for their transformation through new alliances, strategies, and spatiotemporal horizons of action.

It is useful to distinguish between 'one nation' and 'two nations' projects. These terms derive from nineteenth-century conservative political discourse in England[14] and 'nation' signifies an imagined *Staatsvolk* (people-nation) (on other meanings of nation, see chapter 6). A 'one nation' project or vision aims at an expansive and inclusive hegemony, based on widespread popular support mobilized through material concessions and symbolic rewards (as in social imperialism or the KWNS). It is often more rhetorical than real. In contrast, 'two nations' strategies aim explicitly or implicitly at a more limited hegemony, based on the support of strategically significant sectors of the population, and seek to pass the costs of the project to other, excluded sectors (as in fascist and apartheid regimes). During periods of economic crisis and limited scope for material concessions, the prospects for a 'one nation' strategy are restricted (unless it involves an equitable sharing of sacrifice) and 'two nations' strategies are more likely to be pursued. The latter may also be found in relatively stable economies. In both cases, 'two nations' projects require containment, even repression of the 'other nation' (or, continuing the metaphor, 'nations'), and also involve selective access and concessions for the more 'favoured nation'. This is linked to efforts to reorganize political support so that it may reflect a vertical, antagonistic cleavage between the 'productive' and 'parasitic' in economic terms; between the 'loyal' and 'disloyal' in political terms; and between the 'civilized' and 'uncivilized' in terms of civil society (e.g., the discourses of Thatcherism, Stalinism, and apartheid respectively). In short, whereas a 'one nation' strategy involves a pluralistic discourse of difference addressed to groups performing diverse economic functions, expressing different political views, and displaying various lifestyles, a 'two nations' strategy is underpinned by a dichotomous discourse of antagonism (cf. Laclau and Mouffe 1985). Such contrasting strategies must be coupled with appropriate forms of organization, representation, and intervention if they are to provide an adequate social base for exercising state power.

Without a hegemonic vision successfully linking institutional and class unity, politicians and state managers may seek to unify the state around its narrow political function of reproducing the state apparatus itself, at the expense of its general political functions for the wider society. Or, again, the unity of the state might collapse completely. Nothing in the preceding discussion of the six dimensions and their articulation should be taken to imply that the modern state system is inherently capitalist in form or function. This implication is excluded by my remarks on the polymorphy of the state, as well as by the manner in which form problematizes function and, further, by the tendencies of all state forms to experience state failure (chapter 6).

The Paradox of State and Society

In pursuing their wider societal responsibilities, state managers employ available strategic capacities, which are always limited in relation to the tasks facing them. The 'material' basis of the modern state's responsibility to secure general political order, institutional integration, and social cohesion is its constitutional monopoly of violence and the associated capacity to enforce decisions that are binding on the social agents (individuals or organizations) under its jurisdiction. Its 'ideational' basis and motor force is the claim of the state as a juridical subject – and that of state managers as a 'universal class' – to represent society's interests.[15] In neither case does this ensure that state managers actually promote the commonweal rather than their own (or other) particular interests. Yet these fictions affect political expectations and conduct; and so they get honoured in the breach. But, because they are fictions and because the state is just one structurally coupled part of the social formation, it can never play the role expected of it. For it is an institutional ensemble and not a subject; even where consensus emerges about a conception of the common good, it is always a particular conception with partial implications; and the exercise of state powers always encounters structural constraints and resistances that limit its ability to master the social formation. This complex mix of political fiction and political reality continually reproduces both the hubris and the tragedy of the state (Willke 1986, 1992).

This primary paradox is reflected in four other aspects of state–society relations.

1   Although the state has a key role in defining a society's identity, its own identity is in turn contested by forces rooted in other spheres. On the one hand, societies do not preexist the state system but are constituted in part through its activities. As noted, the territory and the society over which a state holds sway come to be identified with that state; and, in external affairs ranging from diplomacy and war to sport and cultural exchanges, the state is widely considered to represent society. On the other hand, a host of nonstate forces within and beyond the political system struggle to (re)build the state and redefine its projects. This produces continuous cycles of definition and redefinition in which states shape society and social forces shape the state.

2   Although the state has its own distinctive dynamic and strategic capacities, so that it is resistant to direct external control, other spheres of society also have their own logics and capacities. Different states develop their own political discourses, own rhythms and temporalities, and own interests and capacities. This ensures that state activities make a difference, are recalcitrant to external control because of their internal complexities, and must therefore be taken into account by agents beyond the state. Other institutional orders have similar degrees of internal complexity, operate with their own modes of calculation, follow their own temporal patterns, and also have distinctive resources and capacities. This renders them in turn recalcitrant to direct control by the state.

3   As the state intervenes more in various spheres of society (suggesting that state power is growing), it is weakened by two other changes. First, its own unity and distinctive identity diminish as it becomes more complex internally, its powers are fragmented across branches and policy networks, and coordination problems multiply. This prompts neoliberals to claim that the state can only be strong if it limits its ambitions and powers. Conversely, as state intervention grows, successful state action depends increasingly on the cooperation of other social forces. So state power becomes more subordinate to, or interlinked with, external forces. This is why some state theorists suggest that the modern state can only become strong if it abandons pretensions to sovereignty (or stops resorting to despotic power) and shares its powers with other forces in order to increase its infrastructural power (e.g., Mann 1984, 2008; Hall and Ikenberry 1989).

4   Even when the state acts in the name of *raison d'état* or invokes
    states of emergency that suspend normal representative mecha-
    nisms, its legitimacy depends on linking state interests and actions
    to those of 'society' and on a credible commitment to 'restore
    normal regime service' as soon as possible. State reason has
    always been linked to claims about the common good, the national
    interest, or both; and states of emergency or periods of dictator-
    ship are normatively expected to lead to an eventual return to
    normality – when competing definitions of the national popular
    interest once again become the common currency of political
    discourse. Thus, alongside the general scope for discursive articu-
    lation, those who engage in political discourse have special reasons
    to integrate issues from beyond the political realm. Conversely,
    state and official discourses can never be self-contained: they are
    liable to disarticulation and disruption by 'external' forces.

Conclusions

The paradoxes that arise from this part–whole relationship entail
dilemmas that require strategic choices. Since any choice privileges
one horn of the dilemma, the problems stemming from neglect of the
other horn tend to grow until a strategic switch is required. This helps
to explain the policy cycles that occur in many areas. For example,
failure to intervene leaves other institutional orders free to pursue
their own logics to the possible detriment of state goals; but intervention can fail because it disrupts other institutional orders and prompts
resistance or other counterproductive effects. One possible solution
is for the state to resort to meta-governance strategies based on prior
consultation with agencies from other systems, to formal or substantive state facilitation of the activities of such agencies where these
activities coincide with agreed objectives, and reliance on these agencies to find the optimal ways to pursue these objectives within the
terms of their own institutional logic. But this form of state intervention is likely to reinforce state fragmentation and disunity unless there
is a wider consensus, not only on state but also on societal objectives.
Such considerations reinforce the relevance of the SRA with its
concern for structural contradictions, part–whole paradoxes, and
other sources of strategic dilemma. I explore the strategic–relational
interplay between strategies and structures in the next chapter.

4

Power, Interests, Domination, State Effects

This chapter builds on the strategic–relational approach (SRA) to address three issues. The first, and conceptually prior, issue is the nature of power and interests. The second concerns the state as a specific institutional expression of power relations. The third is how and how far the state structures power relations and privileges specific interests. Domination has many forms, sites, stakes, and strategies and they cannot all be addressed here. I therefore illustrate the second and third of these issues by asking what difference it makes to focus on 'the capitalist type of state' or on 'the state in capitalist society'. This bears on the controversial topic of the relation between class power and state power in formally democratic societies with a strong institutional separation between the economic and the political system. In terms of the six approaches outlined in chapter 1, studying the capitalist type of state involves a mainly institutionalist account of the state's typical forms, their complementarity, and their adequacy (or otherwise) for securing class domination. For studying the state in capitalist societies, it is more appropriate to adopt a historical and agent-centred account. I then offer some comments on *Ideologiekritik* and end with comments on the limits of a Marxist analysis of the state and state power.

Power as the *explanans* or the *explanandum*?

What is conventionally called 'power' is a complex, overdetermined phenomenon that is ill suited to explain social relations. In part this is caused by confusion about whether power refers to *capacities* to make a difference or to their activation in ways that *actually do* make a difference. Moreover, insofar as power is not just a general term for the production of any and all effects within specific structural constraints, the specific effects of specific agents' exercise of power in specific circumstances constitutes an *explanandum* (something to be explained) rather than an *explanans* (the explanation itself). But the more detailed the specification of the context of a given action is, the less scope there is to attribute effects to the actions that occur in that context. Thus, when conjunctures are well specified, 'power' tends to become a residual category, good to explain only what is left unexplained by contextual factors, including chance or accident. Further, as *explanans*, 'power' lacks independent status in causal analysis. It is *either* a formal concept without content, which cannot explain how particular effects are produced, *or* a place-holding concept, which becomes redundant once research reveals the substantive mechanisms that produce these effects. Failure to recognize this dichotomy leads to a circular reasoning in which the results of the exercise of power are explained by the exercise of power itself. To escape these problems, we must accept that there is no such thing as 'power in general' or 'general power'. So the challenge is to establish the weight of different sets of particular powers and how they combine, if at all, to produce specific structures of domination.

Implicit in the attribution of effects to the exercise of power is the assumption that such actions were freely chosen and causally decisive. Yet the exercise of power does not involve a mechanical clash of wills. It has definite social and material conditions of existence and it is circumscribed through its links with other social determinations. This is why politics is 'the art of the possible'. The analysis of these limits and constraints is logically prior to the study of the actions of the agents involved in a power relation in a given conjuncture. Moreover, unless one asserts that these agents' actions follow from the exercise of unconstrained free will, one must also investigate how the possibilities of action are limited by the specific qualities of these agents. This indicates a need for historical accounts of the combination of social forces, material and symbolic resources, modes of calculation, strategies and tactics, social technologies, and structural constraints and conjunctural opportunities that are necessary or sufficient to produce given effects. Hence the analysis of power must explore how these various factors interact to determine the overall balance of forces and its effects over different spatiotemporal horizons of action.

Similar arguments apply to the notorious concept of 'relative autonomy'. At best, this concept enables its proponents to distinguish their approach from attempts to explain state forms and functions through external causes – or from claims about absolute autonomization, which endows the state with an unconstrained will and the capacity to realize it. When its proponents undertake specific case studies, however, relative autonomy becomes a largely *descriptive* concept, with a content that varies across cases. Thus, like 'power' more generally, relative autonomy cannot be an *explanans*: it is an *explanandum*.

The separation of the state from other institutional orders is, allegedly, crucial for its 'relative autonomy'. However, far from guaranteeing the autonomy needed to pursue the collective interests of capital (a common meaning of state separation in Marxist analysis), the national interest against particular interests (a common conservative and liberal claim), or the national interest against those of other national states (a common meaning in realist and neorealist work), this separation is a serious challenge to such actions. This is due in large measure to the part–whole paradox analysed in the previous chapter. The 'relative autonomy' of actual states is the complex resultant of their form(s) of separation from the economic region and civil society (as the site of 'private', noneconomic relations), of their *sui generis* institutional structure, of their social bases of support and resistance, and of the effectiveness of their policies in achieving defined goals or functions. These points strengthen the case against 'relative autonomy' and state power as abstract, all-purpose principles of explanation.

Interests and Domination

'Interest' is a disguised comparative term (Barry 1965: 173–87). Calculating an agent's interests depends on comparative advantage in particular contexts rather than on absolute advantage regardless of feasibility. Interests must be related to structural constraints and conjunctural opportunities in given circumstances and to potential trade-offs among different sets of interests across different spatiotemporal horizons. So, rather than making blanket assertions about (dis)advantage in general, one must specify which aspects of an agent's interests are being (dis)advantaged in what respects. Moreover, insofar as agents are involved in different sets of relations or have many subjectivities or identities, they may have contradictory sets of interests. These complexities provide the 'rational kernel' to pluralism and to neopluralist analyses of politics and policy – at the expense of ignoring the constraints associated with the configuration of a given polity (or state system). Contradictory interests can lead to wicked (or 'undecidable') problems in strategy making, policymaking, and decision making that, without clear axioms or algorithms for making choices, may lead to procrastination, arbitrary or random choices (with or without learning), the weighing of votes, calculation of the balance of forces, decision making through manipulation or *force majeure*, or a search for new axiological principles.

Analyses of power as domination treat capacities as *socially structured* rather than *socially amorphous* (or random). At stake are systematic, institutionalized, regularly reproduced reciprocal relations rather than one-off and unilateral impositions of will. Power as domination secures the continuity of social relations. Hence, as Jeffrey Isaac notes, 'rather than A getting B to do something B would not otherwise do, social relations of power typically involve both A and B doing what they *ordinarily* do' (Isaac 1987: 96; note the affinities with Foucault's notion of governmentality). Enduring relations involve reciprocal, if often asymmetrical, capacities and vulnerabilities. A common paradigm here is Hegel's master–slave dialectic – in which the slave depends on the master, the master on the slave (Hegel 1977). Used in relation to slavery and colonialism, this paradigm can be elaborated upon in other ways too. For example, some Marxists have related it to class domination; some feminists to patriarchal domination; and some (deep) ecologists to the dialectics of human–nature interactions (e.g., Brennan 2007). This applies particularly to the so-called anthropocene epoch, when human activities have significantly modified global evolution (cf. Crutzen 2006; Steffen et al. 2011; and, for a critique, Moore 2015a, 2015b).

A thoroughgoing SRA would assess interests in terms of potential outcomes, in particular situations, for specific subjects who have internalized specific identities. A multilevel objective–subjective dialectic is at work here. First, objective interests must be related to a particular subjectivity (sense of identity) of an individual or collective actor with a particular place in a given conjuncture. This is because ideal and material interests vary with an actor's identity in a given situation. Whereas 'ideal' interests are linked to other-worldly concerns (such as salvation) and symbolic systems (such as social status), material interests are tied to this-worldly concerns and material advantages. As Max Weber (1978) noted, however, many interests mix ideal and material factors (cf. McIntosh 1977; and Swedberg 2003). This subjective, identity-related aspect does not mean that social agents cannot mistake their interests. For, once given a subjective identity as a reference point, interests are objectively grounded in social relations and value systems rather than dependent solely on a subject's perceptions. This also holds for ideal interests insofar as these are not purely whimsical, idiosyncratic, or amorphous but tied to institutionalized structures.

Second, struggles occur over the redefinition or recombination of subjective identities and their related objective interests in different contexts. This can involve reordering the priority of identities already affirmed by agents and efforts to get the latter to accept new identities, which will often entail other interests. This issue is familiar to students of 'intersectionalism', that is, the differential articulation of class, gender, ethnic, and other identities. It also underpins pluralistic accounts in which diverse ideal and material interests are at play and have different spatiotemporal horizons of action.

In short, the meaning of power and interests must be related to the *relations among social relations* in specific conjunctures. Structural constraints are those elements in a situation that cannot be altered by agent(s) *in a given time period* and vary according to the strategic location of agents in the overall social formation. The latter involves a complex hierarchy of potential powers determined by the range and determinacy of opportunities for influencing elements that constrain other agents. This potential for power depends not only on the relations among positions in the social formation but also on the organization, modes of calculation, and resources of the social forces. The actual balance of power is determined post hoc, through the interaction of the (strategic) actions pursued by these forces within the limits set by structural constraints that vary according to actor and action. The interests thereby affected must also be assessed relationally. They depend on the conjunctural opportunities in a given period, the potential balance of power, and the horizons of action. All this affects the calculation of political strategies over different time periods and highlights the importance of a conjunctural, relational approach to such issues as the nature of state power (chapter 3). I now illustrate these remarks with examples drawn from the efforts of Marxist activists and scholars to examine capitalist states and states in capitalist societies.

The State and Class Domination

Marxist scholars study the linkages between social power and the reproduction of class domination and tend to consider other types of subject, identity, antagonism, and domination mostly in terms of their contingent relevance for, or conditioning by, class domination (for overviews, see Jessop 1982; Barrow 1993; Hirsch 2005; Domhoff 2013). Weberians give equal *analytical* weight to three forms of domination – class, status, and party. A similar position is found in intersectionalist analyses of power and domination as opposed to those of radical feminism, which generally prioritizes patriarchal domination. In contrast, pluralist and neopluralist scholars identify a vast array of resources, identities, and interests, which are deployed in so many potentially cross-cutting and countervailing ways that durable systems of domination are virtually excluded. While Marxist, Weberian, and intersectionalist positions examine the relation between the state and class domination, they differ on how the two are related. In no case, however, do they reify the distinction between 'state' and 'class' power' such that (1) state power would be a property of the state *qua* autonomous subject, which would stand outside and above society and would have its own resources; (2) class power would be anchored wholly in the economy or in civil society; and (3) this stark differentiation between the state and economy or civil society would lead to efforts, especially of a zero-sum character, by agents of one to control the other in an external clash of forces. In rejecting all attempts to distinguish between 'state power' and 'class power' (whether as descriptive concepts or as principles of explanation) on these lines, I do not dismiss the influence of political categories such as the military or bureaucrats, nor deny that states have various organizational capacities and resources that give them specific advantages in exercising power. The key point is that state power is a mediated effect of the changing balance among *all* forces in a given situation. It follows that state power is an *explanandum*, not an explanatory principle (Jessop 1990: 117–18); and, further, that, when we speak as if the state or state action has caused specific effects, this is a shorthand (and a potentially misleading one) for a more complex strategic–relational conjuncture.

More generally, the SRA accepts that class struggle can occur within as well as beyond the state *and* that state agents exercise influence outside as well as inside its formal boundaries. Thus, to study the relation between state and class power, we must consider how state powers are exercised and aligned (or not) with specific class interests in particular societies and conjunctures, and vice versa. Diverse alliances, mixed motives, and ambivalent outcomes may exist – especially as class forces and class interests are not the only factors at play in securing the social bases of state power, in articulating state projects, and in promoting hegemonic visions. Indeed hegemony is secured – to the extent that it is – through the articulation of a wide range of identities, orientations, and interests, many of which are not explicitly tied to class interests (see below).

This suggests that capital accumulation should have two functions in an analysis of the state in capitalist societies: as a point of reference and as an explanatory principle.

- As a reference point, capital accumulation provides a basis for calculating the extent to which the exercise of state powers associated with a particular form of state or regime actually does differentially advance the ideal or the material interests of capital (or both) by comparison to the exercise of powers by other classes and social forces. Let me recall here that such interests are not absolute but relational – a point developed further below. Moreover, taking capital accumulation as a reference point does not require that actors whose actions serve to reproduce it are aware of this outcome.
- As a principle of explanation, capital accumulation can guide research on how the form and the course of differential accumulation and the mobilization of class forces condition and penetrate the form and operations of the state apparatus and circumscribe (without fully determining) the effects of state intervention (cf. Jessop 1982).

The same dual function holds in investigations of the relations between state power and other forms of domination – such as militarism, warlordism, apartheid, ethnic discrimination, centre–periphery relations, theocracy, patriarchy, or heteronormativity.

Marxist scholars mainly pursue four interrelated themes regarding domination. The first concerns power relations as manifestations of a specific mode or configuration of class domination rather than as a purely interpersonal phenomenon lacking deeper social foundations. This does not imply that power and resistance are the preserve of social actors with clear class identities and class interests. Instead this theme focuses on the *class relevance* of, say, distinct forms of polity, politics, and policy – and on this issue rather than on forms and levels of class consciousness. This kind of focus requires explicit accounts of what constitutes class relevance in particular conjunctures (see below). Second, Marxists explore the links (or lack thereof) among economic, political, and ideological forms of class domination. This topic has prompted many theoretical and empirical disagreements. Different approaches ground class power variously in the social relations of production, in control over the state, or in hegemony over hearts and minds. Third, plain or nondogmatic Marxists, a category to which I belong, note that class power and domination are inevitably limited and try to explain this in terms of the contradictions and antagonisms inherent in the capital relation or in the existence of other forms of domination and of competing principles of societal organization (see Jessop 1982, 2002, 2013, 2014a, 2015a). Plain Marxists tend to assume that all forms of social power linked to class domination are fragile, unstable, provisional, and temporary and that continuing struggles are needed to secure class domination, overcome resistance, and naturalize or mystify class power. Fourth, there is interest in the strategies to reproduce, resist, or overthrow class domination in specific periods and conjunctures. An important aspect here is the spatiotemporal dimensions of strategy.

Economic class domination

A mode of production comprises a specific combination of forces and social relations of production. The productive forces comprise raw materials, means of production, the technical division of labour corresponding to given raw materials and means of production, and the relations of interdependence and cooperation among the direct producers in setting the means of production to work. The social relations of production comprise control over the allocation of resources to different productive activities and over the appropriation of any resulting surplus; the social division of labour (or the allocation of workers to different activities across different units of production); and class relations grounded in property relations, ownership of the means of production, and the form of economic exploitation (or appropriation of surplus labour). These relations shape choices among available productive forces and their deployment in production, and also give rise to structural contradictions, the potential for class antagonism, and strategic dilemmas.

The capitalist wage relation illustrates the situation well. For, in voluntarily selling their labour power for a wage, workers transfer its control to the capitalist, who has the right to any surplus. A formally free exchange thereby becomes the contractual basis of workplace despotism (the exercise of management prerogatives) and economic exploitation (the appropriation of surplus labour). The organization of the labour process is the main site of the antagonism between capitalists and workers and is at stake in a wide range of struggles that extend well beyond the workplace. Workers' resistance in labour markets and the labour process indicate that the successful exercise of power is not guaranteed by unequal social relations of production. Marxists also study the overall organization of the production process and its links to other aspects of the capital relation. Relevant concerns include the relative importance of industrial or financial capital, monopoly capital or small and medium enterprises, multinational or national firms, and firms interested in domestic growth or exports. Depending on the focus, capital's ideal and material interests will vary.

These points about economic class domination have been related to a *stylized account* of the modern state. First, individual capitals are prohibited from using direct coercion in the labour process and in their competition with other capitals; and, on the other hand, the state protects private property and the sanctity of contracts on behalf of capital as a whole. This supports capital's formal rights to manage the labour process, appropriate surplus labour, and enforce contracts with other capitals. Second, the rational organization of capitalism requires free wage labour – which the state creates through its role in ending feudal privileges, promoting the enclosure of commons, punishing vagabonds, and imposing an obligation to enter the labour market. It also enables workers to sell their labour power 'freely', secures conditions for the reproduction of wage labour, imposes factory laws, responds to the housing question, secures cheap food, and so on. Third, the modern state does not engage in profitable economic activities on its own account – capital prefers to provide these and gets the state to undertake economically and socially necessary activities that are unprofitable. These vary in time and space (for an exemplary analysis in these terms, see Offe 1972; for further discussion, see Jessop 1982: 78–141). Interestingly, these arguments also occur in Weber's account of the conditions for the maximum formal rationality of capitalist accounting (Weber 1978: 136–40, 150–6, 161–6).

Fourth, as a tax-state (*Steuerstaat*), the modern state derives its income primarily from its monopoly over taxation in an essentially private economic order rather than from profitable management of state-owned or state-controlled property (Goldscheid 1976; Schumpeter 1954; Krätke 1984: 25–6). Its taxing capacity is underpinned in turn by its monopoly of coercion. Moreover, where the state relies on public debt, which is common, this is also backed by the state's taxing powers.

These twin monopolies are typically legitimated on the basis of 'no taxation without representation', which purportedly ensures that the level, incidence, and purposes of taxation match the conceptions of justice and good government held by citizens and other key forces (Krätke 1984: 67; Théret 1992: 133). Alongside its external and internal sovereignty and political legitimacy, the tax state must be able to adapt public finances, in their fiscal (revenue) and expenditure dimensions, to the demands of accumulation as well as to those of political legitimacy (O'Connor 1973; Théret 1992; Streeck 2014). This limits the state's freedom of manoeuvre, as the state is under the permanent (and discursively reinforced) threat of a strike by productive capital or bondholders. Where the tax state uses future taxing powers as security against current and new loans, the views of creditors and credit-rating agencies also matter. Indebted states, notably those with heavy external debts, may seek to negotiate cancellation or rescheduling. Unilateral action, even if possible, would further undermine credibility. This problem is compounded when the state wants to attract inward investment and spur local enterprise. Yet tax holidays, subsidies, and so on could threaten the immediate tax base and the state's legitimacy in the eyes of taxpayers. This reinforces capital's power over the state. Thus the modern state's activities are said to require a healthy and growing (or at least profitable) economy – which ties political programmes to economic imperatives (Offe 1975). Subordinate classes can secure material concessions only within this constraint: if profitability is threatened, concessions must be reversed. In periods of crisis, state dependence on continued private accumulation may even reinforce the power of capital where alternative economic imaginaries are weak and resistance is disorganized. Yet capital cannot press its economic advantages too far without undermining the state's political legitimacy, which in normal conditions requires respect for the rule of law and for public opinion.

Political class domination

Many Marxists who start from the economic bases of domination acknowledge that politics is nonetheless primary because it is crucial to maintaining, reforming, or overthrowing class relations. The state is central not only for political power in narrow terms, but also for class power more generally. This is problematic because of the operational autonomy of the state system (see chapters 1 and 3; also below). Some accounts of political class domination begin with the state's direct and indirect roles in securing the conditions for economic class domination. Many highlight its role in maintaining the overall structural integration and social cohesion of a 'society divided into classes' – without which contradictions and antagonisms might provoke revolutionary crises or lead to 'the mutual ruin of the contending classes' (Marx and Engels 1976b). It is important to repeat that threats to social cohesion are not exclusively grounded in class relations – the challenge is, rather, to maintain social cohesion without threatening the economic and extraeconomic conditions of accumulation and political class domination. This is not guaranteed.

The state is emphasized for various reasons in this regard. Here I mention just three. First, it is argued that, since market forces alone cannot secure all the conditions needed for capital accumulation and are prone to market failure, there is a need for some mechanism standing outside and above the market to underwrite it and to compensate for its failures. Second, economic and political competition between capitals necessitates a force able to organize their collective interests and to limit any damage that might occur from the one-sided pursuit of a single set of capitalist interests. Third, the state is also needed to manage the many and varied repercussions of economic exploitation within the wider society. Only if the state secures sufficient institutional integration and social cohesion can the extraeconomic conditions for rational economic calculation and, a fortiori, accumulation be secured. This allegedly requires a sovereign state that is 'relatively autonomous' from particular class interests – a notion that, as remarked above, is deeply problematic – and can therefore develop and promote projects based on a wider, national popular interest. How such relative autonomy operates in the context of internationalization and transnationalization is an issue addressed in this framework in terms of nodal points in global circuits of capital linked to imperialist states, transnational power networks, and relatively autonomous institutions of global governance (see chapter 8). Where these economic strategies, state projects, and hegemonic visions respect the 'decisive function exercised by the leading group in the decisive nucleus of economic activity' (Gramsci 1971: 161 = Q 13, §18: 1591), the state helps to secure both economic and political class domination. This is deemed more likely to happen in bourgeois democracies than in dictatorial regimes, due to the former's role in mystifying class power and in facilitating the flexible reorganization of power relations in response to changing conditions (see also chapters 3 and 9).

Marx argued that the *form of political organization* corresponds to the *form of economic organization* (Marx 1967: 791). Thus an economic order based on private property, the wage relation, and profit-oriented, market-mediated exchange seems naturally to 'fit' or 'correspond' with a political order based on the rule of law, equality before the law, and a unified sovereign state. This highlights the 'formal adequacy' of bourgeois democracy to a consolidated, profit-oriented, market-mediated capitalism. For, in liberal democratic states, the freedom of economic agents to engage in exchange (a freedom belied by managerial 'despotism' in the labour process) is matched by the political freedom of citizens under the rule of law (a freedom belied by the state's subordination to the logic of capital). Class is therefore absent as an explicit organizing principle of the capitalist type of state – there is no legal monopoly, no exclusivity of political power for the dominant class, whose members or representatives must compete for power on formally equal terms with those of subordinate classes; this is a key point in Evgeny Pashukanis's analysis of the normal bourgeois state (Pashukanis 1978). This encourages the downplaying of antagonistic class interests in political struggle in favour of negotiation around economic–corporate or non-class interests.

In this context, economic struggle normally occurs within the logic of the market (i.e., over wages, hours, working conditions, prices) and political struggle normally occurs within the logic of the representative state, on the basis of the rule of law (i.e., it is oriented to competing definitions of the national interest and aims to reconcile the particular interests of citizens and property owners within an 'illusory' general interest). In broader terms, an important part of the struggle over class domination involves maintaining this fetishized separation of the economic and political spheres and their associated struggles – at least for subordinate classes (cf. Streeck 2013). Yet not all states in capitalist societies have this allegedly adequate form (see the section on 'Limits to Form Analysis' in this chapter; also chapter 9). Nor does formal adequacy guarantee material adequacy, in other words ensure that liberal democracy always and everywhere secures the extraeconomic conditions for continuing accumulation (see Abrams 1988; Barrow 1993; Gramsci 1971; Marx 1978a, 1978b; Moore 1957; Offe 1983; Poulantzas 1978).

This analysis highlights the specificity of the state as a terrain of political struggle vis-à-vis economic class struggle. The separation of the economic and political orders excludes an immediate isomorphism between economic class relations and relations among political categories. Indeed the legitimacy of the modern state would disappear if the state unequivocally served the immediate economic interests of the dominant class(es). It must have a certain apparatus unity and autonomy in order to organize hegemony (see chapter 3). Only then can it impose *short-term economic* sacrifices on the dominant class(es) to secure their *long-term political* domination. Intellectuals and ideological class struggles are crucial here because all social relations in capitalist societies appear as relations of consent, underpinned as necessary through resort to legitimate violence (see next section). This holds not only for political relations between dominant and dominated classes but also for relations among different fractions of the dominant class(es). The diversity of interests indicates the need for work to strategically align them, if a unified power bloc is to emerge and remain relatively stable. This can occur under the hegemony of one fraction of capital; but such hegemony depends in turn on the work of intellectuals, peak associations of capital, natural governing parties, and indeed state managers (e.g., Gramsci 1971; Poulantzas 1973; Portelli 1972; van Apeldoorn 2002).

The linkages between class and political relations depend on the prevailing balance of those forces that are oriented to the exercise of state power in the wider social formation. This poses again the issue of 'relative autonomy'. Marx addressed it in his analysis of the exceptional autonomy of Louis Bonaparte's praetorian regime, which was based on 'the rule of the naked sword' and backed by 600,000 bayonets rather than popular support (Marx 1986: 848). He did not explain this issue in terms of generic features of the capitalist type of state but through the contingencies of class struggle. Specifically, writing of the bourgeoisie, he observed that, 'in order to preserve its social power intact, its political power must be broken... in order to save its purse, it must forfeit the crown' (Marx 1978b: 143). This remark builds on his earlier claim, in *The Class Struggles in France, 1848–1850* (originally published in 1850), that a basic contradiction exists at the heart of a democratic constitution. For, whereas political power is granted via universal suffrage to the classes whose social slavery the constitution is designed to perpetuate, the social power of the bourgeoisie is sustained by the constitutional guarantee of private property rights that mainly benefit the dominant classes (Marx 1978a: 77). In short, liberal bourgeois democracies depend for stability on the self-limitation of what political forces can thematize as a political issue. If the requisite compromise within the power bloc and between dominant and subaltern classes breaks down, there is always the legal or factual possibility of declaring a state of economic or political emergency, of suspending the rule of law, and of limiting the forms, forums, spaces, and methods for expressing political resistance. The alleged demands of national security and of economic recovery then take precedence over 'normal' democratic politics (see chapter 9).

The importance of separation between the economic and the political spheres also explains why Marx rarely resorts to directly economic arguments in explaining the development of specific political regimes or the content of specific state policies – for the specificity of both depends on a specific dynamic of political struggles rather than on immediate economic circumstances. This point was also emphasized by Gramsci:

The claim, presented as an essential postulate of historical materialism, that every fluctuation of politics and ideology can be presented and expounded as an immediate expression of the [economic] structure, must be contested in theory as primitive infantilism, and combated in practice with the authentic testimony of Marx, the author of concrete political and historical works. (Gramsci 1971: 407 = Q7, §24: 869)

In this context, Gramsci noted that (1) the development of political regimes involves what, following evolutionary principles, one might call principles of variation, selection, and retention (and such principles, he insisted, make real-time analysis of the longer-term significance of present tendencies and countertendencies difficult); (2) errors of strategic and tactical calculation are common, leading to trial-and-error learning, often steered by crises and facilitated by the play of forces; and (3) many political actions derive from organizational necessities related to the preservation of state or party unity rather than to class interests (Gramsci 1971: 407–9 = Q7, §24: 869–71). In short, politics cannot be read off directly from changing economic circumstances, economic crises, underlying contradictions, and the like.

Ideological class domination

In *The German Ideology*, Marx and Engels (1976a) alluded to ideological class domination when they wrote that 'the ruling ideas of any age are the ideas of the ruling class' and related this principle to the control exercised by the ruling class over the means of intellectual production. Marx and Engels developed several perspectives on ideological class domination – ranging from the mystifying impact of commodity fetishism, through the individualist attitudes generated by political forms such as citizenship, to the struggles for hearts and minds in civil society. The second of these three perspectives identifies a specific effect of the state form on ideological domination, an effect analogous to the impact of commodity fetishism (see preceding section). Marxist interest in ideological class domination intensified with the rise of democratic government and mass politics in the late nineteenth century and the increasing importance of mass media and popular culture in the twentieth century. This has become a major theme in so-called western Marxism (for useful overviews, see Anderson 1976; Kellner 2005; Therborn 2010; and, on various approaches to ideology, Rehmann 2013).

An inspirational figure here, as indicated several times already, is Antonio Gramsci. His chief concern was to develop an autonomous Marxist science of politics in capitalist societies, distinguish types of state and politics, and identify the conditions for social revolution.

He was especially interested in the specificities of the political situation in the 'west' (Western Europe, United States). In this context, he was most concerned with the prospects for revolution and with the strategies that would be appropriate in the 'west' as opposed to the 'east' (i.e., tsarist Russia and other states in Eastern Europe). His analysis did not start with the territory–apparatus–population triplet – in part because Italy was still a nation-state in the process of formation in these respects and, in many ways, a failed state. He also went beyond a Weberian concern with imperative coordination by a rationally organized administrative apparatus and beyond a Leninist reduction of the state to a largely repressive apparatus. He identified the state in its narrow sense with the politico-juridical apparatus, the constitutional and institutional features of government, its formal decision-making procedures, and its general policies. But he usually focused on 'the state in its inclusive sense' (that is, the *integral state*) as 'political society + civil society' (Gramsci 1971: 263 = Q 6, §88: 763–4). In this context he also defined the state as 'the entire complex of practical and theoretical activities with which the ruling class not only justifies and maintains its dominance but manages to win the active consent of those over whom it rules' (Gramsci 1971: 244 = Q 15, §10: 1765). This approach dethrones or decentres the state as the principal focus of analysis and puts modes of class domination at its heart, thereby reducing the risk of fetishizing the state apparatus or, indeed, its separation and disembedding from the wider society.

Gramsci identified two main modes of class domination: *force* (the use of a coercive apparatus to bring the mass of people into conformity and compliance with the requirements of a specific mode of production) and *hegemony* (the successful mobilization and reproduction of the 'active consent' of dominated groups by the ruling class through its exercise of a political, intellectual, and moral leadership oriented to a 'collective will' or 'national–popular' consensus). Force was not exclusively identified with the state (e.g., Gramsci noted the role of fascist paramilitary terror squads), nor hegemony with civil society (the juridico-political apparatus also has ethical–political functions). Overall, Gramsci argued that the capitalist state should not be seen as a basically coercive apparatus but as an institutional ensemble based on a variable mixture of coercion, fraud–corruption, passive revolution, and active consent. Moreover, rather than treating specific institutions and apparatuses as technical instruments of government, he examined their social bases and stressed how state power is shaped by its links to the economic system and civil society (cf. chapter 3).

Regarding ideological class domination, Gramsci studied ideology as a system of ideas: a conception of the world that is manifest in many aspects of individual and collective life and that translates a worldview into corresponding rules of conduct. Three arguments are especially noteworthy. First, he argued that ethical–political ideas were key elements in the reciprocal shapings of the economic base, the juridico-political superstructure, and the moral and intellectual field. The notion of a 'historical bloc' referred to the resulting structural unity of a social formation. Gramsci studied how this is created and consolidated through specific intellectual, moral, and political practices that translate narrow sectoral, professional, or local interests into broader 'ethical–political' ones (1971: 366–7 = Q 10II, §6i). Ethical–political practices not only co-constitute economic structures but also give them their overall rationale and legitimacy (e.g., via bourgeois notions of property rights, freedom of exchange, and economic justice). Second, for Gramsci, 'hegemonic bloc' denoted a durable alliance of class forces organized by a class (or class fraction) that has proved capable of exercising leadership over subaltern groups as well as among the dominant classes. He also gave a key role here to 'organic intellectuals', that is, intellectuals with an organic link to the ruling or subaltern classes, able to articulate hegemonic projects that express their respective long-term class interests in 'national–popular' terms.

Third, in this context Gramsci also distinguished arbitrary from historically organic 'ideologies'. Ideologies – or, as I would prefer to describe them in the first instance, imaginaries (see the section on 'Social Imaginaries and the Critique of Ideologies') – can be construed in terms of accumulation strategies, state projects, and hegemonic visions (see chapter 3). 'Arbitrary ideologies' or projects are idiosyncratic, wilful speculations with limited (if any) connection with underlying realities and propose alternative futures that are infeasible in a given conjuncture. In contrast, 'organic ideologies' are materially adequate, identify what exists *in potentia* (that is, what could be realized in given spatiotemporal horizons of action), and outline appropriate strategic steps towards putting these possibilities into practice. As such, they help to cement the ideological unity of an entire social bloc at the level of the power bloc and, equally importantly, significant sections of the subaltern groups.

The Articulation of Economic, Political, and Ideological Domination

The preceding arguments indicate the possibilities of disjunction among different forms of class domination (crudely classified for presentational purposes as economic, political, and ideological). Each has its specific social forms, institutional materiality, and logics of action. Yet the overall unity of a social formation, however improbable, depends on a modicum of institutional and ideational coherence across these orders. This need not entail isomorphism or society-wide consensus. Institutional complementarity and a certain self-limitation of social forces to avoid harmful effects for (and resulting blowback from) other forces on which they depend are often more important. Moreover, as Gramsci noted, in capitalist societies hegemony must have a decisive economic nucleus (1971: 161 = Q13, §18: 1591). This invites us to examine in strategic–relational terms how relations among economic, political, and ideological domination depend on the biases of particular forms of domination and the strategies that consolidate (or undermine) these selectivities.

To explore this theme, I will proceed in two steps. First, I present a form-analytical account of the institutional correspondence between the capitalist economy, the juridico-political form of the state, and the latter's implications for political practice. Second, I show that these complementarities do not guarantee the strategic coherence of the economic, political, and social orders. This requires something more – namely specific economic, political, and societal strategies. Thus step two explores what these involve and how they are produced, consolidated, and institutionalized.

Table 4.1 presents six key formal features of the *capitalist type of state*, starting from the basic institutional separation of the economy as a profit-oriented, market-mediated, socially disembedded sphere of activities and the polity considered as a juridico-politically mediated and socially disembedded sphere of political activities oriented to collective goal attainment. The first column identifies significant aspects of the articulation of the economy and state in capitalism, reflected in their separation in unity. The use of this term indicates that this separation is *real* but, if reified, also *illusory* insofar as it is part of a larger social totality, which is tendentially organized in the shadow of profit-oriented, market-mediated accumulation as its dominant principle of societal organization. This separation in unity is grounded in the capital relation, and also aids its reproduction. Further, the distinct economic and political systems have their own operational logics, spatiotemporal dynamics, modes of calculation, and associated practices that are not only dissociated from each other but can also develop in contradictory ways. The two systems are also interdependent, structurally coupled, and coevolve.

The second column identifies some implications of this institutional separation for class relations and for the overall dynamic of

Table 4.1 Some key features of the capitalist type of state

Articulation of economy and state in capitalism	Implications for the economy and class relations	Implications for the state and politics
Institutional separation of market economy, sovereign state, and a public sphere (civil society) that is located beyond market and state	The economy is organized under the dominance of the capitalist law of value, as this is mediated through competition between capitals and economic class struggle	*Raison d'état*, a specialized political rationality,* distinct from profit-and-loss market logic and from religious, moral, or ethical principles
The legitimate or constitutionalized claim to a monopoly of organized coercion within territory controlled by state Role of legality in the legitimation of the state and its activities	Coercion is excluded from the immediate organization of the labour process. The value form and market forces, not coercion, shape the trajectory of capital accumulation	Specialized military-police organs are subject to constitutional control. Force has ideological as well as repressive functions Subject to law, the state may intervene to compensate for market failure in the national interest or for the common good
'The tax state': state revenues derive largely from taxes on economic actors and their activities and from loans advanced by market actors. The state does not have its own property to produce goods and services for its own use and/or to sell in order to generate profits and support itself and its activities Tax capacity depends on legal authority and coercive power	Taxes are a deduction from private revenues but may be used to produce public goods deemed essential to market economy and/or to social cohesion Bourgeois tax form: taxes are a general contribution to government revenue and are levied on a continuing basis that the state can apply freely to legitimate tasks. They should not be specific, ad hoc taxes levied for specific tasks.	The subjects of the state in its territory have a general duty to pay taxes, regardless of whether they approve of specific state activities or not State fiat money is the means of payment for state taxes and therefore circulates more generally in national space (and perhaps beyond) Taxation capacity acts as security against sovereign debt Tax as one of earliest foci of class struggle

Table 4.1 Continued

Articulation of economy and state in capitalism	Implications for the economy and class relations	Implications for the state and politics
Specialized administrative staff, with its own channels of recruitment and training and its distinctive *ésprit de corps* This staff is subject to the authority of the political executive. It forms a social category divided by market and status position	The state occupies a specific place in the overall division between manual and mental labour. Officials and political class specialize in intellectual labour with a close relation between their specialized knowledge and their power Knowledge and intelligence become a major basis of the state's capacities	Official discourse has a key role in the exercise of state power. Public and private intellectuals formulate state and hegemonic projects that define the national and/or the 'national popular' interest The state builds legitimacy by reflecting the national and/or 'national popular' interest
The state is based on the rule of law, which, ideally, involves a division between private law, administrative law, and public law There is no *formal* monopoly of political power in the hands of dominant economic class(es): 'equality before the law' is a key legal principle International law governs the relations between states	Economic agents are formally free and equal owners of commodities, including labour power Private law evolved on the basis of property rights and contract law The state has a key role in securing external conditions for economic exchange and the realization of private profit	The state's formal subjects are individuals endowed with citizenship rights, not feudal estates or collectively organized producer groups or classes. Struggles to extend and defend these rights play a key role in the expansion of state activities. Public law is organized around individual–state, public–private, and national–international distinctions

Continued

Table 4.1   Continued

Articulation of economy and state in capitalism	Implications for the economy and class relations	Implications for the state and politics
Formally sovereign state with a distinct and exclusive territorial domain, in which it is formally free to act without interference from other states Substantively, states are constrained in the exercise of sovereignty by the balance of international forces	There are tensions between the economy as an abstract 'space of flows' in the world market and the economy as a sum of localized activities, with an inevitably politically overdetermined character Particular capitals may seek support in world competition from their respective states	Ideally the state is recognized by other states as sovereign on its territory. but it may need to defend its territorial integrity by force Political and military rivalry is conditioned by the strength of the national economy

Raison d'état refers here to the distinctive modes of calculation that are rooted in the reproduction of the state in its narrow sense and to the conditions for pursuing state projects; it is not used in the restrictive sense of one among several principles of representation, which was introduced in chapter 3.
Source: Jessop 2002: 38–9

the capitalist economy – which, given this separation, is based on profit-oriented, *market-mediated* accumulation (on political capitalism, see chapter 8). The third column presents the results of a similar exercise for the state apparatus, state power, the forms of politics, and political class domination. The issues covered in the second and third columns are, of course, crucial for an analysis of the structural power of capital and class domination and, overall, the table indicates the heuristic potential of form analysis.

From a strategic–relational perspective, this kind of form analysis explores not only the formal constitution and formal adequacy of a given type of state or regime but also its crucial role as a source of strategic selectivity or bias favourable to one or another social agent, identity, interests, spatiotemporal horizons of action, strategies, and so on. The SRA also posits that form, rather than following function, can render it problematic (Jessop 1982). This is one reason why form analysis can be used (1) to consider the problems facing different social forces as they pursue their interests on the strategically selective terrain constituted by a particular set or assemblage of forms; and (2) to identify potential sites of crisis within the state system and within the exercise of state power (see chapters 2, 3, 8, and 9).

However, as noted in chapter 2, the state is polymorphous. Profit-oriented, market-mediated accumulation is one among several alternative orientations to profit (cf. Weber 1961, 1978; see also chapter 8) and, in addition, there are other principles of societal organization besides differential accumulation. Which principle is dominant can influence the form and impact of state power and is itself the contingent outcome of the balance of forces mobilized behind different projects. So there is no guarantee that the modern state will always (or ever) be primarily capitalist in character and, even where capital's representatives and capitalist rationality are deeply embedded in its organizational matrix, state projects typically take account of other functional demands and of civil society in order to promote institutional integration and social cohesion within the territorial boundaries of the state.

The specificity of profit-oriented, market-mediated capital accumulation derives from its character as generalized commodity production and, hence, from the dominance of the value form. The latter comprises a number of interconnected elements that are organically linked at different moments in the overall reproduction of the capital relation. They include such forms as the commodity, the wage, money, prices, taxes, profits of enterprise, interest, rent, and so forth. In their unity as interconnected elements of the value form, these moments define the parameters of accumulation and also delimit the sorts of economic crises that can develop within capitalism. Yet the dominance of the value form does not fully determine the path of capital accumulation. Accumulation depends on capital's ability to valorize wage labour and, hence, on struggles in which the shifting balance of forces is moulded by many factors beyond the value form. Different moments of the value form (see above) have only a formal unity, that is, are unified only as modes of expression of generalized commodity production. The substantive unity and continued reproduction of the circuit of capital depends on successful coordination of its different moments within the limits of the value form. This is achieved post hoc and in anarchic fashion: the circuit can break at many points. A crucial difficulty in analysing the construal and subsequent representation of capital's interests is their indeterminacy. If the substantive unity and the course of capitalist economies are indeterminate, how can one establish capital's interests?

Abstractly, these interests involve the reproduction of the value form (generalized commodity production) along with its various external conditions of existence. This is implicit in the definition of capitalism and might seem tautological. Even at this level of abstraction, however, it is hard to give substantive content to this seeming tautology even at the level of 'capital in general', let alone for particular capitals. For the interests of 'capital in general' consist in the reproduction of a contradictory, dilemmatic, ambivalent, and ill-defined nexus of value and nonvalue forms that are favourable to continued accumulation on a world scale. This nexus is always contested, provisional, and unstable – especially if one extends the analysis beyond trade in free markets and the rational organization of capitalist production (rational capitalism) to include various kinds of political capitalism, as well as financial speculation and traditional commercial capitalism and their articulation in the world market (see chapter 8). 'Capital in general', used here to refer to the overall circuit of capital considered apart from particular capitals, is a real structure with real effects. It lacks agency and calculative powers, however, which can only be exercised by particular capitals. So capital in general as an objective structure-cum-process and particular capitals are interdependent. The former cannot be reproduced without the activities of a set of particular capitals; the latter cannot function outside the economic nexus formed by the circuit of capital. But the reproduction of capital in general requires only *some* – variable – subset of individual capitals; indeed its survival may require the bankruptcy, depreciation, or takeover of other capitals.

In sum, the capital relation is an underdetermined terrain on which diverse agents with diverse interests compete to advance competing accumulation strategies that can reconcile, in different and potentially contradictory and conflictual ways, the tension between – to paraphrase Rousseau's discourse on political economy (1758; see also Rousseau 1792; and Foisneau 2010) – an integrative 'general will' and the pursuit of particular interests that might culminate in an inconsistent 'will of all'. There are three possible ways to secure such an incomplete, provisional, and unstable 'general will'.

The first is through an *anarchically produced* coincidence of the general will with the interests of the most powerful fractions of capital, which impose it on other fractions, through negative or positive coordination (see chapter 7). This is especially unlikely, because the needs of capital in general are not immediately transparent and are probably best served by different particular capitals at different times, in different respects, and in different conjunctures.

The second possibility is that an actual collective capitalist actor emerges to represent the interests of capital in general not merely rhetorically but in practice. Finance capital, the Bilderberg Group, the Trilateral Commission, the European Round Table of Industrialists, the American Chamber of Commerce, the World Economic Forum are among the groups, forums, or associations that have aspired to this role or had it attributed to them (for examples, see respectively, Hilferding 2007; Estulin 2007; Gill 1991; van Apeldoorn 2002; Rupert and Solomon 2006; and Marshall 2015). But there are many competing associations, organizations, think tanks, and strategic forums that seek to aggregate and articulate capitalist interests around different economic strategies; and they are also divided by many other sociospatial interests, especially when we consider this aspect from the viewpoint of the world market rather than of relatively closed national economies. In short, in the absence of a strong strategic bias in the overall articulation of the state system that favoured capital in general on a world scale, they reproduce a pluralist capitalist 'will of all'.

The third, even more remote possibility is that an organ located outside the circuits of capital can act on behalf of capital and impose the 'general will' on actual capitalists. This role is often attributed to the state. It would require the state (or its equivalent) to be so structured that the contradictory demands of particular capitals could be aggregated in and through its operations and rendered compatible with the needs of capital in general. However, as noted, the state has its own interests in reproducing itself as a juridico-political apparatus and in legitimating its authority by advancing state projects and hegemonic visions that do not transparently serve capital's immediate interests.

All three solutions appear even less plausible if we consider the multiple challenges involved in identifying the current – let alone future – interests of 'capital in general' as a reference point for establishing the overall – as opposed to the particular – class relevance of given strategies, projects, and visions (see p. 97 above). This said, four assumptions might make the task easier to achieve: first, there is no inherent directional dynamic to capital accumulation (Postone 1993) – its course is contingent on past and present hegemonic or dominant strategies and on their interaction within the world market; second, strategies are co-constitutive of class interests and alliances, with the result that they can orient action in situations of uncertainty, crisis, or transition and, if consistent with the overall logic of capital, can provide direction; third, muddling through on a favourable strategic terrain is the most likely means in and through which the contingent interests of capital in general and of particular capitals will be discovered (on this third point, see Clarke 1977); and, fourth, crises provide a steering mechanism that indicates where crucial interests have been neglected – though these also pose problems of construing causes and solutions (Jessop 2015b; see also chapter 5 on spatiotemporal fixes).

There considerations suggest another, more contingent solution. This consists in the elaboration of an 'historically organic' accumulation strategy (e.g., state project) that unifies different parts of the circuit of capital (e.g., banking capital, profit-producing capital, commercial capital) under the hegemony of one fraction. Such a solution will not (and cannot) abolish competition or conflicts of interest but can offer a stable framework in which competition can occur, conflicts be worked out, and compromises be reached. The solution depends on a shared, simplified economic imaginary that frames observation, calculation, and governance, is congruent with real-world processes and practices, and is relevant to the objectives of the hegemonic fraction, taken together with a critical mass (number, range, and connectedness) of particular capitals. While leading capitalist interests may play key roles in shaping this strategic orientation, its elaboration and translation into policies requires many technical intellectuals and experts. The aim would be to give some 'homogeneity and awareness' of its economic and political functions to capital, organize relations between value and nonvalue aspects appropriate to accumulation strategies, and perform tasks of political government and social hegemony. These conditions seem more plausible if the state is understood to include 'not only the apparatus of government, but also the "private" apparatus of "hegemony" or civil society' (Gramsci 1971: 261 = Q26, §6: 801). The success of such a strategy also depends on appropriate institutional, spatiotemporal, and social fixes (see chapter 5). In addition, a strategy can be truly 'hegemonic' only where it is accepted by the economically subordinate or exploited classes as well as by the non-hegemonic fractions of capital. This implies in turn that a hegemonic accumulation strategy should be linked to the changing balance of forces between capital and labour as modified from time to time by the influence of other class or nonclass forces (e.g., the traditional petty bourgeoisie, the Christian right, new social movements).

The Limits to Form Analysis and the State in Capitalist Societies

The arguments in the preceding section indicate the scope for another type of analysis, which relies less on the state's formal constitution than on its historical constitution and on the prevailing balance of forces and their strategic orientations and chosen tactics. The potential for this type of analysis is reflected in the common distinction (not always fully understood) between the capitalist type of state and the state in capitalist society. Form analysis is suitable for the former, not for the latter. Moreover, taking membership of the OECD as a proxy for capitalist types of state, there are 34 states that might plausibly be included in this category. Several of these actually fall short of having the key features of this type. For other states, that is, the vast majority, it is better to employ a more historical and agent-centred account of the state as an institutional ensemble and focus on the material adequacy of specific formal and substantive features of the state in its integral sense. Thus analyses will pay more attention to the open struggle among political forces to shape the political process in ways that privilege accumulation over other principles of societalization. The guiding questions are how politics and policies acquire a particular content, mission, aims, and objectives and to what extent they are more or less adequate to securing the economic and extraeconomic conditions that sustain differential accumulation in a given conjuncture or in the medium to long term. This suggests that research on the historical constitution of the *state in capitalist societies* and on the instrumental use of its capacities for capitalist purposes differs from studies of the formal constitution of the *capitalist type of state*, which has an inbuilt, structural privileging of capitalist interests.

Table 4.2 compares the capitalist type of state and states in capitalist societies on six dimensions and indicates relevant theoretical and methodological questions. On the basis of this table, we can conclude that an analysis of the capitalist type of state would begin by identifying its historical specificity and creating a typology and periodization of its various forms. It would study the *formal adequacy* of a given type of state in a pure capitalist social formation, recognize that its form typically problematizes its functionality, and then examine how and to what extent political practices, broadly conceived, *may* overcome such problems in specific periods and conjunctures. In contrast, an analysis of actually existing states in societies that are dominated by capitalist relations of production would begin in relatively more concrete and complex terms and would adopt from the outset a more historical approach, oriented to the changing balance of forces. It would show how political class struggles and their outcomes are mediated and condensed through specific institutional forms in particular periods, stages, and conjunctures regardless of whether these forms corresponded to the capitalist type of state. It would examine

Table 4.2 Capitalist type of state versus state in capitalist society

	Capitalist Type of State	State in Capitalist Society
Historical specificity	Distinguishes capitalist type of state from types associated with other modes of production	Focuses on how inherited state forms may be used in new historical contexts
Dominant axis of societal organization	The logic of capital accumulation is dominant	Either another axis of societal organization is dominant or none
Key approach to the state's development	Focus on *formal constitution* (how state acquires 'formal adequacy') and on how 'form problematizes function'	Focus on *historical constitution* (how state building is mediated by a changing balance of forces oriented to different projects)
Measure of adequacy	Focus on formal adequacy, i.e., on the isomorphic fit or overall complementarity between the state form and other forms of the capital relation, such that the former reinforces the latter	*Focus on functional or material adequacy*, i.e., on the effective exercise of state capacities as these are shaped by the balance of forces with a view to securing key conditions for accumulation and political legitimacy
State power as class power	Class power is structural and opaque. This type of state is more likely to function for capital as a whole (at least nationally) and its functionality also depends less on overt class struggles	Class power is instrumental and transparent. There is a stronger likelihood that the state is used to pursue the interests of particular capitals or other specific interests
Periodization	Phases in formal development, crises in and of the capitalist type of state, alternation between normal and exceptional periods	Phases in historical development, major shifts in institutional design, changes in governments and policies

Source: A substantially reworked version of a table in Jessop 2007a

whether the activities of particular branches, departments, dispositives, power centres, or power networks are *functionally or materially adequate* for capital accumulation and political class domination. And it would investigate how this adequacy is achieved (or not) in specific conjunctures through specific strategies and policies promoted by particular social forces. Both approaches can be useful for specific purposes and both are consistent with the claim that the state is a social relation. The former prioritizes form analysis, the latter privileges work on social forces. To combine them effectively requires more detailed studies of the crucial mediating role of the institutional and organizational forms of politics and their strategic–relational implications for the balance of forces.

On Social Imaginaries and the Critique of Ideologies

Semiosis, discourse, language (and mass media) are key forces in shaping the political imaginaries at the heart of the state and political struggle. Of particular interest here are the assumptions, frames, and structures of feeling inscribed in language and other forms of signification even before specific political strategies are pursued. The 'raw material' of ideological domination is meaning systems and lived experience, and these are articulated into specific 'imaginaries' on the basis of particular articulations of this semiotic raw material (Laclau and Mouffe 1985; Rehmann 2013; Sum and Jessop 2013). These specific imaginaries should in turn be related to specific narrative, rhetorical, or argumentative features of the exercise of state power, as well as to class relations and identity politics (Jessop 2002; Müller et al., 1994; Neocleous 2003). At stake here are the sources and mechanisms that 'bias' lived experience and imaginaries towards specific identities and their changing ideal or material interests in specific conjunctures. This bias does not entail that these are always 'ideological', that is, inevitably related to power and domination, let alone designed to maintain these relations. Indeed, on the latter point, the most powerful ideological effects do not so much stem from immediate conscious action as they derive from their inscription and sedimentation in the form of fetishism, the taken-for-grantedness of the foundational categories of the capitalist mode of production, and so forth (cf. Rehmann 2013).

Thus we must ask how basic categories and general social imaginaries come, more or less durably, to shape, dominate, or hegemonize the world. One aspect is the extent and manner of their connection to, and grounding in, 'lived experience', that is, how actors experience and understand their world(s) as real and meaningful from one or more subject positions and standpoints, and how these basic categories and imaginaries relate to each other. Lived experience never reflects an extrasemiotic reality but involves sense- and meaning-making processes based on the meaningful *pre*-interpretation of the natural-cum-social world.[1] Its form is not pre-given, and this creates space for learning. It is also open to dislocation, contestation, repoliticization, and struggle to restore, alter, or overturn meaning systems, including relevant social imaginaries. Social forces strive to make one or another imaginary the hegemonic or dominant 'frame' in particular contexts or to promote complementary or opposed imaginaries. Key roles in this regard are played by organic and traditional intellectuals and, increasingly, by the mass media. These efforts succeed to the extent that people forget the arbitrary, contested, and constructed nature of the imaginary – with the result that it becomes 'the only...one that makes sense' (Taylor 2001: 2).

These remarks provide the basis for developing a strategic–relational critique of ideology around the sources and mechanisms that 'bias' lived experience and imaginaries towards the promotion of specific identities and interests. This would involve six main steps: (1) recognizing the role of semiosis as a meaning pool in complexity reduction; (2) identifying social imaginaries, that is, specific clusters of meaning (or semiotic) systems, and describing their form and content; (3) exploring the immanent contradictions and inconsistencies in these imaginaries through an immanent critique of texts and discourses; (4) analysing their contingent articulation and functioning in securing the conditions for domination that serve particular interests, ideal or material, in specific conjunctures – which depends in part on contextual knowledge available to the analyst; (5) exploring the semiotic and extrasemiotic mechanisms involved in selecting and consolidating the dominance or the hegemony of some systems of meaning and some ideologies over others (which links to the critique of domination); and (6) distinguishing between cases where these effects are motivated and cases where they are effects of sedimented meaning (for an elaboration, see Sum and Jessop 2013: 164–72).

Conclusions

In terms of the distinctions presented in the introduction, this chapter has developed an institutionalist analysis of the formal constitution of the capitalist type of state and of its implications for economic, political, and ideological class domination. At the same time it has deliberately avoided functionalist claims that form must follow function. I have remarked that a particular structural or institutional form may be formally adequate, that is, isomorphic and complementary to the basic forms of the capital relation. I have also noted that the extent to which this translates into material adequacy (ensures appropriate politics, policies, or equilibrium of forces) depends on the actions of social agents as well as on the wider conjuncture. Indeed, even if capitalist bias is deeply embedded in the matrix of a capitalist type of state, the latter's policies could work against capital as inimical forces capture the state apparatus or pressure it to pursue capitalistically irrational policies (e.g., the final years of the Nazi 'police state', or the national security state promoted by George W. Bush; on exceptional states more generally, see below and chapter 9). It is for this reason that I also distinguished the formal critique of the capitalist type of state from the substantive critique of power relations in states in capitalist societies.

The juxtaposition of these two approaches indicates the strengths and weaknesses of Marxism. First, in privileging class domination, it marginalizes other forms of social domination – patriarchal, ethnic, 'racial', hegemonic masculinities, interstate, regional or territorial, and so on. At best these figure as factors that overdetermine class domination or change in response to changes therein. Second, Marxist analyses may exaggerate the structural coherence of class domination, neglecting its disjunctures, contradictions, countervailing tendencies, and so on. Notions of a unified ruling class belie the messiness of configurations of class power – the frictions within and across its economic, political, and ideological dimensions, the disjunctions between different scales of social organization, the contradictory nature and effects of strategies, tactics, and policies, the probability of state as well as market failures, and the capacity of subaltern forces to engage in resistance. Many empirical analyses reveal this messiness and complexity, but this often goes unremarked in abstract Marxist theorizing. Third, Marxists risk reducing the limits of economic, political, and ideological power to the effect of class contradictions and thereby missing other sources of failure. Fourth, while an emphasis on strategy and tactics is important for avoiding the structuralist fallacy that capital reproduces itself quasi-automatically and without the need for human action, there is a risk of voluntarism if strategy and tactics are examined without reference to specific conjunctures and broader structural contexts.

When taken seriously rather than used as a template to redescribe taken-for-granted dogmatic positions, the SRA provides one means to overcome these limitations. This is where critical reflection on other approaches, entry points, and standpoints is useful – because it highlights possible traps in focusing one-sidedly on the heuristic potential of taking capital accumulation as the primary reference point when analysing the state and state power. This is the reason why the three-element approach to the state – rather than the capitalist type of state – was adopted as the primary entry point for this book. It is also the reason why this approach was supplemented by an emphasis on the 'state idea' – and, by extension, I have emphasized the importance of economic strategies, state projects, and hegemonic visions in this regard. And, lastly, it is the reason why I commented on the important theoretical and methodological differences between studying the capitalist type of state and studying states in capitalist societies.

I close this chapter by identifying four conditions that would justify taking differential accumulation as the privileged entry point into an analysis of the state and state power. The first condition involves a thought experiment, that is, the construction of a rational abstraction or ideal type of state that would be *formally* adequate to the reproduction of capital accumulation and class domination (see Tables 4.1 and 4.2). While the aim of such experiments is to arrive at rational abstractions, the analysis should also draw inspiration from actual cases. The second condition is one where, despite the more complex, polymorphic character of a given state or set of states, they approximate in key respects a formally adequate type of capitalist state for the social formation(s) in question. Attention would then turn to the extent to which and the reason why the structurally inscribed strategic selectivities of such states are actualized in the exercise of state power in a given period or conjuncture. The third condition arises where the dominant principle of societalization is profit-oriented, market-mediated accumulation, but the state is not a typical capitalist state. This rather common condition requires theoretical and methodological tools appropriate to the study of the state in capitalist societies to investigate whether and, if so, how the state system is implicated in the selection and retention of this particular principle of societalization. Fourth and conversely, one might explore the failure of efforts to establish accumulation as the dominant principle of societal organization even when there is a powerful alliance of social forces, internal or external, that seek to establish this dominance; and this is the fourth condition. The question of state failure would be relevant in the other three cases too. I explore some of these possibilities in later chapters.

Part II

On Territory, Apparatus, and Population

5

The State and Space–Time

The strategic–relational approach (SRA) investigates state power not only in terms of the state's basic structure, institutional architecture, and specific organizational forms but also in terms of its strategic capacities within the political system and vis-à-vis the wider nexus of functional systems and the everyday world. These capacities are crucially related to the spatiotemporalities of the state and to their fit or otherwise with other institutional and organizational orders. This invites interest in the spatiotemporal aspects of the structurally inscribed strategic selectivities of a given state system. Time and space are closely related and have both structural aspects (the interrelated temporalities and spatialities of given institutional and organizational orders) *and* strategic aspects (such as specific temporal and spatial horizons of action, wars of position and manoeuvre, and efforts to reorganize social relations in time–space). Addressing such issues builds on the issue of state territory, narrowly conceived, but also takes us well beyond it. Accordingly, this chapter adopts a spatiotemporal entry point to state formation, to the six dimensions of the state considered in chapter 3, and to the questions of domination explored in chapter 4.

First, while all state activities are grounded in particular places and times, their external coordinates in space and time do not exhaust their spatiotemporal features. Such activities are also marked by path-dependent legacies, present spatiotemporal matrices, and future horizons of action. Second, they have their own internal and interiorized spatiotemporalities, which depend in part on the linkages between the spatiotemporal features of the state in its narrow sense and the spatiotemporal features of the social order within which they are embedded. For example, as the world market becomes more integrated, the state's spatial matrix and horizons of action typically change in response to challenges to its territorial sovereignty. Likewise, with the general trend towards social acceleration in the wider society, the temporal sovereignty of the state is being threatened (chapter 7). This creates pressures to speed up political and policy routines, leading to what Peck and Theodore (2015) call 'fast policy'. Third, states have, in turn, spatiotemporal effects on other institutional orders and on everyday life; and the repercussions of state activities, successful or not, spread out in space and time. Fourth, as noted in earlier chapters, states have other material and discursive features that differentiate them as potential objects of governance from other institutional orders. And, fifth, the conditions for the successful performance of state activities nonetheless exceed the times and places susceptible to governance. This poses major questions about governance and governance failure (chapter 6).

Sociospatiality

Space comprises socially produced grids and horizons of social action that divide and organize the material, social, and imaginary world(s) and also orient actions in terms of such divisions. As a product of social practices that appropriate and transform physical and social phenomena and invest them with social significance, space can function as a site, object, and means of governance. Inherited spatial configurations and their opportunity structures are *sites* where governance may be established, contested, and modified. Space is an *object* of governance insofar as it results from the fixing, manipulation, reordering, and lifting of material, social, and symbolic borders, boundaries, frontiers, and liminal spaces. Space can also be a *means of governance* when it defines horizons of action in terms of 'inside', 'outside', and 'liminal' spaces and when it configures possible connections among actors, actions, and events through various spatiotemporal technologies. For boundaries contain *and* connect. They frame interactions selectively, privileging some identities and interests over others; and they structure possible connections to other places and spaces across different scales. While such spatial divisions may generate fundamental antagonisms, they may also facilitate coordination across spaces, places, and scales through solidarity, hierarchy, networks, markets, or other governance mechanisms.

While space is constructed and governed on many scales, ranging from the body and personal space to the planetary level and 'outer space', my focus is on the spatial dimensions of the state, their articulation within state space, their interaction with forms of spatiality beyond the state, and the spatiotemporal imaginaries that provide a discursive–material framework for the six dimensions of statehood. Of particular interest is the relative weight of territory, place, scale, and networks in the overall organization of the state system and in the exercise of state powers (Jessop, Brenner, and Jones 2008; Jones and Jessop 2010; see also below). This is an important issue because, although the territorialization of political power is one of the three defining features of the state, it does not follow that this is the most important aspect of the sociospatial organization of the state – especially if one considers what happens within a state's territorial boundaries rather than focusing on the constitution of those boundaries.

Territorialization and State Formation

We have already encountered territory and territorialization as key statal elements. In chapter 2 the analysis was mainly comparative; here it is more historical. In general, territorialization denotes the enclosure of social relations into relatively bounded, demarcated political units or the attempted reorganization of such units once they are established. The state not only encloses places within territorial borders but also seeks, for a range of purposes, to police social relations that occur within these borders. This informs the 'power container' metaphor noted in chapter 2 – which can nonetheless be misleading when it privileges containment over the connective role of borders.

State formation is not a once-and-for-all process: the state did not emerge in just one place and spread out from there. It was built many times, had its ups and downs, and saw recurrent cycles of centralization and decentralization, fusion and fission, territorialization and deterritorialization. It also assumed many institutional forms – from the mutual recognition by nomadic groups of the boundaries of their respective roaming territories through chiefdoms to early states and city-states, and then on to ancient empires, feudal states, absolutism early modern states, the development of the Westphalian system, and the emergence of so-called postmodern state forms. This is a rich field for political archaeology, political anthropology, historical sociology, comparative politics, evolutionary institutional economics, historical materialism, and international relations. Although the origins of the state have been discussed in various monocausal ways, none of these accounts offers a convincing general explanation (cf. Wright 2006). Marxists focus on the emergence of an economic surplus that enabled the growth of a specialized, economically unproductive political apparatus concerned to secure cohesion in a (class-)divided society (see, classically, Engels 1972); military historians focus on the role of military conquest in state building or on the demands of defending territorial integrity (exemplary here is Hintze 1975; see also Porter 1994; Gorski 2001; Nelson 2006). Others emphasize the role of a specialized priesthood and of organized religion – or other forms of ideological power – in giving symbolic unity to the population governed by the state (see Claessen and Skalnik 1978; and, regarding charismatic authority more generally, Breuer 2014). Feminist theorists examine the role of patriarchy in state formation and the state's continuing role in reproducing gender divisions (e.g., Rapp 1977; Ortner 1978; Gailey 1985). For later periods, yet other scholars focus on the 'imagined political communities' around which nation-states have been constructed (classically, Anderson 1981).

A better approach would be multicausal and multicontextural and would recognize that states change continually, are prone to collapse or partial failure, fusion and fission, hierarchical ordering and resistance thereto, and may be rebuilt in new forms, with new capacities and functions, a new scope and new scales of operation, and so forth. This restructuring often occurs either on the basis of knowledge gained from past experimentation or with the help of lessons drawn from the observation of other cases. The evolution of the state system is also shaped by interactions between state-organized and other types of societies. Such interactions include the intense interactions between nomadic and sedentary populations and the interactions that linked farmers to fishermen, hunter-gatherers to pastoralists, highlanders to lowland peoples (see Scott 2009; Finer 1997b).

A good entry point for understanding state formation is to examine the archaeological evidence on *primary* state formation – that is, cases where a 'state' emerged for the first time and where this process was relatively slow by comparison with cases of so-called secondary state formation, where new states were created in the context of existing ones (on the importance of this distinction, see Service 1962, 1975; Wright 2006; Breuer 2014). Examples include Mesoamerica, Peru, Egypt, Mesopotamia, the Indus Valley, and China. The multiple independent origins of primary states and the subsequent diffusion of state formation across the globe should caution against Eurocentric analyses of statehood. The collapse of primary states, or their integration, through diverse means, into more encompassing political orders also contraindicates an (irreversible) evolutionist approach. Indeed there are recurrent attempts, by populations that have been subjected to state control, to escape it and to regain autonomy in their own spaces (Gledhill, Bender, and Larsen, 1988; Scott 2009). The same caution is justified by the varieties of ancient state traditions and their survival into the modern period. Regarding Europe, for example, given the multiplicity of historical (and geographical) starting points for modern state formation during the early Renaissance period, it is hardly surprising that modern and contemporary states continue to exhibit such divergent institutional and spatial forms, rather than converging around a generic model of the modern bureaucratic–democratic state (Escolar 1997; Dyson 1982; Mann 1986, 1996; Finer 1997a, 1997b, 1997c; Rokkan 1999). Alongside the European tradition we can cite the Chinese state tradition, with its Confucian state project and hegemonic vision and its interactions with nomadic empires and other states; a distinct Indian state tradition dating from the first Mauryan Empire (c. 300 BC), in which the emperor implemented Brahman law and promoted pragmatic realism among local rulers (this tradition is reflected in the *Arthashastra*, which is the Hindu equivalent of Machiavelli's *The Prince*); and the Islamic world, which blurs the line, drawn in Europe after the Peace of Westphalia (1648), between state and religion.

The key to primary state formation is the development of logistical capacities to extend control over a territory and its population and to govern the expanded territory through a multilevel administrative apparatus that had developed an internal specialization of tasks. This suggests that the three-element approach is relevant to state formation as well as to later states and their transformation. Diverse theoretical and historical studies indicate that political evolution has passed through three broad stages.

First are relatively egalitarian societies, with segmentary forms of social organization based on kinship ties or village settlements or both, with a limited surplus allocated on the basis of household membership and reciprocity, and with a wide distribution of relatively simple (often dual-use) tools of combat. Political leadership is decentralized and relatively ephemeral, being based on unusual personal qualities like wisdom or bravery rather than on inheritance; and decision making tends to be collective and to occur in periodic social gatherings linked to natural cycles, specific rituals, or emergencies.

Next come socially stratified societies that have a primitive division of political labour based on institutionalized forms of political authority such as the authority of a chief with a chiefly administrative retinue; these forms survive as *offices* even when individual occupants vacate them, for whatever reason. Thus, if a chief dies, he must be replaced by someone of equivalent standing. There is no formal administrative apparatus or monopoly of coercion, and surplus is allocated through reciprocity and redistribution rather than through market exchange. Indicating the significance of temporality as well as that of spatiality to state formation, centralized authority produces faster decision making than the intermittent pattern of collective deliberation found in segmentary societies. But this depends in turn on the 'infrastructural power' to mobilize resources in order to support chiefly retinues. Thus, while separate chiefdoms frequently interact through exchange or through raiding, in a desire to reinforce chiefly prestige through the acquisition of exotic items or through military success, they rarely engage in the conquest of distant territories and even less often seek to control them for extended periods, as opposed to exacting intermittent tribute. There were two important constraints on such conquest and control. One was the logistical (i.e., spatiotemporal) challenge of exercising expanded control from a single centre when a half-day's travel was limited to 25–30 km by foot. The other was the absence of a division of political labour into multiple, specialized tasks, which made it hard to delegate chiefly authority without risking insubordination, diversion of crucial resources into the hands of subordinates, insurrection, or fission (Wright 1977, 2006; Earle 1997; Pauketat 2007). Together, these factors tended to produce a political cycle marked by an increase in a chief's command over power and resources, followed by a period of decline. This oscillation led to the formation of complex, 'paramount' chiefdoms and to a reversion to simple chiefdoms (Wright 2006). More generally, limited logistical and extractive capacities were a problem for most ancient polities, and not just for chiefdoms (Mann 1984; Finer 1997a, 1997b, 1997c). These comments reinforce Max Weber's emphasis on technologies of long-distance transportation and communication as a crucial precondition of state formation (Weber 1978: 956–1005); other preconditions were literate administrators, writing and record-keeping materials, and coinage).

The third stage involves the emergence of states based on centralized bureaucratic administration that can overcome these spatiotemporal and administrative limits. In all known areas, early states developed from chiefdoms. Not all chiefdoms evolved into states, of course; but it is now widely accepted that all primary state formation – that is, all cases where a first-generation state evolved without contact with preexisting states – involve the development of a more extended, specialized, multilevel administrative apparatus, with more layers of control and a more developed division of 'political' labour (Spencer 2003: 1185; cf. Carneiro 1981; Earle 1997; Wright 2006).

States can be divided into social formations organized on centre–periphery lines and social formations based on functional differentiation, which covers the entire territory of the state (Innis 1951; Polanyi 1957; Fried 1967; Eisenstadt 1963; Flannery 1972, 1999; Service 1975; Luhmann 1989). While chiefdoms use violence but are restrained by the limited development of military technologies (which makes the possession and use of weapons accessible to many subjects too), further developments in warfare and a more specialized political–military division of labour mean that, as states get consolidated, some types of force can be used only by certain categories of state personnel or by allied groups in the wider society. Warfare is especially important in the formation of empires and development of absolute monarchies, given their standing armies, permanent bureaucracy, national taxation, codified law, clear frontiers, and beginnings of a unified market (Anderson 1974a; Goody 1980; Parker 1996; Porter 1994; Rogers 1955).

Samuel Finer's history of government sidesteps what he describes as 'the extremely obscure and contentious question of how states emerge from primeval and tribal societies' in favour of examining how 'states such as we know them today emerged through aggregation from smaller territorial units or the disaggregation of larger territorial units' (Finer 1997a: 9). In fact the evidence on primary state formation is not so murky as Finer suggested. Overall, research on this topic indicates that the process *cannot* be explained in terms of (1) a surplus produced through intensive agriculture; (2) warfare and the conquest of territory and peoples; or (3) the rise of towns and cities. Even if these factors do facilitate the *further* development of the state and the subsequent formation of empires, all three factors long predated primary state formation (Service 1975; Spencer 2003). So they may be enabling factors but cannot trigger state formation. The archaeological record points instead to the role of expanded capacities for economic and political control over areas that lie further than a day's round trip from the political centre or capital. This corresponds to the idea of infrastructural power proposed by Mann (1986, 2008). Territorial expansion in turn mobilized resources through the exaction of surplus in the form of tributary flows to underwrite this administrative transformation, which thereby created a virtuous circle among bureaucratic governance, resource extraction through tribute, and further territorial expansion. Such expansion occurred through penetration into the territories of neighbouring polities, which was easier when they were smaller and weaker (Service

1975; Finer 1997a; Spencer 2010). Like chiefdoms, states usually formed networks based on competitive alliances. Unlike networks of chiefdoms, however, these networks were periodically centralized into a single political unit, which incorporated several polities; and these may be termed 'empires' (Finer 1997a, 1997b; on empires and imperialism, see also below). In addition, competition for control spurred political and administrative and military innovation, and this in turn fed into the state's increased capacities for territorializing political power over larger areas and larger populations (Redmond and Spencer 2012; Wright 1977).

In sum, the key issue in state formation, which takes states beyond chiefdoms, is the ability to extend territorial control through the logistics of space–time distantiation and through the bureaucratization of a central authority.

> A state ruler can dispatch subordinates to locations near and far from the state capital to manage local affairs, and, if the authority of the dispatched official has been defined narrowly enough, this can be done with little risk of insurrection. The ability to delegate partial authority to subordinates gives a state the potential to intrude into local affairs and finance itself with a variety of extractive techniques. (Spencer 2010: 7120)

This involves a hierarchy of administrative offices filled by full-time specialists with specific tasks, in a detailed division of labour (in addition to Weber, see Eisenstadt 1963; Flannery 1999; Fried 1967; Service 1975; Finer 1997a). Detailed delegation enables states to exercise greater territorial control and to develop divide-and-rule strategies. Thus, while chiefdoms usually exhibit no more than three decision-making tiers, states characteristically have four or more (Wright 1977, 2006). Semiotic clues (historical semantics) about this division of labour are found in the archaeological and historical record, in the plethora of named administrative posts in even relatively small states, by comparison with what can be found in chiefdoms (Spencer 2010). The establishment of subsidiary centres of administration often results in a nested lattice of secondary, tertiary, and even quaternary centres with a corresponding hierarchy in population size. In addition, expansion in the levels of decision making and range of delegated tasks requires improvements in record-keeping to link past, present, and future and the development of other capacities to gather, process, and use information in decision making. Power–knowledge relations come into play here. (On forms of communication, record-keeping, and time–space distantiation, see

Innis 1951; Giddens 1981). According to Finer (1997a: 89), it was the Assyrian Empire that first worked out the institutions of imperial rule, that is, the division of conquered lands into provinces governed by centrally appointed officials.

The development of territorialization involves a continuing reorganization of political borders, boundaries, and frontiers. In addition to the forms assumed by simple and complex chiefdoms and early forms of state and empire, political boundaries have also been marked by medieval polymorphy, Westphalian exclusivity, and post-Westphalian complexity. Thus territorial reach remains important for the subsequent constitution and transformation of states. To give an example, the scope of territorial control conditioned the type of political representation that could be sustained in medieval Europe (Blockmans 1978, 1996; Tilly 1992; Finer 1997c; see also Stasavage 2011 on territorial scope, population density, tax capacities, and forms of political representation in the medieval and early modern period in Europe).[1] Likewise, as Marcelo Escolar (1997) shows, the degree of political centralization and state modernization crucially affected the nature of territorial demarcations and their representational practices in different zones of modern state building. From another perspective, the consolidation of capitalism saw the national eclipse of the urban scale, as cities were integrated into national economic systems and subordinated to the political power of national territorial states (Tilly 1992). The national scale has been challenged in turn by global city networks more oriented to other global cities than to national hinterlands (cf. Braudel 1975; Taylor 2000; Brenner 2004).

A related issue is the management of territorial subdivisions with more or less wide-ranging political and administrative powers and some autonomy from the central state apparatus. In addition to the conventional distinction between unitary and federal states, there are further significant differences that shape the 'spatial selectivity' of state forms. These differences provide the framework for cooperation and competition among local and regional authorities as well as for their relations to the national territorial state and, directly or indirectly, to trans- and supranational authorities and institutions. This points to the variable ensemble of technologies and practices that produce, naturalize, and manage territorial space as a bounded container within which political power is wielded to achieve various, more or less consistent, and changing policy objectives.

To examine the strategies and logistics of state power in this way requires concern with a range of problems in government and governance and their solutions. Commenting on the magisterial work of Samuel Finer, one reviewer notes that this kind of concern

> typically obliges him to examine how the government he is analysing copes with five basic challenges of governance: how to maintain territorial boundaries against hostile outside pressure; how to recruit and keep responsive a competent palace staff; how to maintain civilian control over the coercive resources of the military; how to balance sovereign will with the judiciary's responsibilities for adjudication of conflicting claims; and how to manipulate or absorb the potentially competing legitimacy of religious figures. After examining the nominal areal division of governmental responsibility between the central government and the provinces – always a source of tension in imperial regimes in an epoch of weak transport and weaker communication links – he looks, in conclusion, for evidence of the degree to which governmental figures actually succeed in imprinting their societies in accordance with their intentions. (Van der Muhll 2003: 359; see also Finer 1997a: 1–99, 1997b: 603–21, 855–95, and 1997c: 1261–305)

For Finer, the typical form of rule throughout 5,200 years of state formation is monocratic, autocratic rule vested in a single individual and his (occasionally her) court. This leaves open more concrete and complex questions such as 'how these [sovereign] individuals are selected, how their reign is legitimized, what resources they command, how extensively their effective power is dispersed among their courtiers, how liable they are to deposition, and what consequences typically ensue' (van der Muhll 2003: 367). Searching for exceptions, Finer identified one main alternative. This would be the 'Palace-Forum' polity (dating back to the Greek tyrants and Julius Caesar), which was instantiated, inter alia, by certain medieval Italian city-states and represented *de facto* in some modern totalitarian regimes, in which 'the ruler governs in true Palace fashion'. Finer also identifies two minor ideal types: a 'Church' polity and rule by the 'Nobility'. In their pure forms, these would have had only marginal roles in world history. The Vatican and Tibet 1642–1949 would exemplify a pure church polity, eighteenth-century Poland would be a rare example of noble rule, and the thirteenth-century Teutonic Order in the eastern Baltic region would be a unique instance of a church–nobility polity (Finer 1997a: 36–58).

Turning from states to empires, we find, again, quite varied forms, with corresponding problems of definitions. A minimal definition is a very large state comprising several ethnic groups, communities, or territories that is brought into existence through conquest and is governed from a core territorial unit (a city-state, a territorial state, or a modern national state), which forms a centre vis-à-vis one or more peripheries (cf. Finer 1997a: 8). Philip Pomper (2005) notes that definitions of empire range from formal ones, which have a more or less explicit checklist of imperial institutions, to broad ones, which tend to conflate great power and empire. His checklist of key features of historical empires consists of

> military conquest; exploitation of the conquered in the form of, for example, tribute, taxation, and/or conscription; outright seizure and distribution of assets by imperial authorities to landowners and settlers; imperial projects, strategies, and designs continuously pursued by regimes that call themselves empires; proudly displayed imperial symbols, and imperial institutions; imperial elites that educate their children to assume command, but also inspire imitators in other classes, and that find it expedient to recruit administrators and soldiers among the conquered in order to rule effectively; and an imperial club whose elites sometimes cooperate and design the partitions of desirable and conquerable territories, and who sometimes double-cross each other in cutthroat competitions. (Pomper 2005: 2)

There appears to be no determinism to imperial projects. State insiders – for centuries, the court, the oligarchs, and the key councillors – determine whether imperial projects will be pursued, where, with what instruments, and to what ends. Often their decisions are opportunistic and reflect changes in the interstate system, as the strength of other states waxes and wanes and new players enter the great powers' arenas (see Eisenstadt 1963; Finer 1997b, 1997c; Mann 1986, 1996; and Tilly 1975). With the development of capitalism, however, there is an inherent tendency for the capital relation to extend throughout the globe. The world market is the presupposition *and* posit (result) of capital accumulation. This gives a new impetus to imperialism; but, as the historical record shows, it does not always take the form of a rigid division of the world market into distinct territorial blocs, each controlled and exploited by a given great power. On the contrary, direct territorial control of multiple and widely dispersed economic spaces can be costly and counterproductive, especially in an era when rights to national self-determination and democratic rights are being asserted and, for the period between the 1917 Russian Revolution and the collapse of the Soviet Bloc, competition between two rival world systems opened space for political and ideological contestation over how to realize these principles (see also chapter 8).

Table 5.1 Four aspects of sociospatiality

Moment	Basis of sociospatial structuration	Associated sociospatial configurations	Sociospatial contradictions and dilemmas
Territory	Bordering, bounding, parcellization, enclosure	Construction of inside/ outside divides Constitutive role of the outside	Bordered vs cross-border relations (e.g., 'hermit state' vs 'free state')
Place	Proximity, spatial embedding, areal differentiation	Construction of spatial divisions of labour Horizontal distinction 'core' vs 'peripheral' places	Container vs connector (e.g., particularism vs cosmopolitanism)
Scale	Hierarchization, vertical differentiation	Construction of scalar divisions of labour Vertical distinction among 'dominant', 'nodal', and 'marginal' scales	Single scale vs multiscalarity (e.g., unitary city-state vs multiscalar meta-governance regime)
Networks	Interconnectivity, interdependence, transversal or 'rhizomatic' differentiation	Building networks of nodal connectivity Distribution of social relations among nodal points in topological networks	Enclosed network vs networks of networks (e.g., 'functional region' or 'formal region' vs 'unbounded region' or 'virtual region')

Source: Adapted from Jones and Jessop 2010

Territory, Place, Scale, Network

Territorial control is one of statehood's three defining features in the *Staatslehre* tradition and in other major approaches to the state, to which I added the 'idea of the state'. However, besides a territory and its population, states have at least three other primary spatial moments. These are the state's role in place building and place connection; the organizing and reorganizing of the scalar division of labour; and the state's role in (meta-)governing networks. The four aspects – territory, place, scale, network – are subsequently referred to as the TPSN schema. In addition to sociospatial aspects, states also have temporal moments. Thus they involve specific temporal metrics and intertemporal linkages and have their own discursive, strategic, and material temporalities, their own temporal horizons of action, and their logistical implications (see, for example, Innis 1951). These aspects affect all six dimensions of the state introduced in chapter 3, and their relative weight and overall articulation provides another way to characterize and differentiate state forms and political regimes.

Table 5.1 presents the four aspects and their related spatialization principles (cf. Jessop et al., 2008; Jones and Jessop 2010). The first three columns serve mainly definitional purposes. In contrast, column 4 identifies potential sites of structural contradiction and terrains of strategic dilemmas that introduce (1) a dynamic element into socio-spatiality; (2) an entry point for analysing compossibility and incompossibility in strategic–relational terms; (3) a basis for periodization and more robust comparative analysis within and across TPSN configurations; and (4) a means to introduce strategic agency into discussions of the sociospatial transformation of the state. Thus the table is particularly useful for analysing spatiotemporal fixes, contradictions in particular sociospatial configurations, sociospatial strategic contexts, and thinking about transformative strategies.

I discussed *territory* above and will return to it later. Let me just recall the distinction between the terrestrial and territorial. Whereas the former denotes the initial geophysical raw material or substratum for sociospatial relations (and becomes 'second nature' through its sociospatial transformation), territorialization is one form of the sociospatial appropriation and transformation of the terrestrial. Thus, while all social relations occur in terrestrial space (until the rise of telematic or cyberspace),[2] not all social relations occur in territories constituted and controlled by a state apparatus.

Place or *locale* is a more or less bounded, more or less extensive, site of face-to-face relationships among individuals or of other forms of direct interaction among social forces. Place is generally closely tied to everyday life, has temporal depth, and is linked to collective memory and social identity. Places (or locales) provide strategically selective social and institutional settings for direct interactions; they also structure connectivity beyond that place, to other places and spaces, on a range of scales. Place making is an important process: it enframes social relations within spaces of everyday, more or less proximate interaction; place differentiation refers in turn to the horizontal differentiation of various types of place, in a variegated areal landscape. The naming, delimitation, and meaning of places in place making and differentiation are always contested and changeable, and the coordinates of any given physical space can be connected to multiple places with different identities, spatiotemporal boundaries, and social significance. Thus we find significant shifts in the naming, delimitation, and meaning of those places in regard to which place-centred activities are undertaken and in the nature of their material connections. A recent example of the transformation of place can be found in the 'occupy' movements of different continents and countries.

Scale refers to the nested hierarchy of bounded spaces of differing size, e.g., local, regional, national, global. It can denote differences in areal scope (terrestrial or territorial), in spans of organizational or administrative control in a vertical or horizontal division of labour, and in relative dominance in control over more or less significant resources, capacities, and competences. Even if we restrict scale to vertical hierarchies and ignore areal differentiation, there is no single, overarching peak at which multiple scalar hierarchies culminate (e.g., a sovereign world state). On the contrary, multiple scalar orders exist that may be individually tangled or mutually disconnected. Many scales and temporalities of action can be distinguished, but relatively few (although still many) get explicitly institutionalized. How (and how far) this happens depends on the prevailing technologies of power that enable the identification and institutionalization of specific scales of action and temporalities.

Networking is another polyvalent term. We have already encountered parallel power networks. In the present context, however, it has primarily spatial referents. In some recent work it refers to flat, decentred sets of social relations characterized by symmetrical connectivity to centred ensembles of power relations that are organized on functional or flow lines rather than on territorial or scalar principles. This 'flat ontology' perspective runs the risk of neglecting the hierarchical relations that often exist within and among networks. For, even if power relations within all networks were egalitarian and symmetrical, inequality and asymmetry could still occur in network–network relations, as expressed in the uneven capacities of networked agents to pursue their own distinctive strategies and realize their interests. Such asymmetries and inequalities arise from the grounding of networks (global cities or marginal places), the different scales at and across which they operate (dominant, nodal, or marginal – on which see the next paragraph), and the territorial interests with which they are linked (e.g., centre vs periphery or strong vs weak states, imperialism, or empire). Thus an adequate topography of networks must put them in a broader spatiotemporal, strategic–relational context. This is a basic methodological principle of the SRA.

Two further general scalar concepts are useful for the analysis of the state apparatus and state powers: (1) the scalar division of labour; and (2) scale jumping. For Collinge (1999), the former refers to the distribution of different tasks or functions to different scales within a vertical hierarchy of scales. In contrast, the spatial division of labour concerns how the same tasks or functions are divided among different places on the same spatial scale. Often the division of tasks is ordered in both space and scale. The most powerful institutions and actors may not be located at the highest or peak scale. Indeed multilevel or multitier government arrangements are often associated with tangled hierarchies of powers. Thus differential access to scales is one aspect of the sociospatial selectivity of states and political regimes (see below). A case in point is the European Union as a state in the process of formation – where some national states have greater power over the EU level than EU institutions have over them. (This claim must be qualified, of course, by the strategic–relational observation that the state is not a thing or a subject but a social relation – whence it follows both that national interests are asymmetrically represented inside EU institutions and that certain EU principles are interiorized at national level.)

In turn, *scale jumping* occurs when actors seek to make policy, resolve conflicts, exercise power, and so forth at the scale that is most favourable to their material and ideal interests. Scale jumping occurs out of the desire to exploit the structurally inscribed scalar privileging of some forces, some spatial horizons of action, strategies, policies, and so on over others. The scalar division of labour and scale jumping are linked to attempts to redefine and recalibrate that division, engage in interscalar articulation, institute new scales or abolish old ones, and redefine scalar selectivities in order to gain advantage in the jumping game. Scalar strategies are just one set of possible spatial strategies. Others can target other spatial dimensions of social relations.

Following Gramsci's distinction between narrow and integral senses of 'the state' (chapter 4; see Gramsci 1971: 239, 267, and 271 = Q6, §155, Q17, §51, and Q6, §10), we can also explore the latter's narrow and integral spatiotemporal dimensions. State space in its 'narrow' sense refers to spatialities of the state regarded as an ensemble of juridico-political institutions and regulatory capacities grounded in the territorialization of political power. Taken in this sense, spatiality includes, inter alia, the changing meaning and organization of state territoriality; the evolving role of borders, boundaries, and frontiers; and the changing intranational geographies of the state's territorial organization and internal administrative differentiation (cf. Brenner 2004). It likewise includes the state's roles in promoting, addressing, or reversing uneven development in the relation between places, in reorganizing its own internal scalar division of labour, and in managing networks within and beyond the state's juridico-political apparatus. State space in its 'integral' sense denotes the wider sociospatial supports and implications of state space and the sociospatial embedding of particular TPSN configurations of the state apparatus and of state power. It includes the territory-, place-, scale- and network-specific ways in which state institutions are mobilized strategically to regulate and reorganize social and economic relations and, more generally, the changing geographies of state intervention into social and economic processes.

Another key concept in this regard is the spatial imaginary. Spatial imaginaries are discursive phenomena (semiotic ensembles and associated semiotic practices) that distinguish specific places, scales, territories, networks, or spaces in general from the inherently unstructured complexity of a spatialized world. They involve different ways of representing space that, inter alia, give more or less weight to place, scale, territory, or network in that representation. They operate 'through the active simplification of the complex reality of places [and territories] in favour of controllable geopolitical abstractions' (Agnew and Corbridge 1995: 48–9). Competing spatial imaginaries represent state and political spaces in different ways, as a basis for demarcating states from each other, for demarcating the state from the wider political system, and for demarcating the wider political system from the rest of society. Marcelo Escolar (1997) notes the vital role of representational practices in the territorialization of political power that shaped the formation of the modern (inter)state system during the long sixteenth century. He explores the radical reorganization of inherited medieval institutional landscapes, in which borders had served as relatively fluid zones of transition between overlapping, interpenetrating realms of political, religious, military, and other forms of authority. The modern interstate system was not constructed on a terrestrial *tabula rasa* but crystallized rather out of a complex, polymorphic medieval landscape, which was itself inherited from earlier rounds of state building (see, e.g., Finer 1997c; Mann 1996; Poggi 1978; Jones 2007).

Sociospatial imaginaries also provide an important basis for mobilizing territory-, scale-, place-, and network-specific forms of state intervention and for territorial politics within (and against) the state. Henri Lefebvre (1991: 281) argues, for example, that 'each state claims to produce a space wherein something is accomplished – a space, even, where something is brought to perfection: namely, a unified and hence homogeneous society'. He also explores the politics of everyday resistance, the rise of new social movements, and the growth of new, potentially transformative uses of space (Lefebvre 1971, 2004). However, although the modern state may seek to homogenize space partly in order to make it legible for purposes of political control (cf. Scott 1998), this process is disrupted through resistance and through conflicting attempts to appropriate the terrestrial, to challenge borders, to make places, to claim rights to the city, and to escape control (cf. Poulantzas 1978; Roberts 2006; Harvey 2008; Lefebvre 1968; Scott 2009). While many spatial imaginaries involve little more than alternative construals of that world, some have a performative impact through the discursive–material construction of spatiality. Yet even spatial imaginaries that are not 'arbitrary, rationalistic and willed' and have been consolidated in specific spatial orders are prone to instability, because no imaginary can be fully adequate to the complexities of the real world. This is also reflected in changes in popular geographical assumptions about politics, political community, and political struggles.

A final concept is that of *state spatial strategies*. These refer to the historically specific practices through which state institutions and state managers (and the social forces they represent) seek to reorder territories, places, scales, and networks to secure the reproduction of the state in its narrow sense, to reconfigure the sociospatial dimensions of the state in its integral sense, and to promote specific accumulation strategies, state projects, and hegemonic visions. These strategies have important infrastructural as well as despotic dimensions (Mann 1984), are related to specific spatiotemporal imaginaries, and depend on specific technologies and governmental practices. While these strategies are often discussed primarily in terms of economic geographies, they can have many other (mixed) motives, purposes, and effects (Lefebvre 1991; Prescott 1987; Hannah 2000;

Table 5.2   Towards a multidimensional analysis of sociospatiality

Structuring Principles	Fields of Operation			
	TERRITORY	*PLACE*	*SCALE*	*NETWORKS*
Territory	Actually existing frontiers, borders, boundaries that constitute the state as power container	Integrating places into a territory, managing uneven development	Federal systems Multilevel government	Interstate system, state alliances, multiarea government
Place	Core–periphery, borderlands, empires	Locales, milieux, cities, regions localities, globalities	Glocalization, glurbanization (global–local and urban–global articulations)	Local, urban, regional governance or partnerships
Scale	Scalar division of political power (unitary state, federal state, etc.)	Local ↔ global areal (spatial) division of labour	Nested or tangled scalar hierarchies Scale jumping	Parallel power networks, nongovernmental international regimes
Networks	Cross-border region, virtual regions (BRICS, Four Motors, etc.)	Global city networks, poly-nucleated cities, intermeshed sites	Networks of differently scaled places	Networks of networks, spaces of flows

Source: Jessop et al., 2008

Brenner 2004). In this regard, they can also be studied from the viewpoint of sociospatial governance (chapter 6).

These moments of spatiality can be combined to produce more concrete–complex analyses of particular sociospatial configurations, tied to specific substantive relations and processes. Table 5.2 presents some examples of such configurations grounded in the TPSN framework. Sixteen cells are generated by cross-tabulating each sociospatial moment *qua* structuring principle, with all four sociospatial moments as fields of application. This exercise could be extended beyond a two-dimensional matrix; but even this limited version illustrates the complexities of sociospatiality and their implications for the analysis of the state system and state powers.

Specifically, the matrix indicates that each sociospatial concept can be deployed in three ways. For example, territory can be explored:

- *in itself*, as a product of bordering strategies (territory–territory);
- as a *structuring principle* (a causal process or mechanism) that impacts other fields of sociospatial relations (reading the matrix horizontally, hence territory place, territory scale, territory network); and
- as a *structured field*, produced in part through the impact of other sociospatial structuring principles on territorial dynamics (now reading the matrix vertically, focusing on the territory column and considering linkages between place and territory, scale and territory, and network and territory).

Overall, this two-dimensional matrix suggests (1) that the relative significance of territory, place, scale, and networks as structuring principles for sociospatial relations varies with different types of spatiotemporal fix – that sometimes territory, sometimes place, sometimes scale, and sometimes network is more significant in securing the overall coherence of spatiotemporal relations in a given context; in other words, (2) that their relative roles in securing the overall coherence of spatiotemporal relations in capitalist (and other) social formations may vary historically and contextually; (3) that crises, attempts at crisis resolution, and the emergence of new spatiotemporal fixes may be linked to shifts in the most effective sociospatial bases, organizational structures, and strategies for counter-hegemonic projects; and (4) that strategies of crisis resolution could involve attempts to reorder the relative importance of the four dimensions and their associated institutional expressions and, hence, to modify the weight of their role in displacing crisis tendencies and contradictions. Indeed, the cells in Table 5.2 indicate different kinds of sociospatial configurations that could be the objects of sociospatial strategies and fixes. To give just two examples, with increasing internationalization there could be a refocusing of strategies from local government within a national state to governing networks of global cities; or, again, from regulating the state as a territorial power container to building international regimes to govern flows between more porous territories.

Towards new TPSN fixes

Globalization (at least in its currently predominant neoliberal form) has disrupted the nationally focused spatiotemporal fixes inherited from the postwar boom in the circuits of Atlantic Fordism in North America and Europe; from the period of national import–substitution industrialization in Latin America; and from the period of the East Asian economic miracles, which were initially linked to catch-up economic development and export-led growth. The current period of globalization involves a proliferation of spatial scales, their relative dissociation in complex tangled hierarchies (rather than in a simple nesting of scales), and an increasingly convoluted mix of scale strategies, as economic and political forces seek the most favourable conditions for insertion into a changing international order (Jessop 2002). While the national scale has lost its postwar dominance, no other scale of economic and political organization (whether 'global' or 'local', 'urban' or 'triadic') has gained a similar dominance. Instead different economic and political spaces and forces located at different scales compete to become the primary or nodal point of accumulation or state power or both (chapter 8).

The relativization of scale also offers important new opportunities for scale jumping and for struggles over interscalar articulation. This raises the question whether a long-term solution requires a new dominant scale with a complementary set of nodal and marginal scales, or whether the relativization of scale is the new norm and the importance now attached to network forms of coordination is a viable strategic–relational response to this situation.

I now illustrate some of these arguments from the case of Atlantic Fordism. The sociospatial matrix of states in the leading Atlantic Fordist economies constructed after the Second World War was characterized by the primacy of territory and place over scale and network. This does not mean that scale and network were absent – simply that they had a less prominent role in the three formal aspects of the state (representation, institutional architecture, and intervention) and its three strategic aspects (social bases, state projects, and hegemonic visions) (chapter 2). State intervention – designed to secure the conditions for the profitability of capital and the reproduction of the population both as labour force and as a body of national citizens – was stamped by the primacy of national money over international currency and of the individual and social wage as a source of domestic demand over its role as a cost of international production. This was reflected in the primacy of national economies, national welfare states, and national societies managed by national states concerned to unify national territories and to reduce uneven development. In short, in this period, the sociospatial form of the state was marked strongly by the 'nationalization' of economic and political space. The national scale was dominant in a relatively stable scalar division of labour – although, as some scholars note, the national economy, the national state, and the national citizenship regime were embedded in a liberal international order and were supported by the nodal role of local states in delivering certain complementary forms of economic and social policy. Networks also had a key role in representation and in securing the state's social bases. But they were primarily corporatist and clientelist in nature, tied to the Atlantic Fordist accumulation regime and its mode of regulation, and operating within the national Atlantic Fordist economic and political matrix.

The growing internationalization of the world market in the 1960s and 1970s undermined this spatiotemporal fix, with its distinctive TPSN matrix and was accompanied by the crisis of Atlantic Fordism and its various Keynesian welfare national states (KWNSs). In particular, internationalization enhanced the power of international currency and capital flows over national monetary and fiscal policies and prioritized the individual and social wage as a cost of production. This also undermined the complementarity of national economies, national welfare states, national societies, and national state and intensified uneven development across different places and regions – a process that the KWNS sought to remedy through policies that Brenner (2004) has described as 'spatial Keynesianism'. While some theorists are inclined to see internationalization as promoting the deterritorialization of political power or as shifting the scope of territory upwards, to the transnational or global level, or downwards, to the regional or local level, I have argued that recent changes are better understood in terms of a relativization of scale (but see chapter 8). This denotes the absence of a primary scale in the scalar division of political labour and a struggle between representatives of different scalar interests to locate the primary scale at their level. These changes have altered the role of territory, place, scale, and network in the overall architecture of the North Atlantic states in a post-Atlantic Fordist world.[3]

I suggest that the relative primacy of territory and place during Atlantic Fordism has been replaced by a relative primacy of scale and networks. In particular, the post-Fordist relativization of scale has prompted experimentation with network forms of organization that might contribute to the development of a stable, postnational state better able to steer the integration of changing economic and political spaces into an increasingly integrated world market characterized by growing uneven development. Whereas the national state provided the primary scale of political organization in the Fordist period of postwar European and North American boom, the current post-Fordist period is marked by the dispersion of political and policy issues across different scales of organization, none having clear primacy. This development poses problems about securing the inter-scalar coherence of action and leads to a search for new forms and functions of statehood, which can address the crisis of the national territorial state (see chapter 8). With the impact of further crises (especially crises of finance-dominated accumulation in a world market organized in the shadow of neoliberalism), we are witnessing trial-and-error experimentation and contestation about the appropriate ways to reorder a postnational, unevenly developing global economy. Indeed there have been surprising reversals among prominent public intellectuals about the significance and appropriate architecture of the state system and about the most appropriate state projects and hegemonic visions that it should promote (two exemplary cases are Fukuyama 1992, 2011; Friedmann 2005, 2008, 2011).

Domination and Spatiotemporal Fixes

The spatialities and temporalities of the state system are multifaceted and connected in complex ways. I now explore their implications for the state system as a structure of domination. Two aspects merit attention: (1) the articulation of the TPSN matrix of the state system in its narrow and integral senses; and (2) institutional and spatiotemporal fixes as mechanisms in the structuration of power relations.

First, each principle of sociospatial organization has its own forms of inclusion–exclusion and differential capacities to exercise state powers. This creates a strategic field in which different social forces seek to privilege different sociospatial modes of representation, state 'withinputs', and forms of intervention, to reorder state capacities associated with each sociospatial dimension, and to pursue privileged access to territories, places, scales, or networks where the most important capacities are located. Examples include gerrymandering constituency boundaries, voter suppression, promoting or weakening place-based uneven development and centre–periphery inequalities, reordering scalar hierarchies and scale jumping, and organizing parallel power networks that cross-cut formal vertical and horizontal divisions of power within and beyond the state.

Second, given the contradictions and dilemmas associated with basic structural forms (such as the capital relation) and with different sociospatial forms (see Table 5.1), we might explore how these contradictions are managed through spatial displacement or temporal deferral of the direct and indirect costs of efforts to manage them. Two interrelated concepts that highlight the role of structure and strategy here are those of institutional and spatiotemporal fixes. Neither concerns uniquely the state system and state powers. They are nonetheless fundamental features of the state in its narrow and integral senses; and, in addition, the state system and the activation of state powers shape institutional and spatiotemporal fixes more generally.

An institutional fix is a complementary set of institutions that, via institutional design, imitation, imposition, or chance evolution offer (within given parametric limits) a temporary, partial, and relatively stable solution to the coordination problems involved in securing economic, political, or social order. Nonetheless, it is not purely technical and, rather than providing a post hoc solution to pre-given coordination problems, it is partly constitutive of this order. It rests on an institutionalized, unstable equilibrium of compromise or, at worst, on an open use of force. Such a fix can also be examined as a spatiotemporal fix (or STF), and vice versa: a STF can be examined as an institutional fix. STFs establish spatial and temporal boundaries within which the always relative, incomplete, and provisional structural coherence (and hence the institutional complementarities) of a given order are secured – to the extent that this is ever the case. A key contribution of STFs is to externalize the material and social costs of securing such coherence beyond the spatial, temporal, and social boundaries of the institutional fix by *displacing* or *deferring* them (or both). These fixes externalize the material and social costs of securing coherence beyond specific spatial, temporal, and social boundaries, such that zones of relative stability depend on instability elsewhere. Even within 'internal' boundaries, some classes, class fractions, social categories, or other social forces located within these spatiotemporal boundaries are marginalized, excluded, or subject to coercion. STFs thereby only *appear* to harmonize contradictions, which persist in one or another form. Such regimes are partial, provisional, and unstable and attempts to impose them can lead to 'blowback' at home as well as abroad.

While contradictions, dilemmas, and conflicts of ideal and material interests cannot be reconciled permanently *in abstracto*, they can be moderated provisionally and partially through mechanisms and projects that prioritize one aspect of a contradiction, one horn of a dilemma, or just some interests. This can be achieved 'ideally', at least in the short term, through successful presentation of specific, necessarily selective solutions as the embodiment of an (always illusory) general interest. In other cases the 'resolution' will involve more visible, even forcible strategies and tactics. This is a contested process, involving different economic, political, and social forces and diverse strategies and projects. In this context, contradictions and their associated dilemmas may be handled through

- *hierarchization*: treat some contradictions as more important than others;
- *prioritization*: give priority to one aspect of a contradiction or dilemma over the other aspect;
- *spatialization*: rely on different territories, places, scales, and action networks to address one or another contradiction or aspect or to displace the problems associated with the neglected aspect to marginal or liminal territories, places, scales, or networks; and
- *temporalization*: routinely treat one or other aspect of a contradiction in turn or focus one-sidedly on a subset of contradictions, dilemmas, or aspects until it becomes urgent to address what had hitherto been neglected.

The relation among these strategies can be used to explore how institutional and spatiotemporal fixes help to secure particular patterns of domination. In the case of capitalist growth regimes, for example, we can observe differences in the weights attributed to different contradictions and dilemmas (hierarchization), in the importance accorded to their different aspects (prioritization), in the role of different territories, places, scales, and networks in these regards (spatialization), and in the temporal patterns of their treatment (temporalization). Institutional and spatiotemporal fixes are never purely technical but, like other aspects of state power, involve efforts to secure and rework a wider 'unstable equilibrium of compromise', organized around specific objects, techniques, and subjects of government or governance. Regularizing capitalism also involves a 'social fix' that partially compensates for the incompleteness of the pure capital relation and gives it a relative structural coherence through the ways in which it handles contradictions and dilemmas.

Conclusions

The preceding reflections reinforce some well-worn arguments about state formation. Less familiar are the sociospatial and temporal complexities of state formation and transformation. So this chapter has highlighted the articulation of territory, place, scale, and network in the overall structuring of state systems and has indicated some of their strategic–relational implications. It also introduced the concepts of institutional fix and spatiotemporal fix in order to reinforce the general argument that the state system is closely connected to forms of domination. And, although mentioned only in passing, spatial imaginaries of various kinds and their connection to institutional and spatiotemporal fixes are important enough to indicate the relevance of *Ideologiekritik*. Later chapters will explore crisis tendencies in the spatiotemporal matrices of the contemporary state along all four sociospatial dimensions.

6

State and Nation

The question of state and nation relates to the last two elements of the modified four-element approach to the state. The third element is the population (*Staatsvolk*), which is subject to state authority and perhaps endowed with rights against the state. Where rights exist, the people is seen not as a mere population or a threatening mass, plebs, or mob (*mobile vulgus*) that is there to be governed, but as a politically imagined social force – the people (*populus, il popolo*) – regarded as a source of power (Canovan 2005). At stake here is 'people building' as a co-constitutive feature of state building. This links, in turn, to the 'state idea' as the fourth element of the proposed approach. As a source of legitimacy, the people (like the nation) is an imagined community with a certain historical continuity based on a reconstructed past, an imagined present, and an unfolding future. The people serves as the source of political authority in the name of which the state can make decisions that are binding on it indefinitely, if not eternally (Canovan 2005). This tends to endow the people with a corporate personality that is formed as an *unum e pluribus* – a unity formed out of many (ibid.).

A robustly critical reading has been offered by Edmund Morgan, who treats the sovereign people as a 'fiction' that was deliberately invented to challenge and replace another fiction, the divine right of kings. During the English Civil War, 'representatives invented the sovereignty of the people in order to claim it for themselves.... In the name of the people they became all-powerful in government'. (Morgan 1988: 49–50, cited Canovan 2008)

This poses three interesting problems. First, should we restrict the subjects of state power to the 'people' and, if so, should they be understood as individuals, families, communities, 'racialized' subjects, ethnic groups, and so on? Are the subjects of state power any kind of recognized legal persons (including corporations, associations, etc.) that are subject to the rule of law or other forms of state intervention? Or do they comprise any agent or agency that is an object of state intervention or an object of neglect by the state, whether socially constituted or not? At stake here is the question of whether state power is limited to collectively binding decisions (as is usually posited in the definition of the state) or covers all forms of intervention dependent on the use of state capacities that produce structured rather than random, amorphous, ephemeral effects (chapters 2 and 3).

Second and relatedly, if we address population in terms of human subjects, should we consider the state's role in shaping and disciplining individual bodies (Foucault's anatomo-politics), and its role in identifying and tackling basic biopolitical issues such as the overall composition of the population in demographic (narrowly or broadly conceived), economic, identitarian, and other terms (Foucault 2008)? Such governmental activities involve discourses and *dispositifs* concerned with the intergenerational, lifetime, and day-to-day reproduction and recomposition of the *Staatsvolk*. Moreover, reflecting the polymorphy of the state, biopolitics may approach these tasks in terms of several principles of social organization: as political subjects, as citizens, as labour force, as military reserve, as religious community, and so on.

A third issue is the 'nation', which is so often regarded as the basis of the national state. The central theoretical and practical problem here is the referent of 'nation' and the role of the state in constituting the nation in terms of who belongs to the state or has citizenship rights within it and who must obey the state, regardless of citizenship rights or (in some cases) country of residence. I begin with this last question.

National State and Nation-State

Nation and state are distinct concepts that are often combined in the ambiguous concept of 'nation-state' and, less often, in the counter-concept of 'state-nation' (on the latter, see Stepan, Linz, and Yadav 2010: 1–38 and the next paragraph). The nation-state concept is especially confusing because it is often used in ways that conflate two analytically and often empirically distinct types of state. In one sense, it refers to what German state theorists call *the territorial state* – that is, a state that successfully claims a legitimate monopoly of organized coercion *within a relatively large territorial area* that comprises more than one city and its hinterland. For maximum clarity, the territorial state in this German sense is sometimes also called 'national (territorial) state'. City-states such as Singapore and small principalities such as Liechtenstein are thereby excluded, even though both types have formal sovereignty in their respective territories and other states recognize them. Understood in this territorially focused way, the nation-state qua territorial state includes small states (e.g., Denmark, Ireland)[1] as well as quasi-continental states that stretch across many time zones (e.g., Russia, the USA), subcontinental states (e.g., India, China), and archipelagic states (e.g., Indonesia). In another sense, 'nation-state' denotes states that exercise power over a population defined exclusively or primarily through a *shared* identification with an imagined national community whose boundaries largely coincide with that state's frontiers. In other words, here a nation-state is a state with a population that is identified by one or more forms of nationhood. In terms of the extended four-element approach proposed here, whereas the first sense of 'nation-state' (which can also be distinguished as the territorial state, the national state, or, most clearly, the national–territorial state) indicates the *Staatsgebiet* – that is, the specific form of *territorialization* of political power – the second sense of 'nation-state' relates to the composition and identity of the *Staatsvolk* – the nontransient population of the state.

As noted in the preceding paragraph, the terms 'national state' (i.e., territorial state) and 'nation-state' are often used interchangeably and this is particularly troubling when one or the other is the only appropriate term, theoretically or politically. Discussions of how globalization undermines 'the nation-state', for example, generally refer to the ways in which it weakens the territorial sovereignty and security of national states rather than their populations' sense of national identity. Indeed, globalization processes may *strengthen* national identity (e.g., through the declared need to enhance national competitiveness and through perceived threats to national well-being, cultural autonomy, etc.), or they may dilute it thanks to more multiethnic or multicultural populations or divided cross-border loyalties. A similar ambiguity animates debates about the European Union as a territorial state and about the prospects of a European national identity. Finally, the concept of 'state-nation' is used to indicate states that recognize that their population comprises two or more nations and are committed, at least constitutionally, to facilitating their coexistence by making appropriate political arrangements. Well-known modern examples include India, Russia, and Spain (cf. Stepan et al. 2010). This discussion suggests that (1) not all states are territorial states; (2) not all territorial states are nation-states – some have no clear national basis or are multinational; and (3) not all nations are associated with their own nation-state. Situations of this last type could arise when a nation's identity is denied political expression in and through statehood (a denial that can even lead to genocide) or when its members are distributed among several states and are not in a majority in any of them.

The concept of 'national state' (or, for the sake of clarity, national territorial state) should, at this stage in the book, need little discussion. The territorial organization of power long preceded nation formation, and the modern form of national territorial state (sometimes misleadingly described as the Westphalian state) had emerged in Europe by the seventeenth century – although empires and other forms survived for up to another two centuries, even in a broadly European context.

> Three striking things have occurred. First, almost all of Europe has formed into national states with well-defined boundaries and mutual relations. Second, the European system has spread to virtually the entire world. Third, other states, acting in concert, have exerted a growing influence over the organization and territory of new states. The three changes link closely, since Europe's leading states actively spread the system by colonization, conquest, and penetration of non-European states. The creation first of a League of Nations, then of a United Nations, simply ratified and rationalized the organization of all the earth's people into a single state system. (Tilly 1992: 181)

The formal equivalence and equality among sovereign states in the interstate system is expressed in United Nations membership (there are currently 193 members), where member states range from the tiny Tuvalu island state to the 'superpowerful' United States of America. These states nonetheless face different problems at home and abroad; they have different histories; they have different capacities to address these problems and reorganize themselves in response; and, in international encounters as well as in domestic matters, some are more powerful than others. There are crucial inequalities in the United Nations and in other international policy forums and regimes, especially in powerful bodies such as the UN Security Council, the World Bank, the International Monetary Fund, and the World Trade Organization. The same point holds for the European Union. Although the range of member states is more limited, Malta having

Table 6.1 A typology of imagined political communities linked to nation-states

Type of Nation	Simple National Community	Basis of community membership	Plural expression in a state	Possible Decomposed Expression
Volksnation	Ethnos	Blood ties or naturalization	Multiethnic	'Melting-pot society'
Kulturnation	Shared culture	Assimilation, acculturation	Multicultural	Postmodern play of identities
Staatsnation	Constitutional patriotism, civic nationalism	Test of political loyalty	Nested political loyalties to multitiered government	'Flexible citizenship' in transnational space

Source: Amended from Jessop (2002: 173)

the smallest land mass and Germany the largest population, differences in state influence and state capacity shape European policymaking. The latter is further modified by alliances between individual European states and others in the world polity, as well as by the ways in which the EU is inserted into a multiscalar international order.

Nationhood

I now turn to the nation. Many attempts have been made, either for political or for analytical purposes, to establish a primordial criterion for nationhood. Suggestions include consanguinity, language, shared culture, common fate, or some other 'natural' or 'naturalized' property or set of properties. In my view, these are best interpreted as efforts to socially construct a national identity on the basis of such characteristics rather than to establish the 'real' historical existence of a given nation *prior* to its social construction. In short, the primordial nature of nationhood must be narrated or 'invented' and then accepted in the 'daily plebiscite' (Renan 1882) of lived experience, however banal the experience of shared national identity may become even if it was forged in dramatic, possibly traumatic, circumstances.

All this is reflected in Benedict Anderson's acclaimed account of the nation as an 'imagined community'. The latter concept signifies that a nation comprises a group of people so large that its members cannot know each other personally but nonetheless have come to imagine (or been persuaded) that they share important characteristics, which unify them as a nation and justify a claim to political representation and even to national self-determination. The criteria for imagining shared nationhood are quite varied, are often contested, and generally change along with accepted ideas about statehood. Mutual recognition of numerous persons on the basis of supposedly shared attributes that qualify them for membership of the same nation also serves, of course, to distinguish them from others, who are thereby *excluded* from membership of that community. This may involve nothing more than simple difference but could become the basis for rivalry and antagonism, leading ultimately, in the most tragic cases, to campaigns of expulsion and genocide.

Whereas territorial statehood is now almost universal, albeit under challenge, nation-statehood is still far from common. Table 6.1 presents the three main types of nation, the basis for inclusion within (or exclusion from) the corresponding imagined national community, and two further aspects relevant to analysing the changing forms of national statehood and national identity (for a more detailed overview, see Delanty and Krishan 2005). The three main forms are:

- The ethnic nation (*Volksnation*), based on a socially constructed and shared – real or fictive – ethnic identity. To avoid emphasis on ethnicity, which can be controversial, one can substitute it with the alternative German term *Abstammungsgemeinschaft*, which denotes common descent or common roots. An ethnonational state is one based primarily on the imagined identity of a *Volksnation* (for example, Germany), and there are many routes to ethnic nationhood and self-determination (Balibar 1990; Brubaker 1992; Gellner 1983; MacLaughlin 2001; Smith 1986). Fewer than one in ten states are exclusively ethnonational nation-states (Smith 1995: 86). Many national territorial states are either multiethnic in character or, alternatively, have lost a clear sense of ethnic identity through the development of a 'melting pot' society, in which socially constructed ethnic identities are weakened by cumulative interbreeding among differently constituted *ethnē* (heterogamy).
- The cultural nation (*Kulturnation*), based on a shared national culture that may well be defined and actively promoted by the state itself. It could be based on language, shared religion, shared cultural traditions, or other sociocultural expression that stems from intergenerational transmission or the acculturation of new subjects. By analogy, this invocation of shared culture can also inform projects for claims to political identity by other culturally imagined communities (on queer or gay nationalism, for example, see Walker 1997). Returning to the theme of the nation-state, acculturation and assimilation are key factors in nation building. France is often taken as an exemplary case of a cultural nation-state (cf. Brubaker 1992). Conversely, multiculturalism would involve a positive encouragement of or tolerance for cultural diversity based on the coexistence of different cultural traditions. These alternatives could in turn disappear to the extent that distinct cultural traditions (invented or reinvented) are replaced by a postmodern 'play of difference', in which citizens or denizens adopt different cultural identities for different purposes and in different contexts.
- A state or civic nation (*Staatsnation*), based on loyalty to and identification with the constitution and political arrangements of the state. This type of nation is based on a patriotic commitment to the constitution and to the legitimacy of the overall political order. The concept is exemplified by the United States as a

multiethnic, multicultural *Staatsnation* in which loyalty to the flag, the constitution, the office of president, and the principle of representative government are the key tests of citizenship and thereby form the reference point for charges of being 'un-American'. India, with its multiple ethnic, linguistic, religious, and cultural communities, provides another example – although there is a growing countermovement in Hindu nationalism. A civic nation is compatible with loyalty to federal or multilevel government, with decisions based on subsidiarity – that is, with a preference for political decisions to be made as close as possible to citizens in particular places. The same political arrangement can be based on a residual loyalty to the local or regional level, while power is exercised primarily at the national territorial level. This type of nationhood tends to decompose in the face of disputes over the legitimacy of the state, internal wars, the breakdown of political authority due to state failure, or the development of diasporic communities that experience loyalty to two or more states.

Most, if not all real-life cases are mixed. The three analytically distinct forms of nationhood can reinforce each other (as in Denmark, considered as a nation-state), be combined to produce relatively stable hybrid forms of national state and nation-state (mainland Britain has at least three national identities, linked to England, Scotland, and Wales, and, for many, this is nonetheless compatible with a sense of Britishness), or provoke conflicts over the proper basis of the nation-state (as Canada, Spain, or the former Yugoslavia). There are also national territorial states that are the political heartland of nations that have large numbers living in neighbouring states (for example, Hungary or Albania). Pressures may also develop to grant significant autonomy to regionally based national minorities within the existing territorial boundaries of a national state (for example, Spain or mainland Britain) or to establish 'consociational' forms of government in which different nations are guaranteed adequate (or even proportional) representation in the exercise of state power (for example, Belgium or, in the case of aboriginal nations, New Zealand; on consociationalism, see especially Lijphart 1969). Even in relatively stable cases, nationhood often provides the basis for institutionalizing social exclusion within or beyond the territorial boundaries of a given nation-state (cf. Tölölyan 1991). Lastly, there are many cases of nations without corresponding states or regions (e.g., the Roma people), as well as of states without a corresponding nation. Claims to statehood or regional autonomy on the part of stateless nations have been advanced in Europe, where examples include Corse

(Corsica), Kernow (Cornwall), Savoie, Scotland, Südtirol, and Vlaanderen (Flanders). There are many further examples from other regions of the world.

Competing national imaginaries, their selection, and their consolidation in specific nation-states involve more than questions of nationality. In addition to the historical anomaly of the transnational nature of European dynastic rulers with families interlocked through marriage and descent, national identity is shaped by class struggles and also helps to shape class identities and the forms of class struggle. The division of the world market and world society among national territorial states and the constitution of some of these as nation-states affect the forms of politics and the spatiotemporal matrices of specific states. It is reflected, for example, in divisions between national and comprador fractions of the bourgeoisie as well as in the presence of transnational capitalist classes. Likewise, national identities are used to segment labour markets and/or facilitate political divide and rule tactics. The importance of nationalism, internationalism, and cosmopolitanism also varies at different times across different class forces and is overdetermined by other factors (e.g., the growth of nationalism during periods of war or preparation for war or in the aftermath of war).

National imaginaries are also shaped by other types of ideal and material interest and other axes of social conflict (including, notably, gender). Indeed, national states and nation-states have always been gendered states with an 'institutionalized patriarchy where "androcratic" politics flourish[es]' (Ling 1996: 27). The resulting interstate system is premised on masculine rationality, is organized for violence as well as for trade, and typically regards women as the bearers of the nation and of key aspects of its symbolic identity (Anthias and Yuval-Davis 1989; Yuval-Davis 1997). In this regard, as noted in chapter 2, a primary function of the national state is to manage the population, its reproduction, and its patterns of migration, to defend national borders, and to institute and govern welfare and citizenship rights. Each of these characteristics has gender aspects that are likely to attract differential commitment across gender groups as well as across classes, races, urban–rural identities, and so on – commitment, that is, to the national project promoted by the state (Jenson 1986, 2007; Walby 2003). This analysis can be taken further by considering the three main forms of nation: *Volksnation*, *Kulturnation*, and *Staatsnation*. Gender is crucial to the first form, because membership of the 'imagined community' of the nation derives from descent and is inherited through the family. This gives women a key role as maternal 'bearers' of the nation; but it also leads to stricter control over their reproductive role in the name of the 'national' interest (Yuval-Davis 1997). Membership of a *Kulturnation* depends more on acculturation or assimilation. Nonetheless, women still have a key role as socializers, along with state and nonstate ideological apparatuses.[2] The *Staatsnation* is still more open, because inclusion in it depends on loyalty to the constitution and on patriotism. Yet citizenship in early bourgeois democratic states was initially patriarchal in form – being confined to men, associated with military obligations as well as with legal and political rights. Even where citizenship has been extended to women, it tends nonetheless to be premised on the separation of public and private spheres; and this separation tends to operate against the political participation and influence of women (e.g., Lloyd 1983; Pateman 1989; Sauer 1997). Thus women have tended to play a supporting role in definitions of national identity and state projects by virtue of their relative exclusion from participation in formal politics, by virtue of their relative confinement within the private sphere or to the margins of the often segmented labour market, and by virtue of the dominance of the concerns of white heterosexual able-bodied men (WHAMs) in mainstream politics. This state of affairs seems to hold regardless of the specific forms of national identity that are at stake.

The decomposition of each form of nation-state puts a general strain on the role of gender in their reproduction. It also creates opportunities to rethink what it might mean to *belong* to a state in a postnational era, when the ethnic or cultural bases of *nationality* are being dissolved as societies become more multiethnic or 'melting pots', more multicultural or fragmented, or playgrounds for 'hybridic' postmodern identities. These trends undermine the status of women as 'bearers' of the nation and of national identity and have opened political spaces to redefine citizenship, to multiply the spheres of legitimate political action both within and across national borders, and to develop multiple political loyalties, or even cosmopolitan patriotism (for further discussion, see Jessop 2004, 2007b).

Europe as a Territorial State and as a Nation-State

Using the concepts of national state and nation-state enables us to distinguish between the character of the European Union as a territorial state in a continuing, contested process of formation and its future as a potential nation-state. This use is also relevant to discussions about individual member-states. For, regardless of their specific form of nationhood (if any) and of the extent to which national identity is stable or contested, all European states except Luxembourg are national or territorial states. Indeed, secure and undisputed frontiers are a precondition of accession to the European Union, and for this reason full member states must be recognized territorial states (witness current problems over the contested status of the Ukraine). Hence member states face similar pressures to change their territorial form as EU state building develops, and this is reflected in common trends towards the denationalization of statehood and the destatization of politics (see chapter 9). The crisis that emerged in the Eurozone in 2009–14 (and continues at the time of writing, March 2015) poses interesting problems about a return to more national forms of politics or a move to deeper supranational integration based on the centralization of fisco-financial powers. Such issues must be distinguished from the impact of EU state formation on the future of nation-states, whatever the basis of their claims to nationhood and the scope for a European national or postnational identity.

On the one hand, we can inquire into the character of the EU as a form of territorial state. There are at least five different accounts of its character as an emerging form of state. Such a state has been characterized by (1) liberal intergovernmentalism: the European Union is an important site for traditional international conflicts between national states; (2) supranationalism: the European Union is a potentially rescaled national state that is gradually gaining the same capacities and competences as a traditional national state; (3) being a network state: powers in the European Union are being redistributed among diverse official, economic, and civilian actors that must cooperate to produce effective policies; (4) having a multilevel governance: a multitiered, multistakeholder political arrangement has developed in the European Union with a tangled hierarchy of powers with elements of subsidiarity, but also with possible veto points due to the need for joint decision-making; and (5) having a multiscalar meta-governance, in the shadow of postnational statehood (for a critique of the first four views and a preliminary case on behalf of the fifth view, see Jessop 2007b). Some combination of these accounts is better than a 'one size fits all' approach, because different accounts may provide a better entry point for specific *explananda*. They may have differential relevance for different phases in the development of European economic integration and of European statehood, for different policy fields associated with different distributions of legal and political competence, for contingent shifts in the balance of forces and associated state projects and sociospatial strategies, including scale jumping, and for different types of crisis tendency (e.g., Falkner 2005; Zeitlin and Pochet with Magnusson 2005;

Wolf 2011; Ziltener 2001). In any case, such institutional analyses should be linked and explored together with the implications of each type of regime for domination and the ideological implications of the competing imaginaries they are associated and justified with.

Putting aside the intergovernmentalist argument that the European Union comprises little more than a terrain on which national territorial states cooperate to produce mutually beneficial collective goods but nonetheless retain veto powers over European decisions that threaten their national interests, one could see the European Union as a supranational political regime formed through the federation or confederation of a changing number of national territorial states. This development would lead to something like a 'United States' of Europe – analogous to the United States as a quasi-continental territorial state. It would be based on the rescaling upwards of the basic characteristics of the Westphalian state and would occur regardless of the specific character of the European Union's newly formed constituent subunits as nation-states – or, conversely, as states without corresponding nations. At best, a United States of Europe would acquire a new national basis through the development of a strong sense of political identity with the new (con)federal state, a sense based on constitutional patriotism. There is little sign of such a development at present, as is evidenced by the rejection of the European constitution in referenda and by the relative weakness of political loyalties to European political institutions by comparison to national, regional, or local loyalties. Thus any form of *Staatsnation* is likely to involve multilevel political loyalties.

On the other hand, we can ask whether the European Union could develop a distinctive new form of nationhood. Such an identity could hardly be based on a European *Volksnation* grounded in a new imagined ethnic identity, but it could be based on a new form of constitutional patriotism (see preceding paragraph) or on an emerging European cultural identity (*Kulturnation*). The formation of a cultural nation would require cultivation of a strong sense of shared European culture, perhaps with more particularistic national, subnational, or cross-national cultures. The European Union has certainly initiated a series of policies designed to create such an identity – for instance the European common cultural projects or the 'European Cities of Culture' programme, which aims to develop a European consciousness at the same time as it respects the differences among national and regional cultures. These policies reflect the belief that the idea of 'Europe' and a sense of European cultural identity are essential to legitimating the growing power of the European political regime (see, for example, Sassatelli 2002). Nonetheless, whether grounded in an imagined community based on political identification or on one based on cultural identification, the definition of European identity also requires the drawing of boundaries that exclude others from membership of the European 'nation'. Important test cases in this regard are the eligibility of Belarus, Russia, Turkey, and the Ukraine to become part of the European Union, whether on the grounds of their respective political regimes or on the grounds of their cultural traditions.

Towards a World State and a World Society?

Even more challenging than the idea of a European territorial state based on a widely shared and primary European political and cultural identity is the idea of a world state based on a shared global identity. In terms of the future of 'the present state', three possibilities that have been explored are: (1) 'world society' with a corresponding form of government or governance; (2) cosmopolitanism as a distinctive political orientation based on a cosmopolitan identity; and (3) 'global civil society' as the foundation for developing a shared sense of political identity based on a common humanity and common fate.

World society is an increasingly popular social scientific concept and suggests that the ultimate horizon of social action has become truly global, even if much everyday material life remains stubbornly local. This development reflects the weakening of national markets, national states, and national societies (at least as they flourished in the 'first world' of the North) by comparison to their highpoint in the 1960s–1980s. In this context, the notion of world society challenges the idea that we live in an *international* order – that is, in an order formed primarily through interaction among economic, political, and sociocultural entities with clear national territorial boundaries. While this order was always more fictitious than real, the hold of national territorial imaginaries has been further weakened by the multiple processes associated with globalization. These changes also weaken arguments that the world has become more *transnational* – arguments that still treat the national as the benchmark for identifying social transformation. If we reject the relevance of the 'international' or 'transnational' as key concepts for describing world society, is the concept of the 'postnational' a more useful alternative?

The suggestion that world society is developing in a 'postnational' direction gains some credence from the growth of 'melting-pot' societies, the postmodern play of identities, the expansion of diasporic networks and communities, and the rise of multilevel governance. Further credence comes from (1) the relativization of scale (the loss of primacy of the national scale); (2) the territorial rescaling of government powers and authorities; and (3) the resulting increase in variable geometries and tangled hierarchies of political power across a growing range of fields of government action. Nonetheless, while it seems clear that national boundaries and national identity are no longer fundamental premises of economic, political, and sociocultural arrangements, the substantive content of what is 'postnational' remains unclear.

Regarding the state and the interstate system, 'postnational' could involve growing fragmentation as national territorial states become less significant or, alternatively, the development of a stable political order based on regional states, the growing power of a superstate able to wield hard and soft power to promote global cohesion, or even some form of world state (for a well-known but contested claim about the inevitability of a world state, see Wendt 2003). Another line of argument identifies a tendential revival of a *pre-national* form of territorial power, namely new forms of empire and imperialism, which are sometimes strongly endorsed in the guise of liberal empire, sometimes criticized as revamped classical imperialism (e.g., Callinicos 2009; Ferguson 2004; Hardt and Negri 2000). It is unlikely that a global superpower or world state could effectively govern world society, given the inherent complexities of the global order and, more importantly, the limited capacities of any societal subsystem to steer the operations of other subsystems. Even more modest attempts to establish global governance could not be confined to the global level alone and would have to be realized through complex forms of coordination across multiple sites and scales.

The political communities (or publics) around which forces in the political system orient their actions are being reimagined in various ways. Among them are new 'imagined nations' seeking autonomy within, or control of, a defined territory below, above, or transversal to existing national states; a global civil society based on cosmopolitan patriotism, the primacy of human rights over national citizenship, or some other global identity; new 'communities of fate' defined by shared risks regardless of specific territorial location, and perhaps global in character (e.g., communities formed around global warming); and new communities of interest defined by shared identities, interests, and values regardless of specific territorial location (e.g., cybercommunities). Such new territorial or extraterritorial conceptions of the political community are linked to struggles to redefine the nature and purposes of the state, find alternatives to territorialized forms of political power, and redefine the imagined general interest that political power, whether it remains territorial or not, should serve.

These shifts pose problems for the meaning of postnational identity. It could refer to the emergence of another positive identity (e.g., one based on cosmopolitan commitments); to a reversion to more primordial identities; or to a complex, contingent, pluralistic, and hopefully nonantagonistic play of identities. The second possibility was noted in Samuel Huntington's dystopian predictions of a global 'clash of civilizations' (Huntington 1998) and is also discernible in the trend towards internal or cross-border conflicts conducted in the name of ethnic identities, religious beliefs, or other social antagonisms. A major expression of this is fundamentalism: the development of competing, potentially antagonistic, worldviews based on a (reimagined) primordial identity or on claims to a historical mission (Ali 2002; Barber 1995). The third possibility is a growing plurality of values, identities, and interests – primordial as well as postmodern – that are mobilized in different ways for people to cope with the disorienting effects and new opportunities produced through global complexity. These values, identities, and interests range from transnational or cosmopolitan identities through calibrated forms of 'flexible citizenship' (Ong 2000) to localist, 'tribal', or other particularisms.

Cosmopolitanism dates back to ancient Greece and witnessed a revival during the Enlightenment – a context in which it has become identified with universal rights, perpetual peace, and a world state (or, more recently, global governance) (see Fine 2007). Given these historic associations, it is usually juxtaposed to nationalism, internal and external wars, and an anarchic world of national states. Cosmopolitanism comes in many guises (e.g., economic, legal, moral, and political), but this chapter focuses on four of its political expressions (see, in addition, Beck 2005; Habermas 2002). These involve demands to establish (1) a centralized world state (as discussed above); (2) a loose and voluntary global federation with limited power; (3) a more or less expansive and decentralized network of international political regimes with specific remits; and (4) a multitiered form of cosmopolitan democracy (on the last, see, for example, Held 1992). Many of these proposals are normative and aspirational rather than being grounded in realistic analyses of basic tendencies in the world market and world society (see chapters 8 and 10). Nonetheless they help to maintain the belief that 'another world is possible', as opposed to fatalistic resignation in the face of global crises and cynical promotion of new forms of global domination.

Finally for now, *global civil society* can be defined as an emerging space generated by the combination of multiple territorial arrangements and intergovernmental agencies and by a denationalized 'world society', characterized by social identities and by movements concerned with global issues or global action aimed at resolving more localized problems. Hence it serves as a new 'public sphere', which provides an interface among organizations, networks, and movements that represent a wide range of social forces, interests, and values concerned with the state of the world and with action designed to remedy its perceived problems. Many government or intergovernmental bodies recognize the legitimacy of some civil society organizations and social movements and grant them rights of access, representation, and participation in decision making and policy implementation. One expression of global civil society is the expansion of social forums, which often develop independently from economic and intergovernmental forums. They are hailed as a new form of associational democracy, based on continuing dialogue in the context of solidarity, and they provide means of coordinating grassroots and social movements across different sites and scales of action. An important topical example is the rise of global environmental discourses and activism around climate change, natural disasters, species extinctions, and pollution.

Some critics note that global civil society is one more site where global asymmetries are reproduced. This criticism aside, the principal problem that social forums face is to connect particular local struggles, generalize them, and link them to more cosmopolitan or universal projects of social transformation. Moreover, for global civil society to become an influential factor in global governance, it needs to develop the resources, capacities, and collective will to resist hegemonization, domination, or colonization by the institutional logics associated with one particular functional system (e.g., the profit-oriented, market-mediated logic of the capitalist economy, the authority of science, the fetishism of law, the prioritization of military security) or else by the power interests of one superpower or bloc of states. Only then could global civil society provide a space for dialogue so as to develop mutual understandings and coordinate many diverse organizations across many different functional systems and within the wider framework of world society. It would then serve as a reservoir of social energies and 'instincts' (rooted in diverse identities) and social resources that could be mobilized to resist attempts to colonize or dominate a wider social formation. This would provide an alternative to territorial forms of political organization, national identities, and the nation-state.

7

Government + Governance in the Shadow of Hierarchy

This chapter moves beyond a Weberian and Gramscian focus on coercion and hegemony to explore the state apparatus and state power from the perspective of governance and governmentality. Although governance as a more or less distinctive set of political practices has a long history, theoretical interest in 'governance' emerged mostly in the last 40–50 years. This interest reflected a growing perception of the problems generated in this period in advanced capitalist societies by a combination of state and market failure and a decline in social cohesion. The late 1960s and 1970s witnessed growing concern, on the part of national and transnational elites, about various problems in liberal democracies – including governmental overload, state failure, legitimacy crises, and general ungovernability – which prompted a search for political and social arrangements to address these problems. One response was the neoliberal call for 'more market, less state'. Another was attempts to lower popular expectations on what democratic governments can achieve (e.g., Crozier, Huntington, and Watanuki 1975). A third response, more significant for present purposes, was greater interest in the potential of coordination through self-organizing networks, partnerships, and other forms of reflexive collaboration. This has been reflected in claims about an alleged 'shift from govern*ment* to govern*ance*' in the polity and about similar shifts from hierarchical authority to networked or heterarchical coordination in other social fields. This is a topic ripe for investigation from the perspective of historical semantics, which would link the language of governance to growing societal complexity.

Most studies of governance from the late 1970s examined specific practices or regimes oriented to specific objects of governance, linked either to the planning, programming, and regulation of particular policy fields or to issues of economic performance. These practices were often treated as more or less adequate replies to growing societal complexity and/or as providing new ways to overcome old problems that postwar state intervention and the (re)turn to market forces seem to have left unsolved, if not aggravated. (On governance, see, for example, Streeck and Schmitter 1985; Kitschelt 1991; Kooiman 2003; Messner 1998; Pierre 1999; Scharpf 1999; Bevir 2007). As some of the limitations of governance were recognized from the mid-1990s, however, steering optimism was not abandoned but transferred to learning, dialogue, the transfer of best practice, and, more generally, 'meta-governance'.

These shifts in advanced economies coincided with the crises of Atlantic Fordism and the Keynesian welfare national state (KWNS); they were reinforced, in the mid-1990s, as recognition grew of the limited success of an overenthusiastic, fetishistic turn to the market. This was also a period when civil society was celebrated and efforts were made to integrate community organizations and social movements, old and especially new, into policymaking and implementation. Such developments prompted some governance scholars to assert or predict that the sovereign national state was losing authority and influence as governance arrangements were extended and reinforced. The claimed shift from government to governance gained plausibility because such arrangements occurred within and across many social fields and functional systems, at and across different scales of organization, and transversally to the conventional juridico-political boundaries between state and society. In short, the turn to governance seemed to be a more general trend, which extended beyond the state or political system.

This chapter addresses the growing significance of network governance in this mix and its role in the overall coordination of complex social relations. The argument proceeds in six steps: (1) it locates governance within the broad field of coordination practices in the face of societal complexity; (2) it provides a narrow definition of governance that identifies its *differentia specifica* from other modes of coordination; (3) it identifies the forms of governance failure and responses thereto; (4) it introduces 'collibration' as a third-order form of governance, concerned to modulate the relations among other forms of governance and order them in time–space; (5) it relates collibration to governmentality and governmentalization; and (6) it shows how governance, meta-governance, and collibration fit into the more general critique of political economy, forms of domination, and ideology. Overall this argument casts a different light on the state in its integral sense of a political society-cum-civil society.

Governance and Complexity

Whereas statehood (or, less abstractly, authoritative government) pre-supposes a state apparatus, a territory, and a population, the notion of governance lacks this core juridico-political or otherwise relatively fixed institutional reference point. Moreover, whereas statehood relates in the first instance to the polity, governance relates more to politics and policy. It concerns public politics, public policies, or public affairs (Larsson 2013: 107) rather than the state-cum-polity as the framework in which these occur. However, governance is broader in scope because it is not limited to the polity; indeed it is often advocated as a means to avoid the iron fist (even when con-cealed in a velvet glove) of state power. This may partly explain why notions of governance and governmentality appeal to scholars who are critical of reified state concepts, disillusioned with actual states, or interested in particular cases of politics and policy in specific fields that may cross-cut – often deliberately – the dividing lines between the state and its constitutive outside(s).

In broad terms, governance refers to mechanisms and strategies of coordination in the face of complex reciprocal interdependence among operationally autonomous actors, organizations, and func-tional systems. Governance practices range from the expansion of international and supranational regimes through national and regional public–private partnerships to more localized networks of power and decision making and, at least for some scholars, notably Foucauld-ians, to the governance of minds and bodies. Because actors cannot grasp all aspects of this complex world, they must reduce complexity cognitively, through selective sense and meaning making, and simplify governance tasks by isolating some subsets of relations for attention. This requires (1) identifying a subset of relevant features of an inor-dinately complex world that can be governed satisfactorily within a specific spatiotemporal envelope; and (2) developing governance capacities that provide the resources to transform unstructured into structured complexity (cf. Jessop 2009, 2011). Yet these activities often displace current costs elsewhere and store up future governance problems.

Four modes of governance are distinguished here: exchange, command, network, and solidarity (see Table 7.1). The third of these refers to governance in its narrow sense and is also described as dialogic governance, which better reveals its distinctive modus operandi, namely dialogue and negotiation within and across networks. In this context, the strategic–relational approach (SRA) would suggest that, even if we accept the classical three-element account of the state, there is no reason to assume that state power is confined to imperative coordination – that is, to centralized planning or top-down intervention. State power can be exercised not only through coercion, command, planning, and bureaucracy but also through networks, partnerships, appeals to solidarity, and so on. And, in this context, the state (or polity) provides an institutional matrix for political contestation (politics) over how to address specific challenges through governance (policies).

Exchange involves *ex post* coordination based on a formal, procedural rationality that is oriented to the efficient allocation of scarce resources to competing ends. In the case of the literal 'anarchy' of the market, this involves endless 'economizing' efforts at profit maximization. It requires demanding conditions if it is to work efficiently even in its own limited terms, long recognized in theories of market failure and recently illustrated by disillusion with the efficient market hypothesis as a basis for governing finance-dominated accumulation.

Command involves *ex ante* imperative coordination in pursuit of substantive collective goals set from above (hierarchical command in the firm, organization, or state). It prioritizes the 'effective' pursuit of successive policy goals. Like exchange, it has demanding preconditions. For, alongside problems of creating and maintaining appropriate organizational capacities, the algorithms required for effective *ex ante* coordination in a complex and turbulent environment impose heavy cognitive demands. And, like market coordination, command is prey to the problems of bounded rationality, opportunism, and asset specificity (Coulson 1997) – features that apply not only to market-mediated transactions but to many other aspects of social life too.

Dialogue involves a continuing reflexive self-organization based on networks, negotiation, and deliberation that is oriented to redefining goals in the light of changing circumstances around a long-term consensual project, which is taken as the basis for negative and positive coordination of actions. Negative coordination refers to the tacit or explicit agreement to avoid causing problems for other partners or stakeholders when determining one's own course of action. Positive coordination refers to active cooperation in the pursuit of shared goals. This mode of governance has a substantive, procedural

Table 7.1 Modes of governance

	Exchange	Command	Dialogue	Solidarity
Rationality	Formal and procedural	Substantive and goal-oriented	Reflexive and procedural	Unreflexive and value-oriented
Criterion of success	Efficient allocation of resources	Effective goal-attainment	Negotiated consent	Requited commitment
Typical example	Market	State	Network	Love
Stylized mode of calculation	*Homo economicus*	*Homo hierarchicus*	*Homo politicus*	*Homo fidelis*
Spatiotemporal horizons	World market, reversible time	Organizational space, planning	Rescaling, path shaping	Any time, Anywhere
Primary criterion of failure	Economic inefficiency	Ineffectiveness	'Noise', 'talking shop'	Betrayal, mistrust
Secondary criterion of failure	Market inadequacies	Bureaucratism, red tape	Secrecy, distorted communication	Co-dependency asymmetry

Source: Jessop 2007b

rationality that is dialogic rather than monologic, pluralistic rather than monolithic, heterarchic rather than hierarchical or anarchic. It aims to solve specific coordination problems on the basis of continuing dialogue in order to establish the grounds for negotiated consent, resource sharing, and concerted action in mutually beneficial joint projects. It depends on continuing commitment to generate and share information (thereby reducing, without ever eliminating, the problem of bounded rationality); to weaken opportunism by locking partners into a range of interdependent decisions over short-, medium-, and long-term time horizons; and to build on the interdependencies and risks linked to 'asset specificity' by encouraging solidarity among dialogue partners.

Solidarity involves unreflexive, unconditional commitment. Its 'thickest' form is generally confined to small units (e.g., a couple, a family, tight-knit communities of fate, or a *Bund* based on shared sentiments and values, mutual affection, support for a charismatic leader, etc.);[1] the larger the unit, the thinner and less intense solidarity tends to become (e.g., in the case of imagined national communities, or of humanity at large). Eventually solidarity changes into more unilateral forms of 'trust' in the expertise of skilled practitioners, who provide goods and services that their clients cannot procure themselves. (On trust and its failure, see Luhmann 1979; Gambetta 1988; Fukuyama 1995; Misztal 1996; Adler 2001; Nooteboom 2002.)

Governance Failure and Meta-Governance

Each mode of governance has a distinctive primary form of failure and typical secondary forms of failure (see Table 7.1). Failure leads to attempts at meta-governance. This concept has been defined as, *inter alia*, the organization of self-organization, the regulation of self-regulation, the steering of self-steering, the structuring of the game-like interaction within governance networks – and as an interaction among actors with a view to influencing parameter changes to the overall system. In its most basic (but also most eclectic) sense, it denotes the governance of governance. (For a comprehensive review of the theoretical and policy literature on meta-governance, see Meuleman 2008.) If we consider exchange, command, dialogue, and solidarity as four forms of *first-order* coordination or governance, *second-order* governance (see Table 7.2) would involve attempts to modify their institutional conditions and improve their operation in terms of their respective criteria of success when they are judged outdated, dysfunctional, or detrimental in governance terms

Table 7.2 Second-order governance

Meta-exchange	Metacommand	Metadialogue	Metasolidarity
Redesigns individual markets	Organizational redesign	Reorders networks	Develops new identities and loyalties
De- and reregulation	Reorders organizational ecologies	Reorganize conditions of self-organization	From old to new social movements
Reorders market hierarchies	Constitutional change	New forms of dialogue	New forms of solidaristic practice

Source: Jessop 2007b

(cf. Kooiman 1993). Such efforts to redesign each coordination mechanism may focus directly on the mechanism itself or on its facilitating conditions, if not on both.

Market failure is said to occur when markets fail to allocate scarce resources efficiently through the pursuit of monetized private interest; the first-order response might be a further extension of the market mechanism or a reordering of market hierarchies. Command fails in ways that vary with the organizations involved and, in general terms, the first-order response is the reflexive redesign of organizations (Beer 1990), the creation of intermediating organizations, the reordering of interorganizational relations, and the management of organizational ecologies (i.e., a reorganization of the conditions of organizational evolution in a situation where many organizations coexist, compete, cooperate, and coevolve) (cf. Fischer 2009; Hood 1998). More specifically, state failure is said to occur when state managers cannot secure substantive collective goals determined on the basis of their political divination of the (always illusory) public interest. Typical first-order responses to state failure have been attempts to improve juridico-political institutional design, knowledge, or political practice; or a policy of 'more market, less state'.

Network, dialogic, or heterarchic governance – in short, governance in its narrow sense – was once heralded as a 'magic bullet' that supposedly overcomes the problems of market and state failure without creating its own problems. However, dialogue is also prone to failure – albeit for different reasons, in different ways, and with different effects. Insofar as such governance aims to modify goals through ongoing negotiation and reflection, failure would involve the inability to redefine objectives in the face of continuing disagreement about whether the latter are still valid for the various partners. The first-order response to such failures could involve the reflexive organization of the conditions of reflexive self-organization by redefining the framework in which dialogue (or reflexive self-organization) occurs. This can range from providing opportunities for 'spontaneous sociability' (Fukuyama 1995; see also Putnam 2000) through various measures intended to promote networking and negotiation to the introduction of innovations intended to promote 'institutional thickness'.

Finally, solidarity is limited as a generalized mechanism, whatever potential it might have in small-scale social units, local groups, and tight-knit communities of fate (cf. Adler 2001; Nooteboom 2002). A first-order response involves forms of therapeutic action, whether spontaneous or mediated through therapeutic intervention, in order to repair or refocus feelings of loyalty and unconditional commitment.

One term for responses to first- and second-order governance failure is third-order governance (Kooiman 2003). Another term, which avoids confusion with other kinds of governance, is 'collibration', which is also preferable because of its etymological roots as well as its conceptual precision (see above, p. 85). The aim of collibration is to alter the weight of individual modes of governance, so that the overall set of governance arrangements at a higher or more comprehensive level of social organization is better adapted to coordinate complex social relations, in line with the strategic objectives of those engaged in this third-order form of meta-governance (Dunsire 1990: 17). Whereas second-order governance occurs in many arenas and policy fields and need not involve the state (which is primarily concerned in this second-order context with the effectiveness of imperative coordination), third-order governing is more likely to involve the state as an addressee of last instance for appeals to solve societal problems by taking responsibility for the overall balance among modes of governance (cf. Bourdieu 2014 on the state's role in rebalancing the relations among forms of social capital). Indeed, rather than just responding as addressees of last resort to demands from social forces to deal with governance failure, state managers actively promote these new forms of governance as adjuncts to or substitutes for more traditional forms of top-down government. Collibration is one aspect of their actions in this regard. They have sometimes acted this way and promoted these forms in the hope or expectation that policymaking and implementation will become more efficient, effective, transparent, and accountable to relevant stake-holders and moral standards, leading to 'good governance'. But this manner of acting can also serve the interests of the state apparatus and state managers, by facilitating its own reproduction as well as other forms of social domination.

> According to Rosenau, new forms of global governance reflect a disag-gregated, decentred world with new spheres of authority, no single organising principle, and greater flexibility, innovation and experimen-tation in use of control mechanisms. The second part of this claim... is highlighted by the governmentality approach. This makes the world seem disaggregated and decentred. But this disaggregation and decen-tring is, paradoxically, the result of strategies carried out by the domi-nant states. [Yet]... what is mistaken for global governance is a neoliberal form of governmentality pushed *by* states, pushed *on* states and pushed *through* states. (Joseph 2014: 12)

More generally, as a key activity of the state, collibration can be seen as a counter-trend to the shift from government to governance and entails that governments play a major and increasing role in many aspects of meta-governance in areas of societal significance, whether these are formally private or public. Specifically, governments provide the ground rules for governance and the regulatory order through which governance partners can pursue their aims; they ensure the compatibility or coherence of different governance mechanisms and regimes; they create forums for dialogue or act as primary organizers of the dialogue among policy communities; they deploy a relative monopoly of organizational intelligence and information in order to shape cognitive expectations; they serve as courts of appeal for dis-putes arising within and over governance; they seek to rebalance power differentials and strategic bias in regimes by strengthening weaker forces or systems in the interest of system integration and social cohesion; they try to modify the self-understanding of identi-ties, strategic capacities, and interests of individual and collective actors in different strategic contexts, and hence they alter the implica-tions of this self-understanding for preferred strategies and tactics; they organize redundancies and duplication in order to sustain resil-ience through a requisite variety, in response to unexpected problems; they take material and symbolic flanking and supporting measures to stabilize forms of coordination deemed valuable but prone to col-lapse; they subsidize the production of public goods; they organize side payments for those who make sacrifices for the sake of facilitat-ing effective coordination; they contribute to the meshing of short-, medium- and long-term time horizons and temporal rhythms across different sites, scales, and actors, in part to prevent opportunistic exit and entry into governance arrangements; and they also assume political responsibility as addressees of last resort in the event of governance failure in domains that go beyond the state (see Jessop 2002: 219; Bell and Hindmoor 2009).

Governance involves not only institutional design appropriate to different objects of governance but also the transformation of subjects and their orientations to the world. Foucauldian students of governmentality offer more here than students of governance (Lemke 1997). The former are especially interested in the role of power and knowledge in shaping the attributes, capacities, and identities of social agents and, in the context of self-reflexive governance, in enabling these agents to become self-governing and self-transforming (cf. Miller and Rose 2008). This is a productive approach in a period characterized by a shift from government to governance; and it is useful in the study of 'advanced liberalism' (i.e., neoliberal governance beyond the market as well as beyond the state). This state project requires attempts to create entrepreneurial subjects and demanding consumers, aware of their choices and rights as well as of actions that can shift the respective scope and powers of the market mechanism and state intervention.

However, such scholars tend to focus on the logic, rationalities, and practices of government or governmentality in isolation from broader concern with the state's key role as a site in the collibration and institutional integration of power relations, modes of governance, and social domination. In addition to issues of institutional complementarity, this also concerns the distribution of individual and collective capacities to pursue creatively and autonomously appropriate strategies and tactics in order to sustain contrasting modes of governance. This is another area where there is a collibratory role for the state.

In engaging in collibration, the state operates less as the supreme instantiation of command (as a sovereign 'organization' that is not subject to command by another 'organization') than as *primus inter pares* in a complex, heterogeneous, and multilevel network of social relations. This suggests that formal sovereignty is better seen as an interconnected, reinforcing series of symbolic and material state capacities than as an overarching, dominant resource with the monopoly over coercion – a resource that belongs to state as *the* sovereign authority in a single hierarchical command structure. Other stakeholders in collibration contribute other symbolic or material resources (e.g., private money, legitimacy, information, expertise, organizational capacities, or the power of numbers), which are to be combined with states' sovereign and other capacities in order to advance collectively agreed aims and objectives.

From Government to Governance

Five main accounts of the shift from government to governance have been developed since the mid-1970s – the time when the failure of the postwar state in advanced capitalist societies became increasingly evident. In some cases these are alternative descriptions of the same broad set of changes; in other cases they involve a more radical shift in theoretical perspective.

First, there is a tendential *de-hierarchization of the state*. In this process, states or state managers seek to retain or restore their control over society by turning to other forms of governing their territory and population (defined here so as to include collective agents as well as individuals and households), especially through public–private partnerships of various kinds that cooperate in the definition and delivery of state projects and policies. There is also an analogous process whereby political anarchy, which, for realist international relations theorists, is rooted in the absence of a world-state, is replaced by the pooling or sharing of sovereignty through intergovernmental cooperation or through a self-organizing world society. This analogous process might be described as a *heterarchization of the international political arena*.

Second, as an alternative description that highlights other aspects of this process, there is a *recalibration of state power* as government makes more extensive use of networks and other modes of governance as a way of maintaining its political efficacy in the face of growing societal complexity. Here the focus is on the complex, decentred, and pluralistic governance arrangements at stake rather than on the apparently simple fact that the state relies less on imperative coordination based on coercion, law, planning, and hierarchical bureaucratic arrangements.

A third, more common description decentres the state analytically by shifting attention to the more general organization of the polity. It highlights the destatization of politics. This is reflected in a claimed shift from a *hierarchical state* to a *networked polity* (cf. Ansell 2000). Such a shift involves hybrid governance arrangements marked by horizontal and vertical patterns of coordination, multiple public and private sector agents, and the use of resources supplied by different stakeholders according to their respective capacities, competences, and ideal and material interests.

Fourth, going somewhat further, it is suggested that there has been a *depolitization of power*. The meaning of this concept derives from the distinction between polity, politics, and policy. Thus the process refers not just to the state's retreat from the political field as the state invites or allows other political forces to play a bigger role, but also to efforts to define some problems as better suited to nominally *apolitical* forms of decision making. Different forms of marketization are one example; but, for governance theorists, a more interesting form is the growth of *network governance beyond the polity* (as opposed to the expansion of the networked polity, discussed in the preceding paragraph). These arrangements combine resources that are distinctive to the state (e.g., its monopolies on coercion, taxation, and the right to make collectively binding decisions) with resources that are distinctive to other societal subsystems, institutional orders, organizations, or collective actors (such as social movements). This response is more likely to come where governance practices are mainly concerned with managing functional interdependencies, whatever their scope and political geometries, rather than with activities occurring in a defined and delimited territory. It is even more likely to come where governance problems cross-cut territorial boundaries.

Fifth, Foucauldians suggest that there has been a shift to advanced (neo)liberal forms of governmentality, which use various governmental techniques both to mobilize *and* to discipline the energies of civil society and, in so doing, govern social relations at a distance rather than through direct command and control by a sovereign authority. This approach is particularly associated with interest in the development of new kinds of apparatus (*dispositifs*) organized around various discursively constituted problems (*urgences*; Bussolini 2010, summarizing the Foucauldian *problématique* in this regard). For Anglo-Foucauldian scholars, this approach de-emphasizes the role of the state (e.g., Miller and Rose 2008); but for others – especially those influenced by Foucault's later lectures on governmentality, territorialization, and 'state effects' – the *discourse–dispositif* approach provides an alternative account of the modalities of state power and of the role of the state in the strategic codification of power relations (cf. Foucault 1977; Kelly 2009: 61–2; Joseph 2014). Thus it organizes networks of power and promotes 'the statification of government and the governmentalization of the state' (Foucault 2007: 109).

It falls to the state to facilitate collective learning about functional linkages and material interdependencies among different sites and spheres of action. And it falls to politicians – local as well as national – to participate in developing the shared visions that can link complementary forms of governance and maximize their effectiveness. Such tasks are conducted by states not only in terms of their contribution to particular state functions but also in terms of their implications for political class domination and social cohesion. This emerging role means that networking, negotiation, noise reduction, and negative as well as positive coordination occur 'in the shadow of hierarchy'. This phrase was introduced (initially by Fritz Scharpf, 1993) to denote the indirect influence that states may exercise over other actors or forces in political and civil society through the real or imagined threat of an executive or legislative action that draws on the state's unique capacities and powers, including coercion.

Meta-Governance as Politics and Policy

Of particular interest here is the way in which new forms of governance fit into the overall configuration of class power and political domination. Combining Foucauldian and Gramscian perspectives, and mindful of Mitchell's remark that the essence of modern politics is the reproduction of the inherently flexible boundary between state and society (see chapters 2 and 4), I suggest that 'the state in its inclusive sense' can be defined as 'government + governance in the shadow of hierarchy'. This fits well with Gramsci's familiar definition of the state as 'the entire complex of practical and theoretical activities with which the ruling class not only justifies and maintains its dominance, but manages to win the active consent of those over whom it rules' (1971: 244 = Q15, §10: 1765). Overlooking for now its class-reductionist nature, which leads Gramsci to dismiss other aspects of state power as relatively trivial by comparison (ibid.), this definition directs attention from the state as a juridico-political apparatus towards the modalities of the exercise of state power. Thus my proposed redefinition recognizes that state power (1) extends beyond coercion, imperative coordination, and positive law to include the mobilization and allocation of money and credit and the strategic use of intelligence, statistics, and other kinds of knowledge (Willke 1997); (2) depends on the capacity to mobilize active consent or passive compliance from forces situated (or operating) beyond the state in its narrow juridico-political sense; and (3) includes efforts by state agents to strategically rebalance modes of government and governance in order to improve the effectiveness of indirect as well as direct state intervention, including the exercise of power at a distance from the state (cf. Joseph 2012).

In these terms, pursuit of the substantive goals that state managers set from time to time is not confined to the exercise of state capacities that are unique to the state in its narrow sense (e.g., as a constitutionalized monopoly on organized coercion, taxation powers, and legal sovereignty). It also extends to modes of governance or governmentalization such as the market, dialogue, and solidarity, which operate beyond the state. Thus governance straddles the conventional public–private divide and may involve 'tangled hierarchies', parallel power networks, or other linkages across tiers of government or functional domains. Government and governance are often linked through contested practices of meta-governance or collibration, that is, through the rebalancing of different forms of governance within and beyond the state, in the shadow of *hierarchy*. Governance is certainly not a purely technical matter, limited to specific problems defined by the state (or other social forces) and which can be resolved by experts in organizational design, public administration, and public opinion management. It always involves specific objects, techniques, and subjects that are more or less recalcitrant to governance. A fortiori, collibration is also more than a technical, problem-solving fix. Relevant practices involve not only specific political or policy outcomes in particular political and policy fields, but also their broader effects on state capacities. They modify the available mix of government and governance techniques and change the balance of forces. Those engaged in meta-governance may redraw the inherited public–private divide, alter the forms of interpenetration between the political system and other functional systems, and modify the relations between these systems and civil society in the light of their (perceived) impact on state capacities. While collibration is one of the state's main metapolitical activities, an activity where the state has a privileged strategic position, this activity is often hotly contested because of competing meta-governance projects.

Indeed collibration is tied to the management of a wider 'unstable equilibrium of compromise'; and it is typically conducted in the light of the most general function of the state – maintaining social cohesion in a class-divided (or, better, socially divided) society. Thus, although governance mechanisms may acquire specific techno-economic, political, and ideological functions in particular contexts, governance is always conducted under the primacy of the political, that is, the primacy of the state's concern with managing the tension between economic and political advantages and its ultimate responsibility for social cohesion (cf. Poulantzas 1973). This holds both for the political nature of any specific process of problem definition and for the state's monitoring of the effects of specific forms of governance on its institutional integration and ability to pursue its hegemonic or dominant project while maintaining social cohesion in divided societies.

In other words, governance and meta-governance cannot be reduced to questions of how to solve issues of a specific techno-economic, narrowly juridico-political in character, tightly focused social–administrative, or otherwise neatly framed problem. This is not only because of the material interconnections among different problem fields in a complex world, but also because every governance – and, a fortiori, meta-governance – practice affects the balance of forces. This fact plagues liberal prescriptions of an arms-length relationship between the market and the night-watchman state – since states (or at least state managers) are rarely strong enough to resist pressures to intervene when political advantage and social unrest are at stake. More generally, the state reserves to itself the right to open, close, juggle, and rearticulate governance – not only in terms of particular functions, but also from the viewpoint of partisan and general political advantage. As we shall see, this right is related in the last resort to the declaration of states of emergency, which give extraordinary powers to state officials in reordering government and governance arrangements. Even in less extreme situations, this right can often lead state managers to engage in actions designed to protect their particular interests at the expense of the state's overall capacity to pursue an always selective and biased consensual interpretation of the public interest and to promote social cohesion.

Many individual forms of governance (or governmentality) can be interpreted in terms of 'passive revolution' and transformism (*trasformismo*). Passive revolution represents a process of transformation, absorption, and incorporation that translates contentious politics into bureaucratic or technical questions (Gramsci 1971: 105–14, 291 = Q15, §11: 1766–9, 1822–4, Q22, §6: 2155). It also involves creating the conditions for the self-responsibilization of individuals, groups, organizations, or whole 'stakeholder groups' through the adoption of specific technologies of government, which rely on scientific expertise, consultants, expert systems, algorithms, metrology, ratings, bench-marking, contingent rewards for approved behaviour, and so on. (On expertise, see Fischer 2009; on metrology, Barry 2002; on credit rating agencies, Sinclair 2005; on governmentalization, Miller and Rose 2008.) These techniques are sometimes justified in terms of reducing government overload; but they also have affinities with the neoliberal project of a lean state, which depends on various flanking and supporting mechanisms that operate beyond the state and must be coordinated through collibration or meta-governance.

More generally, Gramsci attributed a key role here to the bureaucracy, which served both technical and political functions. Bureaucrats were not confined to the technical administration of things but were also expected to show loyalty to the state and its policies and to know how best to minimize resistance and secure the obedience of the ruled (1971: 144 = Q15, §4: 175). Moreover, with the growing complexity of social life, the bureaucracy expands organically, 'absorbing the great specialists of private enterprise and integrating personnel specialized in the concrete problems of administering the essential practical activities of the great and complex national societies of today' (1971: 27 = Q12, §1: 1532). In this context, technical competence becomes more important than formal–juridical leadership and politics is drained of ideological content. Consent is no longer organized through rhetorical discussion but through the standardization of expectations and norms of conduct (cf. Migliaro and Misuraca 1982: 90). Nowadays one might well posit that the reverse process is occurring. In other words, rather than the statization of governmentality through bureaucratic absorption of technical experts and intellectuals, there is a governmentalization of the state as responsibilities are 'outsourced' in the shadow of governmental hierarchy (cf. Joseph 2012).

In this context, passive revolution is an attempt to absorb the energies and expertise of leading figures in the opposition – an attempt initially limited to parliament but later, with the rise of mass politics, expanded so as to win over entire groups (Gramsci 1995: Q8 §36: 962–7), to defuse a loss of political legitimacy, to recuperate problems of government overload, to turn potential sources of resistance or obstruction into self-responsibilized agents of their own subordination, and to enhance the efficiencies of economic, political, and social domination. Such enhancement is achieved through forms of micromanagement that penetrate into the pores of an increasingly complex social formation, which is intransparent to any single point of observation, command, and control and cannot be left to the invisible but benign hand of market forces.

The Success and Failure of Meta-Governance in the Shadow of Hierarchy

How different modes of coordination operate depends on their relative primacy within the political order (government and governance in the shadow of hierarchy) and on the differential access of their stakeholders to institutional support and resources. Crucial issues here are, *inter alia*, the flanking and supporting measures that are taken by the state; the provision of material and symbolic support;

and the extent of any duplication or counteraction by other coordination mechanisms. Moreover, as both governance and government mechanisms exist on different scales (indeed one of their functions is to bridge scales), success on one scale may well depend on practices and events on other scales. Likewise, coordination mechanisms may have different temporal horizons, and there may well be disjunctions between the temporalities of different governance and government mechanisms that go beyond issues of sequencing, to affect the viability of any given mode of coordination. A further paradox has been identified. Poul Kjaer (2010) notes, concerning the European Union, that, rather than involving contradictory developments, governing and governance are mutually constitutive in that more governing implies more governance and vice versa. In turn, Bengt Larsson (2013) suggests that, whereas the state can enhance its power by using networks to govern, networks depend on sovereign power to maintain the conditions for effective network governance.

While the Gramscian–Foucauldian redefinition above highlights the state's role in collibration, other scholars have suggested that there are functional equivalents to the state's 'shadow' role in this regard. These include (1) the networks' more or less spontaneous, bottom-up development of rules, values, norms, and principles that they then acknowledge and follow (Kooiman and Jentoft 2009); (2) increased deliberation and participation of civil society groups through stakeholder democracy, which puts external pressure on state managers and other elites involved in governance (Bevir 2010); and (3) actions taken by international governmental and nongovernmental agencies to compensate for the inability of failed or weak states to engage in meta-governance (Börzel and Risse 2010) – although this third example seems to involve a rescaling of the shadow of hierarchy, insofar as such actions are typically backed by powerful states (as Börzel and Risse themselves note).

The propensity to failure, whether through governance or meta-governance, is due both to the general problem of 'governability' – that is, to the question of whether a socially and discursively constituted object of governance could ever be manageable, given the complexity and turbulence of the material, social, and spatiotemporal conditions in which it is embedded – and to particular issues of 'governability' associated with particular objects and agents of governance, with particular modes of coordination of reciprocal interdependence, and with the familiar problems of unacknowledged conditions of action and unanticipated consequences. The issue of unacknowledged conditions of action and unanticipated consequences is particularly problematic where the objects of governance are liable to change, or where the environment they are embedded in is turbulent, making strategic learning difficult (see Haas and Haas 1995; Eder 1999; Dierkes et al., 2001). The contemporary dominance of the logic of capital accumulation is a major source of such problems by virtue of the inherent contradictions and antagonisms in the capital relation and by virtue of their generalization through the increasing integration of the world market. It should nonetheless be recognized that, just as the love of money is not the source of all evil, capital is not the source of all governance problems! Different societalization principles are linked to different sets of problems, and this is why the polymorphic nature of the state and governance must be addressed.

Given the tendency for first-order governance to fail, whether from lack of governance capacities or from the inherent contradictoriness and ungovernability of the objects of governance, meta-governance and collibration are also likely to fail. Such failure is more likely to happen where the relevant objects of governance and meta-governance are complicated, interconnected, and perhaps internally or mutually contradictory and where any prior impression of success has depended on displacing certain governance problems beyond the specific spatiotemporal horizons of a given set of social forces. Thus an important aspect of governance success (or, more precisely, creating the appearance of governance success) is the consolidation of specific spatiotemporal fixes within which governance problems appear manageable because certain ungovernable features manifest themselves elsewhere. Two corollaries of this framing are that *current* zones of *stability* imply *future* zones of *instability* and that zones of stability *in this place* imply zones of instability *in other places*. Indeed the capacity to defer and displace problems is one source of the 'steering optimism' in the governance and meta-governance literatures – especially when it is reinforced by the capacity to engage in a *fuite en avant* to produce new spatiotemporal fixes and thereby escape the consequences of past failures. In contrast, 'steering pessimism' tends to look at the underlying long-term structural obstacles to effective governance and meta-governance – neglect of which so often leads to the 'revenge' of problems that get ignored, marginalized, displaced, or deferred. This is especially true during periods of crisis that threaten system integration or social cohesion (see chapter 9). This is where the link between meta-governance and passive revolution is especially strong and major transitions in accumulation regimes, state projects, societal visions, and so forth are likely to occur in the context of crises (Jessop 2015a).

Three further sets of remarks will help to put governance and meta-governance in their place within an SRA. First, in addition to any problems, failure tendencies, and dilemmas inherent in specific modes of coordination, the success of governance is also affected by the dependence of capital accumulation on maintaining a contradictory balance between marketized and nonmarketized organizational forms. Although this was previously understood mainly in terms of the balance between market and state, governance does not introduce a neutral third term but adds another site upon which the balance can be contested. For new forms of governance provide a new meeting ground for the conflicting logics of accumulation and political mobilization. As indicated in chapter 4 and again above, a key aspect of this problem in capitalist social formations is the capacity to develop and consolidate specific spatiotemporal fixes. Strategically, because capitalism's contradictions and dilemmas are insoluble in the abstract, they are resolved – partially and provisionally, if at all – through the formulation–realization of specific accumulation strategies at various economic and political scales in specific spatiotemporal contexts (see chapter 4). Such spatiotemporal fixes delimit the main spatial and temporal boundaries within which structural coherence is secured and externalize certain costs of securing this coherence beyond these boundaries. The primary scales and temporal horizons around which such fixes are built and their relative coherence vary considerably over time. This is reflected in the variable coincidence of different boundaries, borders, or frontiers of action and in the changing primacy of different scales (chapters 1, 4, and 5).

Jonathan Davies (2011) provides a neo-Gramscian approach to governance that complements my proposed redefinition of the integral state but is more tightly focused on the current neoliberal globalizing capitalism. Specifically, he interprets the movement – via markets, he suggests – from hierarchy to governance as an aspect of the continuing struggle for hegemony under neoliberalism (Davies 2011: 128; cf. Provan and Kenis 2008). In this context he emphasizes, against claims that network governance is symmetrical (at least in the sense that it is not hierarchical), that it is strongly asymmetrical and that these asymmetries are rooted in, and also mediate, the wider, contradictory totality of capitalist social formations with their vast concentrations of power and wealth, intensifying competition, and chronic instability. On this basis he outlines a novel typology of forms of network governance *within neoliberalism* that ranges from inclusive governance through sub-hegemonic to counter-hegemonic forms, and he examines the conditions for emancipation through networks. He asks why powerful networks of actors with similar material and cultural endowments have more influence than other types of networks, and why nodal actors in different networks are more closely related than other actors (Davies 2011: 131). He also remarks that network coordination tends to degenerate into hierarchical coordination because networks fail to cultivate governing subjects (he calls them 'connectionist citizen-activists') able to solve policy and management problems in depoliticized, trust-based networks. He concludes that network governance failure moves state power along the Gramscian consensus–coercion continuum from hegemonic leadership towards domination (Davies 2011: 132). In the terms presented above, this could also be described as a reassertion of the shadow of hierarchy – but one tied to a particular class project. This approach need not be confined to neoliberalism but can be extended to the role of governance whenever its objects involve 'wicked problems', rooted in part in social relations of exploitation or domination.

Conclusions

This chapter has drawn on the SRA to facilitate a move beyond mainstream governance studies and the micro-analytical and antistatist bias of governmentality studies. It criticizes the common and one-sided claim that there has been a shift from government to governance on the grounds that this claim rests on a narrow view of the state as a juridico-political apparatus that governs through imperative coordination. Such a view ignores other modalities of state power and implies that, if the state employs other techniques of rule, it must be 'in retreat'. Yet, as part of this shift, states regularly get involved in redesigning markets, in constitutional change and the juridical reregulation of organizational forms and objectives, in organizing the conditions for networked self-organization, in promoting social capital and the self-regulation of the professions and other forms of expertise, and, most importantly, in the collibration of different forms of first-order governance and meta-governance. This is not a new development, even if the concept of governance underwent a major revival in the 1970s and 1980s – which was to be followed in the mid-1990s by a growing interest in governance failure and in the prospects of meta-governance. Meta-governance failure is now increasingly visible too, thanks to the 'wicked complexity' of some governance problems and the inevitable politicization of the state *qua* institutionally mediated material condensation of a shifting balance of forces.

These developments illustrate another facet of the part–whole paradox discussed in chapter 3. For such trends can be read in two ways. On the one hand, a less sovereignty-focused but still state-centric account of governance would examine how the state modifies the relative weight of different modes of governance in order to promote state projects as part of its continuing efforts to preserve state power – if necessary, by sharing it with social agents and with forces from the economy and civil society, or by pooling sovereignty with other states, in various kinds of intergovernmental regimes. Here the state reasserts its role as an apparatus responsible for social cohesion. On the other hand, a more governance-centric approach would consider how the state is enrolled in governance practices in various social fields, not as the prime mover or as *primus inter pares*, but as one actor-cum-stakeholder among others, all endowed with distinctive resources to contribute to governance arrangements and projects that are initiated beyond the state. Here the state is reduced to one part among many.

This is why I also drew on critical political economy to highlight the inherent limitations of steering or governance optimism, which is often exaggerated and indeed utopian, thereby 'creating one of the most important characteristics of ideology, namely, premature harmonization of social contradictions' (Bloch 1986a: 156; cf. 265). For there are some basic challenges rooted in the capital relation or forms of *Herrschaft* that cannot be addressed adequately or at all within an actor-centred institutionalist approach. These include the fundamentally antagonistic nature of certain social relations and their relation to crisis aetiology and dynamics; the social practices involved in constructing pluralistic, nonantagonistic, potentially reconcilable identities and interests as opposed to identities and interests that are regarded as polarized, mutually opposed, and non-negotiable; the asymmetric power to define the nature of collective problems even in liberal democracies (let alone in other political regimes); and the inherent ungovernability of certain 'problems' that can be 'solved' only by displacing or deferring aspects of the problems elsewhere.

Although I have emphasized the intellectual value of combining work on government and governance within a strategic–relational analysis, important differences remain between government and governance regarding modes of economic and social intervention. For, while the sovereign state is essentially a political unit that governs but is not itself governed, self-organization provides the essence of governance. In this context, while the sovereign state mainly governs activities on its own territorial domain and defends its territorial integrity against other states and intrusive forces, governance seeks to manage functional interdependencies, whatever their (often variable) territorial scope. These differences explain the growing interest in forms of governance that operate across scales and coordinate state *and nonstate actors* around particular functional problems, which have a variable territorial geometry. Some theorists emphasize the vertical dimension of coordination (*multilevel government or governance*); others focus on its horizontal dimension (*network governance*). In both cases the state is accorded a continuing role in the reflexive self-organization of multiple stakeholders across several scales of state-territorial organization – and indeed in diverse extra-territorial contexts. This role is that of *primus inter pares* in a complex, heterogeneous, and multilevel network rather than that of *the* sovereign authority in a single hierarchical command structure. Thus formal sovereignty is better seen as a series of symbolic and material state capacities than as an overarching, dominant resource. Other stakeholders contribute other symbolic or material resources (e.g., private money, legitimacy, information, expertise, organizational capacities, or the power of numbers) that can be combined with states' sovereign and other capacities so as to advance collectively agreed aims and objectives. Thus states' involvement in multilevel governance becomes less hierarchical, less centralized, and less directive and, compared to the clear hierarchy of territorial powers theoretically associated with sovereign states, it typically involves tangled hierarchies and a complex interdependence.

Part III

Past and Present (Futures) of the State

Part II

8

The World Market and the World of States

Since the mid-1970s social science research and lay commentary have debated the future of national territorial states in the light of ongoing globalization. Some paradigms predicted the imminent demise of the national territorial state, but such forecasts have not yet been realized. This debate is linked to two others. One is growing interest in a rescaling of the state system, as state powers are transferred upwards, downwards, and sideways from the national territorial level. This process is reflected in the proliferation and density of institutionalized scales at which significant state activities occur – from local through urban and regional to cross-border and continent-wide cooperation, and on to diverse supranational entities. The other debate concerns claims about the transition from government at different scales to networked forms of governance that connect activities at similar scales across several states. This kind of transition reflects the adaptability of state managers and apparatuses, the continued importance of national states in securing the conditions for economic competitiveness, political legitimacy, and social cohesion, and a greater role for national states in coordinating state activities at several scales, including their own. These tasks suggest that the national territorial state is – in certain respects, which will be explored below – nonsubstitutable. The survival of this state form also reflects asymmetrical power relations in wider geoeconomic and geopolitical orders, such that more powerful capitals and states may prefer to exercise influence over politics and policies through the medium of the external and internal balance of forces that shape formally sovereign national states rather than through conquest, occupation, or menace. Overall, then, given the growing integration of the world market and the growing interdependence of world society, the territorial and temporal sovereignty of the classic national territorial state associated with advanced capitalist economies in the 'West' is certainly more constrained now than in the past. This holds even more for territorial states that may have gained national autonomy and formal independence in the past century but have relatively weak state capacities and are associated with dependent capitalist development.

Framing the Problem

Claims that globalization undermines the national state often take as their main reference point a stylized view of the postwar sovereign national territorial state in the 'Anglosphere' and in Western Europe as it existed in the boom years of Atlantic Fordism. This comparison was already reflected in worries expressed in the 1980s and subsequently that the economic and political forces organized through *national* states could no longer act – as they had during the boom years – as if the state's chief economic task at that time were to advance and govern *national* economic performance. Work that adopts this perspective typically focuses on the impact of globalization on these 'advanced' metropolitan states and overlooks how they (or their predecessors) had affected other states and social formations economically, politically, and socially through imperialism and colonialism. An ironic way of reading this view of globalization and of the national state is to take it, in large part, as a 'northern' reaction: initially, to the 'revenge' of spaces freed from direct imperial or colonial rule (plus Japan), as 'eastern' economies and their developmental states gained economic and political power in the world market; and, later, to the efforts of economic and political forces in the 'North' to regain hegemony, or at least dominance, by promoting neoliberal reforms around the world, by imposing structural conditionalities on indebted or crisis-prone states, and by pushing international economic regimes in a neoliberal direction. Many mainstream studies (though not all) also neglect the extent of prior and continuing bilateral and multilateral policy coordination within various blocs with regard to world market integration and the extent of superpower hegemony in various international regimes, institutions, and policy fields.

Two further sets of difficulties in addressing the relation between globalization and the national state are, first, the ahistorical, spatio-temporally impoverished interpretation of globalization and, second, the oversimplified accounts of the state form that globalization is said to affect. I deal with each set of difficulties one by one.

First, globalization is not a single causal mechanism with a universal, unitary logic. It comprises a hypercomplex, continuously evolving result of many events, processes, and transformations – a result that is multicentric, multiscalar, multitemporal, and multiform. Thus, while acknowledging that it has become easier for some – though by no means all – firms, financial institutions, and fractions of capital to operate in real time on a global scale, there are also important continuities with earlier waves of world market integration. For territorial states and urban networks were already integrated to a greater or lesser extent into the world market (and shaped by that experience) before the latest round of globalization began in the 1970s–1980s. Conversely, the most recent wave is distinctive less through the tendential *planetary* reach of capitalism than through the enhanced *speed* of its linkages and their repercussions in real time. Indeed much of the pressure that state managers claim to feel from globalization (sometimes only as a convenient alibi) has less to do with its *spatial extension* than with its *temporal compression*. The more the frictions of national boundaries are reduced through world market integration, high-speed technologies, and the increasing mobility of superfast financial capital, the greater the challenges are, to national states, from the logic of capital. This concerns not only their territorial sovereignty, through the gap that opens between intensified world market integration and the still largely national architecture of many critical state apparatuses, but also their temporal sovereignty, insofar as capital's acceleration undermines normal policy cycles. (On acceleration, see Rosa 2013; on time–space compression, see Harvey 1996; and on fast policy, see Peck and Theodore 2015.) Of course, other factors and forces are also challenging the territorial and temporal sovereignty of states; and I address the resulting problems for the polity, politics, and policy in the closing section of this chapter.

Drawing on the territory–place–scale–network framework presented in chapter 5, the dynamic of the world market can be seen to involve more than a space of flows. It has crucial territorial dimensions; engages different places to different degrees, leading to uneven development; unfolds on different scales in often tangled hierarchies; and is mediated by different types of networks as well as by other governance mechanisms. Both the structural power of capital, rooted as it is in the impersonal logic of the circuits of capital, and the strategic power of mobile, competitive capitals increase as the world market becomes more closely integrated in real time through new forms of economic exploitation and political domination, the closer articulation of their institutional supports in other systems, and the interdependence of their diverse governance regimes. This phenomenon generates uneven geographical development, affects the spatial and scalar division of labour, alters the scope for networking of different kinds, and reorders the spatial aspects of economic domination. It also intensifies competitive pressures on capital and labour through the widening, deepening, and intensification of global competition and, in addition, it subjects state managers to various pressures. These complexities get ignored when the question is framed in terms of zero-sum market–state relations where the influence of one can only increase at the expense of the other (see below).

Second, regarding the national state, a search for easy generalization leads to neglect of the variety of state forms and political regimes that might be affected by globalization. It also supports the one-sided but still common assumption that states function primarily as 'power' or 'wealth' containers. Yet states also serve as 'power connectors' in networks of states plus nonterritorial forms of political organization – networks that reflect and refract the balance of forces in their respective political space. Such connectivity means that local, regional, and national states were already differentially integrated into the world market (and other international relations) before being affected by recent patterns of globalization. Different effects follow from different modes of insertion into the world market (e.g., rentier oil states like the United Arab Emirates; small, open economies based on a rich ecology of industrial and postindustrial regional clusters and strong local and regional authorities like Switzerland; quasi-continental economies like the United States; or low-tech, low-wage exporting economies like Cambodia).

States should not be seen as somehow set apart from their respective economies, as if they existed in separate spheres and had only external relations with each other (see chapter 2). On the contrary, normal states are, typically, heavily involved – actively, passively, or by default (in the case of 'rogue' and 'failed' states) – and in many respects, in shaping the institutions and practices that constitute the economy. This involvement often includes actively promoting, or at least passively accepting, world market integration – either directly at a global level or through forms of regional integration, through their second-, third-, and nth-order connections. Moreover, globalization is linked to processes on other scales (see p. 191) – such as regionalization, triadization (linking the so-called triad regions of North America, Europe, and East Asia), global city network-building, the formation of virtual intercontinental regions (such as the growing but still uneven links between Brazil, Russia, India, China, and South Africa – the BRICS), international localization (a global strategy of adapting products and services to local markets), and cross-borderization. Thus states and state managers and the forces they represent seek to promote, modify, or resist these other sociospatial processes too. This contributes indirectly to the shaping of globalization or, as a plain Marxist might say, to the formation of the world market. For the latter comprises a complex assemblage of heterogeneous territories, unevenly connected places, tangled scalar hierarchies, and asymmetric networks rather than a level surface for the free play of market forces. Even neoliberal forms of economic globalization continue to depend on political institutions and policy initiatives to roll out neoliberalism and to maintain it in the face of market failures, crisis tendencies, and resistance. This is especially evident in the responses to the North Atlantic financial crisis, which first became publicly evident in 2006–7 but whose causes date back much further and whose effects have spread unevenly, through contagion, to other parts of the world market.

Whereas some political elites try to resist the forces and processes associated with globalization in order to preserve some measure of formal sovereignty or in order to protect infant industries or other economic interests, other elites actively promote globalization as being in their perceived national interest, and may also hope thereby to enhance state capacities. The most important example of this latter strategy is, of course, that pursued by the US federal state, which has been the most vocal and forceful advocate of neoliberal globalization for many years. The United Kingdom is another major example. In contrast, Germany pursues a more neo-mercantilist approach to world market integration, which is based on its specialization in the production of capital goods (especially for making capital goods) and high-value-added, design-intensive, high-quality consumer durables. In response to the Eurozone crisis, however, Germany has also been advocating neoliberal austerity for indebted states in Southern Europe. China's neo-mercantilist strategies have a very different basis in its role as the 'factory of the world' – although China is also pursuing several upgrading strategies, extending its global economic and financial reach, and promoting domestic consumption.

Moreover, since these pressures are reflected inside the state as a result of its character as a social relation, globalization modifies not only the balance of economic and political forces (including relations between fractions of capital and capital–labour relations), but also the relation between market and state. These changes are reflected in turn in the state itself and its policies. Globalization also prompts countermovements against allegedly unbridled market forces, with their inherent tendencies to spatial expansion and acceleration of the rhythms of social life (see below).

Theoretical Debates on the World Market and World of States

At stake in the above-mentioned theoretical debates is a more fundamental problem, namely the question of how best to interpret the structural coupling and coevolution of the world market and the world of states. There are two opposed and equally inadequate theoretical approaches here. One is to treat them as if they were distinct *elements* with their own logics that engage in purely external, quasi-mechanical relations; the other is to treat them as if they were the interdependent economic and political *moments* of the dialectical 'unity in separation' of an overarching capital relation, with a logic that ascribes to each its own role in securing the conditions for capital accumulation. The first alternative understates the interdependence of these apparently separate elements; the second exaggerates the unity of the two (and only two) posited moments. A strategic–relational perspective indicates the need for the proverbial 'third way', that is, an account of the semantic, institutional, and spatiotemporal fixes that might secure for a time the contingently necessary conditions for a relatively stable differential accumulation on a world scale (see chapter 4). It also indicates that different concepts would be required and different answers would be supplied should the question concern conditions for peaceful coexistence among states in the global political order, for resolving the challenge of climate change, or for devising the appropriate institutional and strategic solution to another urgent problem.

The complexities of this necessarily contingent relationship have prompted vigorous debates among heterodox scholars about how best to approach, describe, and explain it. These debates can be distinguished in terms of their primary focus on capital-theoretical, class-theoretical, or state-theoretical issues. One focus of debate concerns competing capital-theoretical positions on world market integration. These disagree on the extent to which one or more of the following logics are at play: (1) a singular global dynamic, grounded in the logic of an emerging ultra- or super-imperialism or in that of a well-established world system (on ultra-imperialism, see Kautsky 1914; on world systems theory, see Wallerstein 2000 and Arrighi

1994); (2) the interaction of different national varieties of capitalism (VoC) that are initially examined individually, without regard for their respective strengths and weaknesses in a global context (for a modern classic, see Hall and Soskice 2001); or, as I prefer, (3) the development, on a world scale, of a variegated capitalism with a contingent, emergent logic that may be organized in the shadow of, under the guidance of, or subject to the dominance of a fraction of capital with global reach, an accumulation strategy with global impact, or a hegemonic or dominant variety of capitalism (Jessop 2011, 2014b, and 2015a). The problem with the varieties of capitalism literature (and its equivalents in the study of national economic regulation-cum-governance) is that it tends to fetishize *national* models or distinctions, treating them as rivals or competitors, ignoring potential complementarities and issues of compossibility within a wider international or global division of labour. If we pay heed to these complementarities and compossibilities, the constraints imposed by globalization on varieties of capitalism become much greater. At the level of the world market, variegation is currently being reconfigured in the shadow of neoliberalism. Within European economic space, however, it is the shadow of German neo-mercantilism that is dominant (for further discussion, see Jessop 2014c). It is also essential to recognize the 'varieties of state' that are involved, whether as perpetrators or as victims, in the realization of globalization. By analogy with the varieties of capitalism versus variegated capitalism debate, it would also be more appropriate, instead of talking simply of a world of states, to explore a variegated interstate system or a global political system that is organized along imperialist lines and increasingly characterized by governance failure (see chapter 7).

A second focus of debate concerns competing class-theoretical positions on world market integration. The two poles of this debate are (1) a more theoretically informed focus on how, how far, and why historically specific forms of the capital relation and their distinctive institutional supports affect economic and political struggles in specific periods, especially when the bourgeoisie enjoys a significant measure of hegemony; and (2) a more politically motivated stress, reflecting the standpoint of subaltern groups, on the potential for globalization to produce a generalized class struggle, or the broader mobilization of a pluralistic 'multitude' of the oppressed and marginal to overthrow all forms and moments of the capital relation – and to do so with the strategic priority given to linking up struggles globally. Each pole in this debate has strengths and weaknesses. The first tends to be more detailed and to draw on a wide range of nuanced case studies and theoretical reflections; but it risks losing sight of the wood of differential accumulation on a global scale for the trees of individual case studies. The second highlights the interconnectedness of the capital relation and global crisis tendencies and, in particular, the reformist consequences of channelling struggles into separate, fetishized economic and political institutional forms with distinctive logics (see also chapter 4). But it achieves this result at the risk of adopting essentialist forms of argumentation and neglecting the uneven development of class struggle, its defensive and offensive phases, and the challenges of coalition-building across such a wide range of social forces.

A third point of focus in this debate (and one that is particularly relevant to the present book) concerns the changing character of the world of states and their place within the global political system, understood in the triple sense of polity, politics, and policy. Thus arguments focus on whether this system mainly comprises (1) a world of national states acting on behalf of their respective national capitals, in an internationalizing economy (e.g., Weiss 1998); (2) an emerging set of subnational or cross-national regional states with their respective hinterlands (e.g., Ohmae 1995); (3) a series of interconnected but partially competing national states that represent capitalist enterprises, foreign as well as domestic, that operate within their respective economic spaces and may reproduce relations of economic dependency or subordination vis-à-vis more competitive economies (e.g., Poulantzas 1975, 1978); (4) some form of multilevel conglomerate or hemispheric state with a leading organizational role for the United States (e.g., Shaw 2000); (5) the primacy of a postwar US imperial state that assumes responsibility for organizing the international and, more recently, transnational integration of the world market (e.g., Panitch 2000; Panitch and Gindin 2012); (6) an emerging transnational state that connects national states, international institutions, and transnational networks (Robinson 2004); and (7) an emerging empire that transcends even a powerful US state thanks to its networked nature (Hardt & Negri 2000). This list is incomplete not only in its own terms (there are more nuanced and hybrid positions) but also in terms of the wider range of debates that touch on globalization and the national state, the nation-state, or both.

World Market Integration and the State System

A first point to make is that, given the complexities of globalization and the differences among states, the growing integration of the world market does not (and could not) put pressure on *the state* (sovereign or otherwise) as a general transhistorical form of political organization. The many social forces and mechanisms that generate globalization can only exert pressure on – or indeed strengthen – particular forms of state with particular state capacities and liabilities. Each state will be affected in many different ways by these complexities. In affecting states this way, the pressures of globalization also modify the balance of forces within states. For any differential loss or strengthening of capacities will favour some economic, political, and social forces over others; and will also create space for, and prompt, struggles to reorganize state forms and capacities in order to meet these challenges. States vary greatly in their capacities to exploit, to absorb, resist, or counteract pressures from globalization in all its forms. No individual state combines an effective global reach with the ability to compress its routines so as to match the time–space of fast hypermobile capital. Even the more powerful states still encounter external pressures from other states, power centres, and the logic of the world market, as well as from the internal impact of their own policies and the blowback and resistance that these generate. The humbling of the Unites States as a superpower in recent years, financially, economically, militarily, and geopolitically, illustrates this truth – although the fragility of its main rivals in the Western hemisphere means that it retains the capacity to compensate for lost hegemony by stepping up its attempts at securing full-spectrum dominance and at reorganizing the governance of the world market in the interests of transnational capital.

The many social forces and mechanisms that generate globalization put pressure on *particular* forms of state, which have *particular* state capacities and liabilities and different unstable equilibria of forces. Not all of these territorial states are national states (as defined in chapters 3 and 5). In addition to city-states and their hinterlands, which are alleged to be well positioned to compete as 'regional states', there are many island states or small states that function as sovereign 'offshore' bases for various 'unproductive' capitalist operations and thereby play a key role in global accumulation. Some states and some populations are badly harmed by the world market (notably in its neo-liberal form) as existing state capacities are undermined, some states fail, and spaces are opened for warlordism, narco-fiefdoms, *nomenklatura* asset seizure, and so on. Other states and populations may benefit from integration into the world market, from pressures for good governance, and so on.

Moreover, in shaping state capacities, the world market also modifies the balance of forces within states – an outcome that is consistent with strategic–relational assumptions. For any differential loss of (or gain in) capacities will favour some economic, political, and social forces over others; will create space for, and prompt, struggles to alter state forms and capacities, to promote globalization, redirect it, or resist it. To research these issues requires serious engagement with the modalities of globalization and with the specificities of state forms and political regimes. These aspects are often associated, because different kinds of state favour different modalities of globalization, which are based on inherited modes of insertion into the world market and are typically linked to the recomposition of power blocs and class compromises. Likewise, the differential and uneven dynamic of globalization will have different impacts on metropolitan capitalist states, export-oriented developmental states, rentier oil states, post-colonial states, postsocialist states, and so on.

These theoretical observations exclude a zero-sum approach to world market integration and state power – especially when such an approach is posed in terms of a *singular emergent borderless flow-based economy operating in timeless time*, which is expanding at the expense of a *plurality of traditional national territorial states operating as 'power containers' that control fixed territorial boundaries*. On the one hand, this zero-sum approach would oversimplify the world market's complexities and contradictory dynamic, would ignore the extent to which it depends on changing place-based competitive advantages, would neglect the general dependence of economic activities on extraeconomic supports that are place- and time-bound, and, of course, would overstate the extent to which a truly global economy has already emerged, even in regard to financial capital, let alone industrial and commercial capital. It would also ignore the extent to which the unfolding economic logic (and illogic) of globalization constrains individual firms, branches, and clusters, as well the operations of the political system. On the other hand, despite the formal equivalence among sovereign states in the modern state system, such a zero-sum approach tends to ignore the fact that not all states are equally capable of exercising power – internally, internationally, or both. They face different problems at home and abroad; they have different histories and different capacities to address these problems and reorganize in response; and, in international encounters as well as in domestic matters, some states are more powerful than others.

Three conclusions follow from these reflections. First, the dynamic of the world market is irreducible to flows – whether of merchandise, productive capital, interest-bearing capital, or variable capital (i.e., flows in the migration of labour power). It has important territorial dimensions (reflected in concepts such as industrial districts, agglomeration economies, global cities, and regional or national capitalisms).

Second, states are more than 'power connectors' or 'power containers'. Third, because the impact of globalization on states is mediated through state capacities and the changing balance of forces, one cannot say that globalization diminishes the power of states unless one knows how and to what end political forces (choose to) exercise state capacities and, in addition, how state capacities might be changed so as to be enhanced, adapted, or reduced vis-à-vis market forces. Thus we should focus on the changing organization of politics and economics and of their respective institutional embodiments and see frontiers and borders as actively reproduced and contingent rather than as pre-given and fixed. All three conclusions can be illuminated through the adoption of a strategic-relational approach (SRA) that focuses on the ways in which capital and the state as social relations condense the changing balances of force as mediated through their respective social forms and institutional frameworks.

The Growing Dominance of the Logic of Capital

This section adopts a capital- *and* class-theoretical perspective. World market integration enhances the economic and political power of capital insofar as (1) it weakens the capacity of organized labour to resist economic exploitation through concerted subaltern action in the economic, political, and ideological fields – action for which the 'multitude' alone is not an effective substitute (on this, see Hardt and Negri 2000); and (2) it undermines the power of national states to regulate economic activities within mainly national frameworks. Neoliberal measures designed to extend and deepen world market integration reinforce the exchange value over the use value moments of the capital relation. They privilege value in motion (i.e., liquid capital), the treatment of workers as disposable and substitutable factors of production, the wage as a cost of (international) production, money as international currency (especially due to the increased importance of derivatives), nature as a commodity, and knowledge as intellectual property. Moreover, as capital is increasingly freed from the constraints of national power containers and increasingly disembedded from other systems, unrestrained competition to lower socially necessary labour time, socially necessary turnover time, and naturally necessary production time (i.e., the reproduction time of 'nature' as a source of wealth) becomes an ever more powerful driving force in the dynamic of capital accumulation.

Overall, this forces states to try, at different scales, to manage the tension between (1) potentially mobile capital's interest in reducing

its own place dependency and in freeing itself from temporal constraints and (2) the state's interest in fixing (allegedly beneficial)
capital in its own territory and in rendering capital's temporal horizons and rhythms compatible with statal and political routines, temporalities, and crisis tendencies. An important response to such
pressures is the development, at different scales, of 'competition
states' (Altvater 1994; Hirsch 1995; Cerny 1997, 2010). These not
only promote economic competitiveness narrowly conceived but also
seek to subordinate many areas previously seen as 'extraeconomic'
to the currently alleged imperatives of accumulation (Jessop 2002:
95–139). The consolidation of such states is accompanied by the rise
of an authoritarian statism that strengthens executive authority, reinforces the mediatization of politics, and extends the parallel power
networks that connect state power to capitalist interests (chapter 9).

Mainstream discussion tends to view these trends in narrowly
state-theoretical terms. Thus viewed, they appear as threats to the
territorial and temporal sovereignty of the *national* state as guardian
of the national interest – or, more narrowly, as responses to problems
confronting the national state as an apparatus with its own logic and
interests. Seen in capital- or class-theoretical terms, however, they
might appear as a means to rearticulate the economic and political
moments of the capital relation (and, a fortiori, the generalization
and intensification of the contradictions and crisis tendencies inherent
in the capital relation) in response to world market integration or as
part of a broader drive, led by powerful class forces, to reorganize
the market–state relation to their advantage (and, of course, in recent
decades notably in the interests of international financial capital and
other transnational capitals).

Trends and Counter-trends in State Responses

I now adopt a more state-theoretical – but not state-centric – perspective. Just as globalization does not generate a single set of pressures
that affect all states equally, there is no common response of all states
to the multiple forms assumed by globalization. Nonetheless, the
restructuring of the national territorial state is characterized by three
general trends – which vary across states and regimes – in the transformation and refunctionalization of the advanced contemporary
capitalist state. In this context, trends refers to stylized facts about
empirically observable changes in the three forms of the state identified in chapter 2, especially in the institutional architecture of the
state; they do not refer to causal mechanisms or laws of tendency

grounded in more fundamental features of the political economy of capital or in the form and functions of the state. In this sense, to describe trends is to capture commonalities in a rather heterogeneous series of changes and to link them to core features of a given state form or political regime as the basis for further theoretical and empirical research. In discussing trends, I will refer to the postwar territorial state in advanced capitalism, considered in isolation from its role in extending colonial, neocolonial, or imperial domination and without concern for any claims to extraterritorial powers. Taking dependent capitalist states as a reference point would involve identifying different trends. The three trends to be explored here comprise the denationalization of statehood, the destatization of politics, and the internationalization of policy regimes and policymaking (see Table 8.1). There are also three counter-trends: the enhanced role of the state in interscalar articulation, the shift from government to meta-governance to continually reorder the relationship among different forms of governance, and the increased struggle for hegemony and dominance over international policy regimes and policy implementation. The combination of the shift from government to governance and from government to meta-governance is another illustration of how the part–whole paradox gets reworked. The combination of trends and counter-trends implies that the national state remains an

Table 8.1   Three trends and counter-trends in state transformation

Trends	*Counter-trends*
• Denationalization of the state as powers are transferred upwards, sideways, and downwards • Destatization of politics consequent upon shift from government to different forms of nonhierarchical governance beyond the state • Internationalization of policy regimes to address issues arising from increasing integration of world society and its growing functional, sociospatial, and operational complexity	• Increased scope for the state to engage in interscalar articulation • Increased role of the state at different levels of governance, especially collibration • Contesting the forms, relative importance, and implementation of international regimes to advance national interests or the international interests with which a given state is allied

Source: Original compilation based on this chapter

important political force in a changing world order (for good overviews, see Weiss 1998; Nordhaug 2002).

Denationalization of statehood

'National' refers here to territorial institutional arrangements rather
than to an imagined national community. This essentially affects the
rearticulation of the *territorial* boundaries of states and entails a
diminishing role for national frontiers. This trend involves some
capacities, previously located at the *national* level, moving up to a
growing number of pan-regional, supraregional, plurinational, or
international bodies with a widening range of powers; others are
devolved downwards, to restructured local or regional states within
a national state framework; and others are passed outwards to, or
usurped by, emerging horizontal networks of power – local, metropolitan, and regional – that bypass central states and connect locali-
ties or regions in several nations. The development of new forms of
multilevel govern*ment* would fit in here, especially where there is a
tangled hierarchy of scales such that the peak of the hierarchy may
not always be dominant (see chapter 5). Somewhat more complex
are cases of multilevel govern*ance*, that is, new forms of public
authority that not only link different territorial scales above and
below the national level but also mobilize functional actors whose
operations may not coincide with territorial boundaries, as well as
actors with ties to one or more territorial scales (see chapter 8). New
state powers have also been allocated to various political scales. This
is sometimes justified in terms of the need to recalibrate state powers
so as to match the global scale of the market economy or the need
to penetrate microsocial relations in order to enhance competitiveness
and manage uneven development.

To interpret all this as state decline in the face of globalization is
doubly misleading. On the one hand, such an interpretation would
fetishize one particular form and scale of statehood, the national
territorial state, when the capital relation merely requires some
form of separation of a profit-oriented, market-mediated 'economy'
from a juridico-political order that secures key extraeconomic conditions for accumulation and social cohesion. The 'new constitutionalism' could offer such an external order. On the other hand,
there is considerable evidence across many sites of action that
national states seek to exercise some residual power over the movement of interscalar powers and still serve as an addressee of last
resort in demands for decisive action in the face of crises or other
urgent problems. These responses involve the recalibration of state

capacities and can be understood, in part, as forms of meta-governance and collibration (chapter 6).

This said, the process of de- and reterritorialization of specific state powers weakens national territorial states *qua* mutually exclusive, formally sovereign, spatially segmented entities in the modern interstate system. It may also enhance states' operational autonomies and strategic capacities through the pooling and redistribution of formal sovereignty. Not all states are equal in this regard, of course; within each regional bloc there is usually one hegemon. In the European Union, for example, this force is conventionally regarded as Germany, with France as a key rival and partner. Indeed, from a variegated capitalism perspective, the Eurozone economy can be seen as being organized in the shadow of German neo-mercantilism, and its regulation as dominated by the German state and its allies (cf. Jessop 2014b). In the global order, the United States plays the hegemonic role and, analogously, the world market can be seen as organized in the shadow of a neoliberalism orchestrated by the US imperial state through hard and soft power. Thus de- and renationalization are essentially concerned with the *territorial* boundaries of state power and the extent to which these coincide with the frontiers of mutually recognizing territorial (or national) sovereign states. They do not directly affect states in their aspect, if any, of nation-statehood. Nonetheless, these processes may be triggered by struggles over the form and future of the nation-state that may lead to secession, federalism, *revanchisme*, and so on, which also redraw state boundaries.

Destatization of polity, politics, and policy

While denationalization concerns the *territorial dispersion and recalibration* of state activities away from the national level, destatization redraws the boundaries between state and nonstate apparatuses and activities. As such it alters the 'public–private' divide and reduces the authority of the sovereign state in the fields of politics and policy. This is sometimes referred to as a shift from government to governance (see chapter 7). In this guise it is a process that removes issues from the purview of a territorial state (national or non-national) – whether in the form of electoral politics, legislative deliberation, executive decision, bureaucratic administration, or judicial determination – and moves them into an ill-defined political sphere in which 'stakeholders', 'social partners', or a congeries of social forces deliberate and negotiate about societal steering in areas of mutual interest. But destatization is not confined to facilitating or enhancing societal steering. It concerns the more general organization of politics and policy, whether concerned with collective problem solving or with the clash of private material and ideal interests.

This trend is reflected in a shift from the predominance of government to greater reliance on governance or self-governance on various territorial scales and across various functional domains that bypasses or circumvents state power. This shift may reflect demands by social forces dissatisfied with state and market failure, or initiatives by state managers to supplement or replace more traditional forms of top-down government to better serve relevant 'publics'. In this respect, governance straddles the conventional public–private divide and may involve 'tangled hierarchies', parallel power networks, or other linkages across tiers of government and functional domains. Such innovations engender new forms of interpenetration between the political system and other functional systems and modify relations among systems, the public sphere, civil society, and everyday life, as the latter three social fields impact the nature and exercise of state power. New forms of governance are especially significant in the management of flows. These arrangements bypass or circumvent states through new forms of international regime and extraterritorial networks. Some of the functions (technical, economic, fisco-financial, juridico-political, ideological, etc.) performed by states (on any scale) get transferred entirely to or shared with parastatal, nongovernmental, private, or commercial actors, institutional arrangements, or regimes in order to coordinate economic and social relations. This process blurs the division between public and private, expands and reinforces the principle of subsidiarity, strengthens the informal sector as well as private enterprise (especially in delivering welfare and collective consumption), and reinforces mechanisms such as 'regulated self-regulation' and 'private-interest government'. It is also linked to the state's growing involvement in decentred societal guidance strategies based on growing recognition of functional interdependencies, the division of knowledge, and the need for mutual learning, reflexivity, and negotiated coordination.

Even where the state remains active in these arrangements, it is, at best, first among equals. This trend sometimes occurs at the behest of state managers, as a way of reducing 'overload' (something highlighted in several state-theoretical accounts of this trend). In these cases, although the trend is often taken to imply a diminution in state capacities, this need not, however, entail a loss in the overall power of government, as if power were a zero-sum resource. For resort to governance could enable states to project their influence further and secure their objectives by mobilizing knowledge and power resources from influential nongovernmental partners or stakeholders. In such cases, the state may reserve the right to repatriate authority to itself in one way or another. In other cases, however, it may also be imposed through force majeure (e.g., through structural adjustment, or as part of bilateral or multilateral negotiations with more powerful states), or indeed, 'behind the backs' of state managers, through the accumulation of molecular shifts. These second cases, as well as the first, can also be seen as a way to free capital (or some capitals) from the frictions of state control and to promote an international order more favourable to world market integration.

Internationalization of policy regimes

This trend has three aspects. The international context of domestic state action (whether national, regional, or local) now includes a widening range of extraterritorial or transnational factors and processes; the international context has become more significant strategically for domestic policy; and key players in policy regimes have expanded to include foreign agents and institutions as sources of policy ideas, policy design, and policy implementation. These changes affect local and regional states below the national level as well as supranational state formations and international regimes – witness the growth of interregional and cross-border linkages among local and regional authorities and governance regimes in different national formations. This is especially evident in the enormous expansion of international regimes of varying kinds, as well as in the development of international nongovernmental and civil society organizations (cf. Drori, Meyer, and Hwang, 2006; Meyer et al., 1997).

These three trends are analytically distinct but can be combined in different ways. Two contrasting examples are (1) the growing importance of international regimes with public and private representatives for the relative stabilization of a globalizing economy and (2) the rise of cybernetworks in an extraterritorial, telematic space allegedly beyond state control – although cyberspace is being rapidly recolonized, monitored, and controlled by states (see chapter 9).

Three sets of counter-trends

Each trend is also associated with a counter-trend that both qualifies and transforms its significance for the form of the state, politics, and policies. This combination of trend and counter-trend involves more than the presence of complex 'conservation–dissolution' effects associated with successive stages in societal development. Such effects certainly exist, insofar as past forms and functions are conserved or dissolved as the state is transformed. The counter-trends noted above are specific reactions to the new trends rather than survivals of earlier patterns. This is why they are better seen as counter-trends to the trends than vice versa.

Countering the denationalization of statehood are the increased attempts of national states to retain control over the articulation of different spatial scales in the face of an emerging 'relativization of scale'. As we noted in chapter 5, the postwar period saw the primacy of the national level of economic and political organization in many different states. The current globalization–regionalization dynamic has seen the national scale lose its taken-for-granted primacy without another scale acquiring a similar primacy. Nonetheless, in the absence of a supranational state with powers equivalent to those of the national state, the denationalization of statehood is linked to constantly renewed attempts by national states to reclaim power by managing the relationship among different scales of economic and political organization.

Countering the shift towards governance is government's increased role in *meta-governance*. This should not be confused with the survival of state sovereignty as the highest instance of government or with the emergence of some form of 'mega-partnership' to which all other partnerships are somehow subordinated. Rather, governments (on various scales) are becoming more involved in organizing the self-organization of markets, partnerships, networks, and governance regimes. In other words, states enact various forms of 'governance in the shadow of hierarchy'. States are not confined to hierarchical command but combine all four forms of governance in different ways. They also monitor how these mechanisms are working and may seek to modify the combinations accordingly (see chapter 7).

Somewhat ambiguously countering yet reinforcing the internationalization of policy regimes is the growing *interiorization* of international constraints, as the latter become integrated into the policy paradigms and cognitive models of domestic policymakers. This process is not confined to the level of the national state: it is also evident at the local, regional, cross-border, and interregional levels as well as in the activities of so-called 'entrepreneurial cities' (e.g., Paul 2003). The relativization of scale makes such identification of international norms, conventions, and regimes significant at all levels of economic and political organization and indeed leads to concerns with the complex dialectics of spatial articulations, which is reflected in such phenomena as 'glocalization'. At the same time there are increasing struggles by states (in their own name and on behalf of their respective power blocs or national popular forces) to shape the form of international regimes and the manner in which they operate.

This applies especially to the more powerful states in the state system and is one of the factors behind the formation of regional blocs. This tendency is, once again, especially clear in the context of the global economic crisis as the search for a new global financial and economic architecture proceeds apace.

To conclude this section, which reflects on the interaction of trends and counter-trends, we can state that, insofar as states, regardless of other activities they may perform, remain integral moments in the expanded reproduction of the capital relation, any loss of formal *territorial* sovereignty by national states through the upward, downward, and sideways transfer of powers may be compensated by pooling sovereignty and enhanced capacities to shape events through interscalar coordination. This process concerns the role of national states not only in multilevel governance, but also in producing and regulating (or not) extraterritorial spaces such as offshore financial centres, tax havens, export processing zones, and toxic waste sites and in accepting practices such as 'flagging out' – the operation of commercial vessels under flags of convenience. States at other levels also engage in interscalar management, of course; but even the European Union – the most advanced supranational political apparatus – still lacks powers and legitimacy to match those of its member states, especially larger ones, like France and Germany; and those powers that it does have result from a multilevel strategic game that involves powerful economic and political forces pursuing their interests on the most favourable political terrain. State policies are never determined purely by the logic of the state or by the interests of state managers but are linked to economic strategies and state projects that reflect a multiscalar equilibrium of compromise, shaped by a changing balance of forces.

Loss of Temporal Sovereignty

Cross-cutting the trends and counter-trends identified above is another important change: the relative loss of temporal sovereignty. While the development of the world market and its associated space of flows challenge the state's territorial sovereignty, its temporal sovereignty is challenged by the acceleration of time (see Rosa 2013).[1] States increasingly face temporal pressures in their policymaking and implementation due to new forms of time–space distantiation, compression, and differentiation. For example, as the temporal rhythms of the economy accelerate vis-à-vis those of the state, which occurs on many scales from the local to the global, the state has less time to determine and coordinate political responses to economic events, shocks, and crises – whether these responses are formulated by the national state (or states at other scales), by public–private partnerships or private-interest government, or by international regimes. This situation reinforces conflicts between the time(s) of the market and the time(s) of the state. One solution to the state's loss of time sovereignty is a laissez-faire retreat from areas where states are too slow to make a difference or would become overloaded if they tried to keep pace. States abandon attempts to control short-term economic calculation, activities, and movements. Deregulation and liberalization are examples of this response. However, by freeing up the movement of superfast or hypermobile capital, this response can reinforce the destabilizing impact of deregulated financial markets and economic crises, as seen in the global financial crisis – both in its initial dynamic and in its subsequent contagious effects around the globe.

Another solution is for states to seek to compress their own decision-making cycles by resorting to fast policymaking and fast-tracking policy implementation, so that they can make more timely and appropriate interventions. This strategy increases pressures to make decisions on the basis of unreliable information, insufficient consultation, lack of participation, and the like, even as state managers continue to believe that policies are taking too long to negotiate, formulate, enact, adjudicate, determine, and implement. Indeed the rhetoric of crisis can be invoked, whether with justification or not, to create a climate for emergency measures and exceptional rule. This resorting to 'fast policy' is reflected in the shortening of policy development cycles, fast-tracking decision making, rapid programme rollout, continuing policy experimentation, and the relentless revision of guidelines and benchmarks (cf. Rosa 2013; Peck and Theodore 2015). Fast policy privileges those who can operate within compressed time scales, narrows the range of participants in the policy process, and limits the scope for deliberation, consultation, and negotiation. A scholar inspired by the Frankfurt School, Bill Scheuerman (2000), summarized some of these trends in terms of a general shift to 'economic states of emergency' characterized by executive dominance and constant legal change and dynamism (on states of emergency, see also chapter 9).

This response has important implications for the structure and operations of the state. Its capital- and class-theoretical impact depends, of course, on the changing balance of forces. Fast policy is antagonistic to corporatism, stakeholding, the rule of law, formal bureaucracy, and to the routines and cycles of democratic politics more generally. It privileges the executive over the legislature and the judiciary, finance over industrial capital, consumption over long-term investment. In general, resorting to fast policy undermines the power of decision makers, who have longer decision-taking cycles – because they lose the capacity to make decisions according to their own routines and procedures, having to adapt to the speed of fast thinkers and fast policymakers. Such undermining can significantly affect the choice of policies, the initial targets of policy, the sites where policy is implemented, and the criteria adopted to demonstrate success. This is especially evident in the recent global financial crisis, where the pressure to act forced states to rescue banks that were deemed 'too big to fail' and led to the concentration of decision-making power in the hands of a small financial elite – which had played a key role in creating the crisis in the first instance.

An alternative strategy is not to compress *absolute* political time but to create *relative* political time by slowing the circuits of capital. A well-known recommendation here is for a modest tax on financial transactions (the so-called Tobin tax), which would decelerate the flow of superfast and hypermobile financial capital and would limit its distorting impact on the real economy. Another important field of struggle is climate change. Here we see continuing conflicts between national states about the timing, speed, and nature of the response, along with well-funded and vocal opposition from firms and sectors with vested interests in continued economic expansion that could cost the earth. In this sense, rather than being a general problem that affects all equally, the differential causation and uneven impact of the environmental crisis and the struggles over appropriate responses and over the distribution of costs of adjustment have a strong class aspect (Burkett 1999; Moore 2015a).

Conclusions

The overall impact of increasing the integration of the world market along primarily neoliberal lines has been to strengthen international financial capital at the expense of productive capitals that must be valorized in particular times and places. Nonetheless, the latter also benefit from deregulation and flexibilization at the expense of subordinate classes and wider public interests. This does not mean that finance can postpone forever its overall dependence on the continued valorization of productive capital or escape crisis tendencies rooted in capital accumulation on a world scale. The revenge of the 'real economy' can be seen in the continuing (as of mid-2015) liquidity, credit, and financial crises and in their role in forcibly reimposing the unity of the circuits of capital by deflating the associated bubbles. The crisis of neoliberalism shows that the national state generally remains the addressee of last resort in appeals to resolve economic, political, and social problems.

Paradoxically, even as neoliberal capital and its allies demand decisive state intervention, neoliberalism has undermined the territorial and temporal sovereignty of states and their capacity to resolve these crises. National states cannot coordinate their interests in forums such as the NAFTA, the European Union, the G8, the G20, the IMF, or other forms of summitry. Whereas the promotion of the microsocial conditions for capital accumulation in these changing circumstances may well be better handled at other levels than the national, problems of territorial integration, social cohesion, and social exclusion are currently still best handled at the level of the large territorial national state. For the latter is still currently irreplaceable, given its fisco-financial powers and its scope for redistributive politics in rearranging the balance of forces and in securing new social compromises. This is especially evident in the massive subsidies and bailouts that were given to failed and failing financial institutions in the economies that went furthest down the neoliberal road and in the efforts of other economies that made neoliberal policy adjustments but have since been caught up in the generalization of the contradictions of neoliberalism on a global scale in an integrated world market.

We can provisionally conclude that the establishment of a new spatiotemporal fix – with its own institutional architecture, within which accumulation could be reregularized – has not (yet) been seen. In the late 1990s it seemed that the new scale would become the triad. This rescaling was expected to take different forms in each triadic region: the consolidation of an already overwhelming US dominance within the North American Free Trade Association and its further extension into Central and South America and the Caribbean (where a series of regional alliances are also being consolidated); multilevel governance within a broadened and deepened European Union and the extension of EU influence to North Africa and the Middle East; and, most problematically, the consolidation of open regionalism in East Asia. From 2000 onwards, however, the prognosis has become more complicated – thanks to the declining hegemony (as opposed to dominance) of the United States, the apparent political paralysis of the European Union (seen in the failed Lisbon Agenda and in the Eurozone crisis), the rise of the BRICS (Brazil, Russia, India, China, and South Africa), and China's influence not only in East Asia but also in Africa, Latin America, and the Middle East and its moves to reconnect the Eurasian heartland.

9

Liberal Democracy, Exceptional States, and the New Normal

This chapter addresses democracy, its crisis, and exceptional regimes as well as the trend towards the normalization of an authoritarian statist polity that displays strong elements of exceptionalism. It starts from the claim that liberal bourgeois democracy is the 'normal' form of capitalist state, that is, the formally adequate form of state in societies where not only does rationally organized capitalism prevail but profit-oriented, market-mediated accumulation is also the dominant principle of societal organization. This does not mean that liberal democracy exists in most states in capitalist societies – a whole series of empirical indicators developed by political scientists, think tanks, and other researchers show that this is false. It does imply that capitalism would be less open to challenge if liberal democracy were established and it operated according to substantive democratic principles. For, as noted in chapter 4, this form of political regime disguises the nature of class power more effectively than when the state apparatus is more openly controlled by dominant classes (or class fractions) or by state managers who are closely allied with predatory capital or are running openly kleptocratic regimes for personal enrichment.

On this basis some scholars, orthodox and heterodox alike, distinguish normal states and exceptional regimes in terms of conformity to democratic institutions and hegemonic class leadership. Normal states characterize conjunctures in which bourgeois hegemony is stable and secure; and exceptional regimes develop in response to crises of hegemony. An unstated premise in these analyses is that, where political and ideological crises cannot be resolved through the normal democratic play of class and other social forces, democratic institutions must be suspended or eliminated and crises resolved through an open 'war of manoeuvre' that ignores constitutional niceties. Thus, while consent predominates over constitutionalized violence in normal states, exceptional states intensify physical repression and conduct an 'open war' against the dominated classes or other subaltern or marginal forces. This analysis draws, as we shall see, on constitutional law literature devoted to temporary states of emergency and the institution of commissarial dictatorship (see below). Related literature also points to the possibility of more enduring forms of dictatorship, and this possibility in turn provides the basis for analyses of Bonapartism, Caesarism, authoritarianism, and totalitarianism. This possibility is further reflected in two recent lines of state-theoretical analysis: a soft thesis about the continuing decline of liberal democracy and a strong thesis about the irresistible rise of authoritarian statism. (Compare, for example, Crouch 2004 and Streeck 2014 with Poulantzas 1978, Bruff 2013, and Oberndorfer 2015; for further discussion, see below.) Whereas the former thesis tends to focus on symptoms at the level of the political scene, the latter tends to ground its analysis in more fundamental shifts in contemporary capitalism and challenges to national security.

I address these issues in six steps: (1) the elective affinity between capitalism and democracy; (2) the major determinants of that affinity; (3) the effects of democratic forms on political struggle based on class interests or other major lines of social cleavage; (4) political crises and states of emergency; (5) the differences between normal states and exceptional regimes; (6) the normalization of key features that are typical of exceptional regimes in the emerging authoritarian statism in contemporary capitalist societies, such that the exception is becoming the norm. I conclude that the conditions in which democracy might be regarded as the best possible political shell for capitalism are historically circumscribed (economically, politically, and in other ways) and that the authoritarian statist trends are becoming entrenched features of the modern state.

'The Best Possible Political Shell'?[1]

Capitalism is often described as a system of commodity production that is characterized by private property, private control over the means of production, and the principle of free labour (also described as the generalization of the commodity form to labour power and the treatment of workers *as if* they were commodities).

In this context, capital accumulation is based on the profit-oriented and market-mediated production, circulation, and exchange of commodities. On the basis of his historical studies of capitalist development, Max Weber distinguished six ideal–typical modes of orientation to profit. Two were classified as instances of rational capitalism, namely free trade in markets and the rational organization of capitalist production; and trade and speculation in money, currency, loans, and credit markets. Weber also identified three ideal–typical, albeit internally heterogeneous, *modes of political capitalism.* These derive their profits, respectively, from predatory activities, force and domination, and 'unusual deals with political authority'.[2] He also noted a sixth type, which gets its profits from traditional commercial transactions (Weber 1978, 1961; see also Swedberg 1998). This typology is well grounded historically and remains relevant to today's world market. It also provides a basis for a more nuanced account of the relation between varieties of capitalism and forms of political regime.

Arguments for the elective affinity of capitalism and democracy tend, intentionally or not, to focus on the relation between formally rational capitalism and the democratic features of the modern national territorial state based on the rule of law. This relation has so far been investigated mostly in terms of the isomorphism or complementarity of social forms (formal constitution) and not in terms of actual, historical trajectories of economic and political institutions and their practices (historical constitution). The diverse contradictions, paradoxes, and dilemmas of capitalism and democracy appear most obviously in historical analysis – and there rather than in formal analysis. The affinity becomes less evident when one turns to other periods or kinds of capitalism or to the implications of the denationalization of statehood (on this, see chapter 8).

Liberal democracy has specific legal preconditions. These include specific institutionalized political freedoms (e.g., freedom of association, freedom of speech, free elections), a competitive party system, the (potential) circulation of natural governing parties (see chapter 3), alone or in coalition, in government office, parliamentary (or equivalent) control over the executive and over state administration, and responsiveness of legislators and of the executive to the electorate and public opinion. Popular–democratic struggles aim to extend the sphere of validity of citizens' rights, to include more of the population within the category of citizens, and to initiate and consolidate the legal framework for creating and maintaining the social conditions and an unstable equilibrium of forces in which the people can monitor and safeguard these preconditions.

Democratic institutions thereby inhibit major ruptures or breaks in social cohesion and, hence, in the system of political class domination. However, if political and ideological crises cannot be resolved through the normal, democratic play of class and other social forces, there are growing pressures to suspend or eliminate democratic institutions and to resolve the crises through an open 'war of manoeuvre' that ignores constitutional niceties. Yet the very act of abolishing democratic institutions tends to congeal the balance of forces that prevails when the exceptional state is established. As Hannah Arendt noted, once they have seized power, dictatorships tend to become routinized, predictable, and domesticated (Arendt 1956: 407). This freezing of a particular conjuncture makes it harder to resolve new crises and contradictions through routine and gradual policy adjustments and to secure a new equilibrium of compromise (Poulantzas 1974, 1976). In short, the alleged strength of an exceptional regime actually hides its brittleness. This nonetheless varies by type of exceptional regime (see below).

Another source of variation is the periodization of capitalism. The origins of capitalism were tied to mercantilism and absolutism and to the role of the state in creating the conditions under which 'exploitation' could take the form of exchange. When these conditions were established, liberal capitalism became possible (at least for the first wave of capitalist economies), and this facilitated the development of a state based on the rule of law and the consolidation of a parliamentary government – if not yet a liberal democratic state that meets the above-mentioned conditions – that was able to maintain the conditions for free trade in markets and capitalist production and to compensate for market failures. This created the conditions for the legitimacy of bourgeois domination through the illusion of formal equality among citizens and among participants in the market economy. A third stage emerged as crisis tendencies became more evident and monopoly capitalism expanded at the expense of liberal, competitive capitalism. Late developing economies may also be characterized by large banks' and the state's stronger ties to industrial capital (cf. Gerschenkron 1962). Even if we accept this crude three-stage model, it is clear that it holds primarily for first-wave capitalist economies such as England, the Netherlands, Belgium, and the United States. Even in these cases we see the impact of Weber's three kinds of political capitalism (e.g., slavery, colonialism, imperial conquest, robber barons). Moreover, as the latest trends in capitalism are rooted in the dominance of neoliberalism and finance-dominated accumulation, the relation between free markets and democracy is further undermined. For, as Michael Hudson (2011) notes, for neoliberals, 'a free market is one free *for* a tax-favoured *rentier* class to extract interest, economic rent and monopoly prices'. This kind of free market is incompatible even with the stripped-down formal and elitist democracy that has prevailed in the last century, and especially in the last four decades.

Capitalism's elective affinity with liberal democracy is weakened when profits derived from financial speculation and risk-taking start to exceed those that come from the financial intermediation and risk-management activities that are essential to the circuits of productive capital. The affinity is further weakened where finance-dominated accumulation leads to growing inequalities in income and wealth due to deregulation, liberalization, and the interpenetration of economic (especially financial) and political power. And it is even less sustainable when the dominant forms of orientation to profit depend on predatory political profits (including kleptocracy and primitive accumulation based on dispossession), on profits that are largely derived from force and domination (e.g., from the use of state power to impose neoliberal rules, institutions, and practices on other accumulation regimes and to open up new fields of accumulation),[3] or on 'unusual deals' with state managers and political authorities (such as financial contributions in exchange for special legislative, administrative, judicial, fisco-financial or commercial decisions that privilege particular capitals and fall well outside the normal definition of the rule of law). These observations indicate why capitalism and democracy do not always coincide. Indeed, as a rule of thumb, one might propose that, where political forms of profit making are dominant, authoritarian rule is the norm rather than the exception.

Overall, these remarks confirm Marx's account of the contradiction at the heart of bourgeois democracy, namely that subaltern classes can participate in the political process on condition that they do not use their political (read electoral and parliamentary) power to challenge the social (read economic, political, and ideological) power of the dominant classes – which, in turn, can enjoy these more basic forms of power on condition that they tolerate the short-term vagaries of democratic rule (see chapters 3 and 4). Unsurprisingly, this contradiction creates a whole series of tensions within the liberal democratic state. A potential resolution is suggested by Gramsci, among others, in his account of struggles over political, intellectual, and moral leadership through the elaboration of state projects and hegemonic visions that partially reconcile the particular interests of different economic, social, and other categories in an 'illusory' general interest (see chapter 4). 'Natural governing parties' have a key role to play here, to the extent that they can reconcile the interests of a substantial part of the electorate and key sections or fractions of the dominant classes (see also Gamble 1973). Where this is not achieved, a representational crisis will emerge and there may also be threats to the legitimacy of the state system. To explore what is at stake here, I turn first to the relation between states of emergency and dictatorship.

States of Emergency and Exceptional Regimes

Constitutional historians distinguish two main types of exceptional regime that emerge in response to states of siege, states of emergency, or other urgent threats to the state. One type is seen in the Roman pattern of *commissarial* (or delegated) dictatorship. Three features characterized the original Roman model: (1) one authority (the Senate) entrusted power temporarily, via a second party (consuls), to a third and special authority, namely the dictator; (2) the dictator exercised power outside the ordinary constitutional structure for the duration of an emergency that threatened the territorial integrity of the state, the survival of the state apparatus, or the security of the population; (3) he then returned it to the normal authorities, which immediately resumed 'political business as usual'. In the second type, which Ferejohn and Pasquino (2004) term 'neo-Roman', emergency powers are exercised by a branch of the regular government, normally the popularly elected executive, which is granted special prerogatives (*pleins pouvoirs, Diktaturgewalt*, etc.) for as long as the emergency lasts. As in the original model, once the emergency ends, this branch of government reverts to operating within normal constitutional rules. A variant of the neo-Roman model occurs where the decisions of the emergency authority are subject to *ex post* judicial control by courts and can be reversed in real time. By the time of Oliver Cromwell (after the English Civil War) and Napoleon Bonaparte (after the French Revolution), dictators assumed control in the name of the people (McCormick 2004: 198). This pattern is found in semi-presidential systems in Europe and in Latin American cases where the president gains popular legitimacy through direct election (Ferejohn and Pasquino 2004: 334–8).

The preceding description of commissarial dictatorship is framed in constitutional terms, as if its declaration were principally a matter of legislative or judicial decision about an imminent existential threat to the survival of the state, such as war or invasion. Even this is problematic; but matters become more complex when the threat is manufactured (e.g., the *casus belli* is a false flag operation, war is declared on terror, an enemy within is discovered, or a general strike or financial crisis creates an economic state of emergency). In such cases, declarations of a state of emergency often provide cover for open or covert action to weaken social forces that oppose *crisis-induced* – or at least *crisis-legitimated* – policies (on the distinction between real and fictitious states of emergency, see the discussion in Agamben 2005: 3–5, 59–63).[4] In addition, dictatorial regimes can result from the creeping erosion of normal constitutional rules as they are subject to growing restrictions, longer periods of exceptional rule, and the normalization of the exception (cf. Rossiter 1948; Lasswell 1950; Morgenthau 1954). The same phenomenon emerges with the national security state, especially when the threats to security are extended from an imminent external military danger to economic security, domestic political subversion, and cultural erosion (see below).

A radical break with commissarial dictatorship occurred under the Roman generals Lucius Cornelius Sulla (138–78 BC) and Gaius Julius Caesar (100–44 BC). They seized power unconstitutionally and established *sovereign* dictatorships, using their emergency powers to change Rome's constitutional order so as to make their power permanent. The German legal theorist Carl Schmitt, who described these events in his book on *Dictatorship* (2013), strongly advocated this kind of sovereign dictatorship as a response to the interwar crisis of parliamentary democracy – notably for the Weimar Republic (Schmitt 1988) – and considered that it should be subject only to confirmation in plebiscites. He critiqued parliamentary democracy for becoming an ineffective talking shop, unable to act decisively in an emergency. What is important constitutionally about sovereign dictatorship is that it reverses the relation between norm and exception: first, the dictator determines the nature and timing of the exception, expands its scope, and may make it permanent; and, second, subject to the dictator's personal decision alone, his unlimited sovereign powers may be used at any time and may thereby also become permanent (cf. Gross 2000: 1845). In short, the exception becomes the norm. Authoritarian measures justified in the name of security may then range between redesigning the architecture of the state, reordering the capital relation, waging external or civil war, and pursuing genocidal aims (Neocleous 2006). Reviewing cases in the American hemisphere, Claudio Grossman observes:

> the majority of cases of states of emergency in the hemisphere indicate that the probability of complete restoration of human rights by those who declared the original states of emergency is inversely proportional

to the magnitude of human rights violations perpetrated during the emergencies. (Grossman 1986: 37)

Political Crisis and States of Emergency

States of emergency are declared, commissarial dictatorships are appointed, or (quasi-)sovereign dictatorships seize power in response to threats to the state. But they may also be instituted in response to economic and political crises that are not so urgent and acute and represent threats to the government or to the dominant classes and other leading social forces whose ideal and material interests they represent. Economic crisis alone does not cause political and state crises. Indeed the flexibility inscribed in the normal democratic state, especially through the turnover of political parties and coalitions, often provides the basis for crisis management, or at least the capacity for a *fuite en avant* – that is, a continual game of blame, displacement, and renewed disappointment. It is where this flexibility is blocked through political crisis, whether in the form of a catastrophic equilibrium of compromise or of a severe breakdown in the effectiveness of political institutions, that capitalist states become less open and democratic and increasingly coercive and an exceptional regime becomes more likely. Political crises may also occur where the scope for material concessions to subaltern groups shrinks on a long-term basis and limits the flexibility of parties and governments to play this game. This is especially likely to happen where there are close ties between the primary mechanisms of differential accumulation (orientation to profit) and the state apparatus; and, in turn, the latter is more likely to happen where the types of political capitalism are major sources of profit for accumulation, appropriation of public goods for private gain, or conspicuous consumption. Political crises may also occur when the institutional separation between economic and political struggles necessary to the smooth and legitimate functioning of liberal democracies breaks down (e.g., through a general strike with political objectives, or through the use of political power to expropriate capital or challenge its prerogatives).

In his analysis of normal states and exceptional regimes, Poulantzas (1973, 1974, 1976, 1978), whose analysis I follow closely here, contrasted them in terms of four sets of institutional and operational differences (see Table 9.1).

- Whereas the normal state has representative democratic institutions with universal suffrage and competing political parties,

Table 9.1   Normal states and exceptional regimes

Normal States	Exceptional Regimes
• Liberal democracy with universal suffrage and formally free elections	• Suspend elections (except for plebiscites and referenda)
• Power is transferred between parties and/or governments in a stable way, in line with the rule of law	• No legal regulation of power transfer ('might is right', state of exception, state of siege)
• Pluralistic series of ideological apparatuses operate relatively independently of the state	• Ideological apparatuses are integrated into the official state to legitimate its enhanced power
• Separation of powers	• Concentration of powers
• Power circulates organically, which facilitates a flexible reorganization of power	• These regimes congeal the balance of forces existing at the time when an exceptional regime is introduced

Source: Based on Poulantzas 1974, 1976, and 1978 and on material presented in this chapter

those who control exceptional states end the plural party system and employ plebiscites or referenda closely controlled from above.
- While constitutional and legal rules govern the transfer of power in normal states, exceptional regimes suspend the rule of law in order to facilitate changes deemed necessary for solving economic, political, and hegemonic crises.
- Whereas ideological apparatuses in normal states typically have 'private' legal status and largely escape direct government control, in exceptional regimes they are mobilized to legitimate increased coercion and to help overcome the ideological crisis that accompanies a crisis of hegemony.
- The formal separation of powers is also reduced through the infiltration of subordinate branches and power centres by the dominant branch or through extensive use of parallel power networks and transmission belts that connect different branches and centres. This centralizes political control and multiplies its points of application, thereby serving to reorganize hegemony, counteract internal divisions, short-circuit internal resistances, and facilitate flexibility (Poulantzas 1973: 123, 130, 226–7, 311; 1974: 314–18, 320–30; 1976: 42, 50, 91–2, 100–1, 113–14; 1978: 87–92; for more extended discussion, see Jessop 1985: 90–103).

Poulantzas also suggested that only one type of political crisis produces an exceptional political regime, namely a crisis of hegemony within the power bloc. This occurs when no class or fraction can impose its 'leadership' on other members of the power bloc, whether by its own political organizations or through the 'parliamentary democratic' state. This is typically related to a general crisis of hegemony over the whole society. Such crises are reflected in the political scene and in the state system. Symptoms include a crisis of party representation – that is, a split between different classes or fractions and their parties; attempts by various social forces to bypass political parties and influence the state directly; and efforts by different state apparatuses to impose political order independently of the decisions coming through formal channels of power. Such phenomena can undermine the institutional and class unity of the state even where it continues to function and provoke splits between top echelons in the state system and lower ranks. The state may also lose its monopoly of violence (see Poulantzas 1974: passim; 1976: 28).

Poulantzas was firmly of the opinion that the normal form of the capitalist type of state – at least in advanced, metropolitan capitalist social formations – was liberal democracy. This opinion was informed by the legal justification for commissarial states of emergency – namely that they were limited in duration, being dissolved when a temporary crisis was overcome – as well as by the general experience of the instability of most exceptional regimes in Europe, from which his observations were largely drawn. Accordingly, he talked about *normal states* and *exceptional regimes*. He nonetheless discerned important differences among exceptional regimes; and he was particularly impressed by the flexibility and manoeuvrability of fascism. In contrast, military dictatorship is the least flexible type, and Bonapartism is located halfway between these extremes (for further discussion, see Jessop 1985: 229–83). Hannah Arendt drew a similar distinction between dictatorships, which tended to stagnate, and totalitarian states, which were in a constant state of movement, transgressing barriers and being engaged in permanent revolution (cf. Canovan 2004).

This relative rigidity is especially true, Poulantzas argued, where exceptional regimes lack specialized politico-ideological apparatuses to channel and control mass support and are thereby isolated from the masses. They are marked by a rigid apportionment of state power among distinct political clans linked to each apparatus. They have no ideology that can forge state unity and also secure national–popular cohesion. This condition produces a muddle of inconsistent policies toward the masses as the exceptional regime attempts to neutralize their opposition. It also leads to purely mechanical compromises, tactical alliances and a settling of accounts among 'economic–corporate' interests among the dominant classes and fractions. In turn, the ensuing situation intensifies the internal contradictions of the state apparatus and reduces its flexibility in the face of economic and political crises (Poulantzas 1976). These features make exceptional states vulnerable to sudden collapse as contradictions and pressures accumulate, such that the transition to democracy will also be ruptural and crisis-prone.

Thus, just as the movement from a normal state to an exceptional regime involves political crises and ruptures rather than taking a continuous, linear path, so the transition in the opposite direction will also involve a series of breaks and crises rather than a simple process of self-transformation. This places a premium on the political class struggle to achieve hegemony over the democratization process. Indeed Poulantzas insisted that the institutional form and the class character of the normal state will vary significantly with the outcome of this struggle (1976: 90–7, 124, and passim). The collapse of the military dictatorships in Southern Europe in the mid-1970s (Greece, Portugal, and Spain) or of the socialist states in Central and Eastern Europe (think especially of Romania) are exemplary here and led to very different outcomes, depending on the balance of forces prevailing at the time of the collapse. (See, from contrasting theoretical perspectives that take account of classes, other social forces, and elements of the state apparatus, Chilcote et al., 1990; Ivanes 2002; Poulantzas 1976; Przeworski 1993; Linz and Stepan 1996.)

Fragile states, failed states, and rogue states

Depending on the configuration of capacities, on state managers' ability to project power beyond the state's multiple boundaries, and on the prevailing challenges, state strength varies considerably – and indeed, in extreme cases, states may disintegrate or show other signs of what is often described as 'state failure'. All states fail in certain respects, and normal politics is an important mechanism for learning from, and adapting to, failure. In contrast, 'failed states' lack the capacity to reinvent or reorient their activities in the face of recurrent state failure in order to maintain 'normal political service' in domestic policies. The discourse of 'failed states' is often used for stigmatizing some regimes as part of interstate as well as domestic politics. This description is probably justified in the case of predatory states, that is, states whose officials 'live off' the surplus and other resources of specific classes, or of the population

more generally, without securing the conditions for expanded reproduction. Other names for this phenomenon are 'kleptocracy' and
'vampire state'. A judicious mix of good governance and liberal
market reforms is often recommended in such cases, but this is not
a universal panacea. As in other cases of external pressure or external intervention, it is internal state capacities and the internal balance
of forces (as modified by external factors) that are the primary determinant of transformation. While there are some successes of 'good
governance' policies (e.g., Rwanda), there are many examples of
serious and continuing failures (e.g., Afghanistan, Zimbabwe, the
former Belgian Congo).

Similarly, the label 'rogue state' serves to denigrate states whose
actions are considered by hegemonic or dominant states, notably by
the United States, to threaten the prevailing international order. The
US State Department used four criteria to identify such states:
(1) they are authoritarian regimes; (2) they sponsor terrorism;
(3) they seek to proliferate weapons of mass destruction; (4) they are
guilty of serious abuses of human rights at home. In 2000 the State
Department replaced 'rogue state' in its official discourse with 'states
of concern'. Whereas some 'rogue states' are also 'failed states',
others are strong but brittle exceptional states (e.g., North Korea,
Myanmar). The labelling of rogue states has invited the counter-
hegemonic critical response that the United States itself has been the
worst rogue state for many years (e.g., Blum 2001; Chomsky 2001).
Charges and countercharges of this kind indicate that terms such as
'failed' and 'rogue' states are heavily contested – but this does not
mean that the validity of claims cannot be tested against specific
criteria. A similar label is 'pariah state', which is applied to states
that abuse human rights at home but do not threaten world peace
(e.g., Myanmar, Zimbabwe).

Authoritarian Statism

Notions such as Bonapartism and Caesarism were integral parts of
the nineteenth-century European political discourse and provided a
focus, alongside democracy, for exploring the relation between political authority and the popular will. This theme continued into the
twentieth century, especially during the interwar period, around dictatorship and totalitarianism. The theme of authoritarian rule was
revived again after the end of the Second World War – especially in
the context of the Cold War and in association with the rise of the
national security state – and after the crisis of the postwar Atlantic

Fordist mode of growth, which had combined rising prosperity with strong support for catchall parties and for an expanding welfare state.

There are several important accounts that suggest that 'authoritarian' forms of rule are characteristic of mature capitalism and not just found in the period of primitive accumulation and late development or in dependent and peripheral capitalisms. Examples include the ideas of first-generation Frankfurt School theorists on trends towards a strong, bureaucratic state – whether authoritarian or totalitarian in form – in the context of economic crisis and the emergence of state capitalism (see Dubiel and Söllner 1981; Scheuerman 1996; and the discussion in Scheuerman 2008). These early Frankfurt School theorists argued that this state form was linked to the rise of organized or state capitalism, which relied increasingly on the mass media for its ideological power and either integrated the labour movement as a political support or smashed it as part of the consolidation of totalitarian rule.

Among postwar theorists one might mention Jürgen Habermas's arguments (1989) on the decline of the public sphere in late capitalism. Other examples include Joachim Hirsch (1980) on the rise of the *Sicherheitsstaat* (security state) in the context of postwar Fordism; various arguments about the tendency towards the 'strong state' (*starker Staat*), the 'garrison state', 'friendly fascism', and so forth. Such arguments typically concern states in advanced European and North American capitalist societies. Peripheral capitalism poses the issue of statism even more acutely, insofar as statism is assimilated to the developmental state (e.g., Kemal Atatürk's Turkey, Lee Kwan-Yiu's Singapore). As well as these more 'normal' forms of developmental statism, we find exceptional 'developmental' states (e.g., the early stages of the South Korean and Taiwanese developmental states, with their strong national security regimes presided over by dictatorships – before democratization occurred, due to divisions among capital fractions and growing popular pressure).

In the immediate postwar period, Hans Morgenthau, the realist international relations theorist, described the US state as an assemblage formed by a 'regular state hierarchy' that acts by the rule of law and a more hidden 'security hierarchy' that monitors and controls the regular state, limiting the influence of democracy and provoking demands for protection by cultivating fear of enemies without and within. More recently, developing but qualifying Martin Shaw's notion of the western conglomerate state (Shaw 2000), Ola Tunander argues that the US *Reich* has divided the western state (which he also refers to as the western *Großraum*) into two: a series of regular democratic or public national states that operate under the rule of law; and a covert transnational security state that can veto its decisions and 'securitize' regular politics by construing certain activities as fundamental threats to national or international security, resorting in some cases to terrorism to justify military coups or coup attempts (Tunander 2009: 56–7 and passim).

The idea of security hierarchy or security state is also reflected, more recently, in a growing interest in the 'deep state'. This phrase, 'deep state', was coined in Turkey (its equivalent in Turkish is *derin devlet*) to denote a system composed of high-level elements within the intelligence services, military, security, judiciary, and organized crime (see, e.g., Park 2008; Söyler 2013). Similar networks have been revealed in Egypt and the Ukraine, Spain and Colombia, Italy and Israel, and many other countries. For Mike Lofgren, who wrote an insider's exposé on the George W. Bush administration in these terms, the deep state comprises 'a hybrid association of elements of government and parts of top-level finance and industry that is effectively able to govern the United States without reference to the consent of the governed as expressed through the formal political process' (Lofgren 2014).

In similar vein, Jason Lindsey (2013) distinguishes the *shallow state* from the *dark state*. The shallow state is the public face of the state – it forms the front stage of the political scene: speeches, elections, party politics, and the like; in contrast, the deep state is increasingly concealed from public gaze (or 'hidden in plain sight') and comprises networks of officials, private firms, media outlets, think tanks, foundations, NGOs, interest groups, and other forces that attend to the needs of capital, not of everyday life. Indeed, it is more and more concealed under the aegis of and through practices of neoliberalism: deregulation, privatization, and the myth of waning sovereignty – which mask the many ways in which the public–private divide serves the interlocking interests of capital and the state. Tom Engelhardt, a radical journalist, refers to it as 'the Fourth Branch' of US government, alongside legislature, executive, and judiciary; for him, it comprises an ever more unchecked and unaccountable centre in Washington, working behind a veil of secrecy (Engelhardt 2014).

In addition to his analyses of parallel power networks and the role of the 'bunker' as the hard core of exceptional regimes, Poulantzas came to argue that features of the political order that were previously exceptional and temporary were more and more becoming normalized in what he called the authoritarian statist type of capitalist state. For, as the world market has become more integrated, its contradictions have been generalized and its crisis tendencies have become more evident. This makes it harder to displace or defer crises, and they have become a permanent feature of contemporary capitalism. Thus significant 'exceptional' features coexist with and modify 'normal' features of the capitalist type of state, as they become orchestrated into a permanent structure that runs parallel to the official state system. This process involves a constant symbiosis and functional intersecting of normal and exceptional structures under the control of the commanding heights of the state apparatus and the dominant party (Poulantzas 1978).

Thus Poulantzas argued that the capitalist type of state is now *permanently and structurally characterized by a peculiar sharpening of the generic elements of political crisis and state crisis*. This reflected the long-term structural economic crisis of contemporary capitalism that was manifest in the 1970s and its condensation in a variety of political and ideological crises that were fracturing the social bases of the interventionist state, such as the decomposition of the traditional alliance between the bourgeoisie and the old and new petty bourgeoisie; the growing militancy of rank-and-file trade unionists and other subaltern groups; the ideological crisis accompanying the growth of new social movements on erstwhile 'secondary' fronts; and the contradictions within the power bloc, which sharpened under the impact of internationalization on the relations between fractions of capital (Poulantzas 1978: 210–14, 219, 221). These symptoms reflect the crisis of Atlantic Fordism, but analogous symptoms can be seen in the export-oriented knowledge-based economies and neoliberal finance-dominated economies of the 1990s and of the first two decades of the present century. Moreover, reflecting the much greater integration of the world market now than in the mid-1970s, crisis tendencies have become more multiform, more multiscalar, and more polycentric than Poulantzas envisaged and are motivated by many more cleavages, material and ideal interests, and identities.

While the details of Poulantzas's analysis reflected the conjuncture in which he was writing, his description of the newly emerging 'normal' form of the capitalist type of state is quite prescient. He described the basic developmental tendency of 'authoritarian statism' as 'intensified state control over every sphere of socioeconomic life combined with radical decline of the institutions of political democracy and with draconian and multiform curtailment of so-called "formal" liberties' (1978: 203–4). More specifically, the main elements of authoritarian statism and their implications for representative democracy comprise:

- A transfer of power from the legislature to the executive and administrative system and the concentration of real power within the latter, which seals itself off from the serious influence of parties and parliaments, considered as representatives of the people. Indeed politics is increasingly concentrated in the staff office of a president or prime minister. Standing at the apex of the administration, this office appears as a purely personalistic presidential–prime-ministerial system. This does not involve a genuine Bonapartist dictator who concentrates despotic powers in his (or her) hands; it rather involves the search for a charismatic frontman who can give a sense of strategic direction to the complexities of politics – both for the dominant classes and, in more plebiscitary fashion, for the popular masses. Personalism actually condenses many contradictory pressures and works to rebalance conflicting forces and popular interests that still surface in the form of contradictions inside the administration (1978; cf. Poulantzas 1974: 311–14).

- An accelerated fusion between the legislature, the executive, and the judiciary, accompanied by a decline in the rule of law. Parliaments and parties are now simple electoral 'registration chambers' with very limited powers – where their deputies may well become 'owned' by campaign funders, lobbyists, and potential future employers in the revolving doors of contemporary politics. So it is the state administration, guided by the political executive, which has become the main site for developing state policy. These changes also transform the parties of power (or the 'natural parties of government', in contrast to those parties destined for a permanent oppositional role) into a single (or duopolistic) authoritarian mass party whose task is more to mobilize mass support for state policies in a plebiscitary fashion than to directly articulate and represent popular interests and demands to the state. This massively politicizes the administration and risks its fragmentation behind a formal façade of bureaucratic hierarchy and unity (Poulantzas 1978: 236). The existence of this trend is corroborated by Katz and Mair's (1994) analysis of how a shift in party elite strategies, together with the changing dynamic of party competition, has led to the ascendancy of 'the party in public office' at the expense of grassroots members and national party executives (see also chapter 3).
- The functional decline of political parties as the leading channels for a political dialogue with the administration and as the major forces in organizing hegemony. There are also changes among the parties in power 'that seek to participate, and do participate, in government according to a pattern of regular alternation that is organically fixed and anticipated by the existing state institutions

as a whole (and not just by constitutional rules)' (Poulantzas 1978: 220). Their ties of representation to the power bloc become looser because monopoly capital finds it harder to organize its hegemony through parliamentary parties and therefore concentrates its lobbying on the administration (Poulantzas 1973; 1974; 1978: 221–3). Thus the parties no longer fulfil their traditional functions in policymaking (through compromise and alliances around a common party programme) or in political legitimation (through electoral competition for a national–popular mandate). They are now little more than transmission belts for official decisions and merely differ in the aspects of official policy that they choose to popularize (Poulantzas 1978: 229–30, 237). In turn, political legitimation is redirected through channels that are based on plebiscitary and manipulative techniques dominated by the executive and amplified through the mass media (1978: 229; see also chapter 3).

- The growth of parallel power networks, which cross-cut the formal organization of the state and hold a decisive share in its various activities (Poulantzas 1974, 1978). More precisely, authoritarian statism involves enhanced roles for the executive branch, its dominant 'state party' (which serves as a transmission belt from the state to the people rather than from the people to the state), and a new, antidemocratic ideology. This further undermines the already limited involvement of the masses in political decision-making, severely weakens the organic functioning of the party system (even where a plurality of parties survives intact), and saps the vitality of democratic forms of political discourse. Accordingly, there are fewer obstacles to the continuing penetration of authoritarian–statist forms into all areas of social life – especially, one might add, where this penetration is justified in the name of (national) security and war on terrorism. Indeed Poulantzas actually claims, hyperbolically, that 'all contemporary power is functional to authoritarian statism' (1978: 239).

In fact Poulantzas retreated somewhat from this claim when he noted that the activities of the state administration continually run up against limits inherent in its own political structure and operation. These limits are particularly clear in the internal divisions between different administrative coteries, clans, and factions and in the reproduction, inside the state system, of class conflicts and contradictions. Thus we must ask how the administration overcomes these tensions so as to act effectively on behalf of monopoly capital. Exceptional states achieve this through a political apparatus (such as the fascist party, the army, or the political police) that is distinct from the administration. In the normal form of representative democracy, the same is achieved through the organic functioning of a plural party system located beyond the central administrative apparatus (1978; cf. Poulantzas 1974).

The question arises how this organic functioning can be realized under authoritarian statism. Poulantzas suggested that it is achieved through the transformation of the dominant mass party into a dominant state party. This party now functions as a parallel network that acts as a political commissar at the heart of the administration, developing a material and ideological community of interest with key civil servants and representing the state to the masses rather than vice versa. It also transmits the state ideology to the popular masses and reinforces the plebiscitary legitimation of authoritarian statism (Poulantzas 1978: 236–7). Such a highly unified and structured mass party is most likely to develop over a long period during which there is no alternation among the governing parties. Similar functions can be performed by a single interparty 'centre' that dominates the alternating parties of power (1978: 232, 235–6).

Poulantzas related this 'irresistible rise of the state administration' mainly to the state's growing *economic* role, as modified by the political situation. Again, his account is marked by the conjuncture of the 1970s but can be reworked for the current period of neoliberal regime shifts, pragmatic neoliberal policy adjustments, and externally imposed neoliberal structural adjustment policies.

For state intervention means that law can no longer be confined to general, formal, and universal norms whose enactment is the preserve of parliament as the embodiment of the general will of the people-nation. Recent research on the US case shows that economic elites and organized groups representing business interests have substantial independent impacts on US government policy, while ordinary citizens and mass-based interest groups have little or no independent influence (Gilens and Page 2014; see also Ferguson 1995; Hacker and Pierson 2011). Legislation is also increasingly initiated by the administration rather than by parliament – and often in consultation with business interests or business lobbies such as the American Legislative Exchange Council (ALEC), which prepares boilerplate model legislation for rolling out at state level in the United States. Likewise, legal norms are increasingly modified and elaborated by the administration to suit particular conjunctures, situations, and interests (Poulantzas 1978: 218–19; cf. Scheuerman 2003). The decline of the rule of law also affects the political sphere. One sign of this is the increasing emphasis on preemptive policing of the potentially disloyal and deviant rather than the judicial punishment of clearly defined offences against the law (Poulantzas 1978: 219–20; cf. Boukalas 2014). More generally, the crisis of hegemony means that state administration becomes the *central* site where the 'unstable equilibrium of compromise' within the power bloc is elaborated, thanks to an increasingly dense network of cross-cutting ties between big business and the central administrative apparatuses of the state (especially the economic apparatuses) and to a general increase in political and administrative centralism.

Yet this centralization of administrative power at the expense of parliament, popular parties, and democratic liberties does not mean that the state has been enormously strengthened. On the contrary, the authoritarian state finds it hard to manage the growing intensity, interconnectedness, and global scope of economic contradictions and of crisis tendencies and to deal with new forms of popular struggle. It must either allow economic crises to run their course or assume responsibility for managing them and for displacing or deferring their effects without eliminating them. It has also become much harder for the dominant fraction to sacrifice its short-term economic–corporate interests in order to promote its long-term political hegemony. The administration also finds it much harder than a flexible plural party system to organize hegemony and manage the unstable equilibrium of class compromise; likewise, the state's growing involvement in hitherto marginal areas of social life politicizes the popular masses – especially as postwar social policy commitments exclude spending cuts, austerity, and recommodification and the resulting legitimation crisis leads the masses to confront the state directly and threaten its stability. Any failure to intervene in these areas would undermine the social reproduction of labour power. The state's growing role in promoting the internationalization of capital also causes problems for national unity. This is especially clear from its impact on less developed regions and national minorities (Poulantzas 1978).

Similar ideas have been developed by other critical commentators, from the right as well as from the centre and the left, especially in the context of the recent and continuing financial crisis and its broader economic repercussions. For example, Greg Albo and Carlo Fanelli refer to a new phase of bipartisan or pluripartisan 'disciplinary democracy' as the political form of 'permanent austerity' (Albo and Fanelli 2014; cf. Rasmus 2010; Stützle 2013). Ian Bruff refers to neoliberal authoritarian constitutionalism (Bruff 2013); Ingar Solty (2013) identifies an 'authoritarian crisis constitutionalism' oriented to the economic governance of competitive austerity (Solty 2013); and Lukas Oberndorfer describes the development of authoritarian competitive statism (Oberndorfer 2015). From a social democratic perspective, Wolfgang Streeck refers to a move from the welfare state to the consolidation state (Streeck 2013); and a (former) Fabian Socialist, Colin Crouch, describes the transition to postdemocracy (Crouch 2004). On the libertarian right, there is condemnation of the strong and repressive state – the kind of state that emerges from allegedly unconstitutional intervention to shore up finance capital and police dissent (e.g. Stockman 2014). Such claims prompt the question whether these are short-term aberrations, conjunctural states of emergency, or precursors of a 'new normal'.

Largely neglected by Poulantzas, who wrote in the mid-1970s, is the development of authoritarian statist tendencies at the transnational level. Developments here involve scale jumping for capital (see chapter 5), which is coordinated through parallel power networks and oriented to securing the conditions for a 'new constitutionalism' (Gill 1995). The latter provides superprotection for capital as neoliberalism is rolled out globally and limits the territorial and temporal sovereignty of national states. The secret negotiations between national (and EU) administrations, representatives of capital, and post-Washington Consensus international economic institutions around the Trans-Pacific Partnership (TPP), Transatlantic Trade and Investment Partnership (TTIP), and Trade in Services Agreement (TiSA) illustrate this trend. They aim to rescale quasi-constitutional protections for capitalist enterprises and their activities to the international level, thus removing them from the more contentious field of national politics; to allocate adjudication over disputes, including disputes with states, to private tribunals, experts, lawyers, and other ostensibly nonpolitical forums and figures; and – surprisingly (or not) in allegedly democratic regimes – to limit the power of elected governments to introduce legislation or administrative rules that would harm the anticipated profits of transnational enterprises under the threat of financial penalties.[5]

The growing popular hostility to TPP, TTIP, and TiSA as details leak into the public domain is one example of the limits of the power of the transnational deep state. Another is the growing concern, among economic and political elites, about the backlash from growing inequalities of wealth and income and the obvious bias in favour of financial capital in managing the North Atlantic financial crisis and the Eurozone crisis. Thus the rise of 'authoritarian statism' involves a paradox. While this phenomenon clearly strengthens state power at the expense of liberal representative democracy, it also weakens its capacities to secure bourgeois hegemony (Poulantzas 1978: 241, 263–5; Bruff 2013).

The European Union

These trends are even more evident in the European Union. Thus we observe that the executives of member states are represented in the legislative branch of the Union through the Council of Ministers and the European Council; that the power of the European Commission as an executive body is continually expanding; and that this body is also the principal site for the fusion of executive, legislative, and some judicial powers. It is also more decoupled from the national interests of member states (witness the shift to qualified majority voting). The European Parliament remains insignificant and party blocs are weak, with no direct election of European-wide parties on a common platform. In addition, the role of informal networks, working groups, committees, and so forth gets stronger – producer groups being especially influential (CEO 2004; ALTER-EU 2010; Cronin 2013). We are no longer dealing with a material condensation of an intergovernmental mode where national interests compete with each other. Rather, the Commission now officially claims that it 'represents and upholds the interests of the EU as a whole' and thereby asserts a transnational *raison d'état* over normal representative principles (Kaczyinski 2014: 5).

By way of illustration, Wolfram Elsner suggests:

> The EU '*Economic and Financial Governance (or Government)*' by the President of the EU Commission, the ECB president, the heads of IMF and ESM, the Council of Economic and Finance Ministers, and top bankers, may easily become the *postdemocratic prototype* and even a pre-dictatorial governance structure against national sovereignty and democracies. (Elsner 2012: 158)

Department of Homeland Security

The development of authoritarian statism is associated with a reordering of the departments and branches of the state. This linkage can be seen in the increasing importance of the (national) security apparatus, the manner in which its operations cross-cut formal bounds and boundaries within the state, and the fact that it is linked through parallel power networks to important forces, formally located beyond the state. Many crucial activities are conducted behind the cloak of official secrecy, intransparency, and the 'need to know' principle. The population is excluded from shaping policy or controlling its operations other than through populist ventriloquism coordinated with the fourth estate, which also plays on fears of insecurity. Some of the strategies and tactics adopted in the security apparatus have been pioneered in colonies, on the (semi-)periphery, or in occupied countries (e.g., McCoy 2009; Grandin 2007). The threat of terrorism is invoked in order to roll out the state, with the result that 'the only way...terrorism affects our daily lives is through counterterrorism' (Boukalas 2014a: 2).

An egregious example of these institutions and practices is the US Department of Homeland Security (DHS) in the US. This is a further development of the national security bureaucracy considered as a comprehensive system of interdependent institutions, which emerged after the Second World War and was established through the omnibus 1947 National Security Act; and it created all of the leading institutions of the US national security bureaucracy, except for the Department of State. Just as the ground for the 1947 legislation was provided by the Japanese attack on Pearl Harbour and the security lessons drawn therefrom, the USA PATRIOT Act and the DHS were introduced in the wake of the attack on the World Trade Center. The 1947 Act established the 'Pearl Harbor system' (Stuart 2008), where national security was an overriding purpose of the state – or a state project – based on the projection of global military power and backed by nuclear weaponry. In turn, 9/11 has provided the basis for what one might call the 'Homeland Security system': a complex of 'counter-terrorism law (Patriot, Homeland Security, and Intelligence Reform Acts, and their epigones) and para-legislation (Executive and Military Orders)' directed against the inherently political crime of domestic terrorism (Boukalas 2014a: 8). If we add all this to the president's powers as commander-in-chief, we witness the decline of the separation of powers and individual rights at home and, abroad, the construction of an international as well as national state of emergency – which requires other countries to make exceptions to international law and to their own constitutional orders (Scheppele 2004).

For Christos Boukalas, another Greek political scientist, this marks a third phase in the development of authoritarian statism. Statism in this phase alters the relations between the executive, Congress, and the courts; concentrates power in the executive; alters the structure and operation of the policing mechanism and the spatiality and temporality of policing; and extends the powers of the state over the population – whether citizens, 'aliens', or 'enemy combatants'. These powers are also deployed in support of managing the repercussions of economic emergencies, 9/11 provisions being used to criminalize popular politics – including by methods such as preemption, suspicion, and entrapment. Popular movements far removed from any conventional definition of terrorism – antiwar, Occupy, environmental and animal rights movements – are now targeted; journalists and individual dissenters are under suspicion, surveillance, and intimidation. The result is that there is pluralism for dominant capital and despotism for the rest of the population (Boukalas 2014b). It is a state form that results from the state's need to combat economic and political crises in some variable mix of the interest of the state in reproducing its apparatus, restoring the conditions for differential accumulation and social cohesion, and appeasing popular pressures. But it is also a form that generates crises and thereby creates the conditions for further extensions of the security state!

Towards an Enduring Austerity State

While austerity policies differ across 'varieties of capitalism' (as the latter reflect the former's specific economic profiles and imaginaries), they are also shaped by interdependencies that result from interstate relations, including forms of regional and global governance, from foreign trade and other features of world market integration, and from the prevailing logic of the world market. This highlights the need to examine austerity in terms of the basic forms and institutional architecture of the economic and the political field, the relations between these fields, and their mediation through the changing balance of forces.

The policy–politics–polity triplet introduced in chapter 2 suggests that austerity can be studied in three ways. First, there are *conjunctural austerity policies*, which are introduced in the first instance as temporary measures in response to short-term or immediate problems. As the conjuncture becomes favourable again, these policies are suspended or reversed. Second, there is the *enduring politics of austerity* (often called 'permanent austerity' in the relevant literature),[6] which is promoted in response to a 'chronic' crisis, real or manufactured, in the fisco-financial domain or in the economy more generally. This enduring politics of austerity, as noted above, is intended to bring about a more lasting reorganization of the balance of forces in favour of capital rather than to make policy adjustments to safeguard existing economic and political arrangements. Third, there is the *austerity polity*. This results from a continuing and fundamental institutional reorganization of the relations between the economic and the political in capitalist formations. It can be an unintended cumulative result of the enduring politics of austerity, especially where this politics aggravates the underlying causes of fisco-financial crisis. It can also result from a deliberate strategy to subordinate the polity more directly and durably to the 'imperatives' of the world market as these are construed in neoliberal discourse, with its one-sided emphasis on the logic of exchange value. And, given the political, ideological, hegemonic, and organic crises that have developed in the context of the financial, economic, and fisco-financial crises, it can also be an authoritarian response to growing popular unrest – which can take the form of right-wing extremism – about the technocratic and plutocratic nature of crisis responses.

Whereas conjunctural policies are found in the pattern of neoliberal policy adjustment and are associated with targeted cuts in specific areas, an enduring politics of austerity is characteristic of neoliberal regime shifts and assumes the form of general fisco-financial restraint, putting downward pressure on most areas of expenditure, especially discretionary ones (Pierson 2002; Ferrera 2008; Seymour 2014). This pattern can occur in normal forms of politics, in states of economic emergency, or even in lasting states of exception. It can be triggered by an obvious and real crisis, by one that is deliberately exaggerated, or by one 'manufactured' for political purposes. Indeed in neoliberal regimes, whatever the state of the economy, it seems that it is always the right time to reduce public expenditure (except for corporate welfare) through an appropriately crafted (and crafty) politics of austerity. This involves far more than quantitative cuts in spending, because it is also intended to have qualitative, transformative effects. It is pursued as a means to consolidate and extend the power of capital, especially interest-bearing capital, and to subsume ever wider areas of social life under the logic of differential accumulation. It becomes a major vector of the colonization, commodification, and, eventually, financialization of everyday life – processes subject to friction, resistance, and tendency to crisis.

Seymour (2014) explains this well. He argues that austerity involves something much broader and more complex than spending cuts – thanks to its role in restructuring, recalibrating, and reorienting state expenditure. Indeed, for him, austerity is the dominant *political* articulation of the global economic crisis in Europe and North America. Its strategy has seven aspects: austerity (1) rebalances the economy from wage-led to finance-led growth; (2) redistributes the income from wage earners to capital; (3) promotes 'precarity' in all areas of life as a disciplinary mechanism and means to reinforce the financialization of everyday life; (4) recomposes social classes, widening the inequality in income and wealth between them and the stratification within classes; (5) facilitates the penetration of the state by corporations; (6) accelerates the turn from a Keynesian welfare state based on shared citizenship rights to a workfare regime that relies on coercion, casual sadism, and, especially in the United States, penality; and (7) promotes the values of hierarchy and competitiveness (Seymour 2014: 2–4). In many respects, these aspects were already inscribed in the politics of neoliberal regime shifts; but, for Seymour, they were reinforced after the 2007–9 financial and economic crisis. This can be explained in part by the fact that the painful measures already taken to consolidate budgets in the 1990s and up to the 2010s were wiped out by the impact of the North Atlantic financial crisis and the Eurozone crisis, as governments took on more debt to bail out banks or to create stimulus packages (Rasmus 2010; Hudson 2012).

This ramping up of the politics of austerity occurred in part because the response of financial capital to this crisis intensified the state's fisco-financial crisis. Measures were taken to rescue interest-bearing capital from the effects of its Ponzi dynamic and from the inherently unsustainable drive for financial profits (see above; also Demirović and Sablowski 2013). This created a debt–default–deflation dynamic that has worsened public finances as well as the private sector (Rasmus 2010). In addition, as Seymour (among others) notes, the politics of permanent austerity is a response not just to economic crisis but also to political and ideological crises – and indeed to an organic crisis of the capitalist social order (Seymour 2014: 4; cf. Gramsci 1971: 210–18, 318 = Q13, §23*, Q22, §15; Bruff 2013). This fact is used to justify a state of economic emergency that is presented initially as a 'temporary' response to immediate or chronic problems but then acquires more permanent form through cumulative and mutually reinforcing institutional change, routinization of exceptional measures, and habituation.

The politics of austerity can be interpreted as a long-term strategic offensive designed to reorganize the institutional matrix and balance of forces in favour of capital. It aims to rearticulate relations between (1) the social power of money as capital and of capital as property and (2) the political power of the state. *Inter alia*, this involves a politics aimed at *disorganizing* subaltern classes and *reorganizing* the capitalist power bloc around interest-bearing capital (in neoliberal regimes) and export-based profit-producing capital (in economies where neoliberal policy adjustments prevailed). In the Eurozone, for example, we are witnessing the emergence of an 'authoritarian crisis constitutionalism' (Solty 2013: 75), that is, the further entrenchment of neoliberal constitutionalism in a more authoritarian direction, in order to reinforce the ability of states at different scales to manage economic and political crises. The central goals of this juridico-political response is to deepen EU integration on neoliberal terms and to govern through competitive austerity, pitting economic spaces and political regimes at different scales against each other in terms of their willingness to undertake austerity. In both finance-dominated and export-oriented regimes, the overall approach can switch between offensive and defensive tactics (an example of the latter is the 'Third Way', with its flanking and supporting mechanisms to maintain the overall momentum of neoliberal transformation). The successful pursuit of this strategy, which cannot be taken for granted, leads to an *austerity state* embedded in a political system (polity) that institutionalizes a 'permanent' politics of austerity.

Conclusions

The exceptional features of authoritarian statism are articulated under the dominance of the normal elements. In chapter 8 I explored the extent to which there has been a transnationalization of the state – taken in the sense of government + governmentality in the shadow of hierarchy; and, in exploring exceptional regimes in this chapter, I noted how this transnationalization now involves not only exceptional measures at home but also the organization of an exceptional state across advanced capitalist states and in the vast majority of other states – either as an offensive or as a defensive measure in geopolitical and geoeconomic fields. The intensification of national security issues, economic states of emergency, and the war on terrorism illustrate, in different ways, the principle that 'no nation that oppresses another can ever be free', that world market integration generalizes and intensifies the contradictions of capitalism, and that counterterrorism can produce blow-back effects that increase terrorism and so on, in a vicious spiral.

The postdemocratic, authoritarian state of political emergency that is being constructed in this conjuncture will continue as the 'best possible political shell' for a predatory, finance-dominated accumulation regime, even if – and even when – the financial crisis is resolved. For, as noted above, the survival of this new bloc depends heavily on Weber's three forms of political capitalism. The longer it survives, the more harmful its effects on the 'real economy', human flourishing, and the natural environment. Crises do not engender their own solutions but are objectively overdetermined moments of subjective indeterminacy. How they are resolved, if at all, depends on the balance of forces in each case. The manner and form of the resolution determines the forms of presentation of subsequent crises. It remains to see whether the many fragmented forms of resistance can be linked up horizontally, vertically, and transversally to provide an effective challenge to this new bloc, its finance-dominated accumulation regime, and its 'new normal' state form by exploiting the bloc's fragilities. This will require connecting economic and political power in ways that are 'proscribed' by the democratic rules of the game but are realized continually, in nondemocratic ways, by the new transnational financial bloc.

10

The Future of States and Statehood

This book has reviewed some key themes in mainstream and hetero-dox approaches to the state from a variety of disciplines. It has presented a four-element approach to the state, considered as one form of the territorialization of political power; has provided some conceptual frameworks for exploring the main formal and substantive features of the state and state power; and has commented on the history and present condition of the state. Whereas the analysis of primary state formation drew on a wide geographical range of cases, which reflects the multiple and dispersed nature of the phenomenon, the analysis of the present state has been largely confined to advanced capitalist social formations and their forms of government and gov-ernmentality. This focus reflects the author's expertise – but also the nature of the 'world of states' (*Staatenwelt*), in which the United States and Western Europe are still, for good or ill, powerful influences in the overall dynamic of a variegated global political order. But this bias in addressing the selectivities of the state also reflects a more general weakness in theorization about the state.

Is State Theory Eurocentric?

State theory has tended to be too influenced by the experience of the North. Charles Tilly, the historical sociologist, suggested that the state developed in Western Europe and spread out from there (Tilly 1992); and this view is quite common (cf. Lachmann 2010). It is reflected in state theory, especially given the close links between political philosophy, normative political theory, and the development of the state. This makes it hard to assess the relevance of state theory to the many states at the semi-periphery or periphery of world society that are less likely to have 'normal' (or bourgeois democratic) forms of capitalist state and where it is in consequence more appropriate to study states as 'states in capitalist societies' – assuming that one or another of Weber's six modes of orientation to profit is the dominant basis of the formal economic organization – and not as instances of the 'capitalist type of state' (see chapter 4). This point is reinforced when we recall the polymorphous nature of the state: the state can take different forms according to the dominant principles of societal organization or according to the most immediate problems, crises, or *urgences* (to use Foucault's French term) in particular conjunctures. A related problem is that states in advanced capitalism cannot be isolated from the interstate system, which is more than the anarchic sum of individual territorial states: rather it reflects their co-evolution, their structural coupling, and – equally significantly, theoretically and in practice – various forces' strategic attempts (often abortive, failure-prone, and subject to blowback) to reorder interstate relations and to re-create the hierarchical nature of a variegated global political system through force, law, money, information, and other state resources (Willke 1997). In short, states in advanced capitalist social formations reflect the interstate system to which they belong as well as the more general nature of a still emerging world society.

Unsurprisingly, then, different (and differently related) economic and political institutions are said to characterize social formations in the 'South' by comparison with the liberal democratic market econo-mies of the 'North'. In North East Asia and in parts of South (East) Asia, this division is reflected in work on the developmental state; and, in Latin America and in parts of North and South Africa, in studies of the dependent capitalist state (Amin-Khan 2012; Canak 1984; Ebenau 2012; Larrain 1986; McMichael 1996; Robinson 2012; Woo 1991). This is not just a question of incomplete modern-ization, to be overcome as laggard economies catch up and converge on some western version of modern capitalism. More generally, many states in the South have been described as exceptional (or nondemo-cratic) regimes and, in some cases, as failed or rogue states. It is already clear that a third or fourth wave of democratization has not remedied this: despite the cheerleading and triumphalism of neocon-servatives and neoliberals when the Soviet bloc collapsed, the various 'colour' revolutions were promoted and guided by western powers and led in most cases to dependent capitalist development and, in several, to weak states. Likewise, popular uprisings occurred in states in the Middle East and North Africa (MENA) and in other social formations but, more often than not, have been blocked or reversed, or have ended (at the time of writing) in failed states.

This should prompt us to consider whether state theory is inherently Eurocentric or can be developed in a more general way. This is especially problematic in dealing with societies that lack their own concepts for a 'state' in its Westphalian sense and conceive of the prevailing institutions and conjunctural issues of political authority as being deeply embedded within the wider social formation.

Some problems of applying Eurocentric categories and theories to the 'South' can be illustrated from the analysis of East Asian economic growth. Three accounts dominated in the late 1990s and early 2000s: market-centred, developmentalist, and culturalist. The first is closely related to the neoliberal policy orientation of the International Monetary Fund (IMF) and World Bank. It is based on neoclassical theory, which argues that 'the market takes center stage in economic life and governments play a minor role' (World Bank 1993: 82) and, hence, that the most efficient allocation of resources will only occur if market forces are allowed free play and if the state has a minimalist, night-watchman role in economic development. While correctly rejecting the idea that there is a single East Asian export-oriented model of economic growth, the World Bank argued that, in all cases, states skilfully tapped into the private sector's strengths. The basic mechanisms were: (1) a virtuous cycle of high investment, high economic growth, and high savings rates; (2) good-quality labour and an increasing labour participation rate; and (3) rising production efficiency on the basis of import of foreign capital and technology (World Bank 1993). Criticizing this approach, state-centred studies argue that East Asia's 'economic miracles' depended crucially on wide and effective state intervention, on targeted industrial policies, and on the primacy of substantive criteria of economic performance over the formal rationality of market forces. This state-centred explanation is the second account. The third one invokes specific cultural factors and is exemplified by – but certainly not limited to – the confused, overextended idea of 'Confucian capitalism'. None of these accounts is satisfactory individually and, together, they reproduce the problematic Enlightenment conceptual triplet of market–state–civil society, which is often quite inappropriate for analysing other social formations. These accounts owe more to European thinking, then, than to East Asian specificities. (For studies that touch on some of these dimensions, see H. J. Chang 2007; D. O. Chang 2009; Chibber 2003; Evans 1995, 2011; Kang 2002; Kohli 2004; Mazzucato 2013; Routley 2014; Weiss 2013; Weiss and Hobson 1995.)

The problem with these accounts is that East Asian societies are not characterized by a distinct realm of market forces, a hierarchically organized and institutionally distinct sovereign state, or a bourgeois civil society. Markets are heavily linked to networks that control economic, political, and social resources; states are not institutionally demarcated but have blurred boundaries and may be organized into fiefdoms and other kinds of networks invested with parallel power; and citizenship and individualism are linked to collectivities, ethnicity, and so on. Thus Enlightenment categories are not well suited to grasping the complexity and interdependence of economic and extraeconomic activities, organizations, and institutions. Indeed, there are also good grounds for arguing that, even in the West, these categories are fetishistic and inadequate – as the analysis of growth poles like Silicon Valley or the Third Italy, the different forms of governance that characterize so-called 'varieties of capitalism', or the semantic content of general terms like 'military–industrial complex', 'knowledge-based economy', or 'global city networks' might indicate. To avoid these problems, one should place developmental states in the context of the world market, interstate system, and the emergence of world society as a horizon of action.

Another issue concerns states that do not share many of the characteristics of the modern state (which here includes developmental states). In the Middle East, Africa, and Central Asia, kinship and tribal loyalties often count for more than typical institutions of the modern state or plausible simulacra of such institutions. In these regions states sometimes operate in a kleptocratic manner, as warlords, mafias, and predatory bodies that collect tribute or 'loot' from local, regional, national, or international trade in natural resources, for instance in oil, coltan, diamonds, and drugs. Some dynastic regimes still exist – notably Saudi Arabia and other Middle East oil monarchies (on these, see, for example, Kostiner 2000 and Gause III 2013). And in the Middle East there is a widespread religious revival linked to emergent national identities, many of which underpin aspirations to independent statehood (e.g. Shiites in southern Lebanon, Palestinians in Gaza, Kurds divided among four post-Ottoman states).

First, apart from the common assumption that the state involves the territorialization of political power, there are many unanswered questions about state forms and interstate relations, their functional necessity or historical contingency, and their articulation with wider sets of social relations. In part this arises because of the tendency to focus on one or two forms of state (e.g., the Westphalian state, the Weberian modern state) as if these were typical of all states – or else to retreat into detailed ethnographic studies or highly specific historical analyses that do not lend themselves to systematic comparison and theory construction and testing. Second and closely linked to this set of issues (and reinforcing them) is the inherent polymorphy and pluri-functionality of the state apparatus. States have been organized to pursue very different economic strategies, state projects, and societal visions and it is important to integrate this feature into theories of the state. One major implication of this point is that the capitalist nature of the state cannot be taken for granted even in societies where capitalist relations of production are dominant. Third, there are major issues about the future of the state as a core institutional arrangement in complex social formations – with advances and retreats, transformations and revivals, changing functions and new forms of public–private partnership that are evident on a continuing basis. Fourth, while some regard state failure as an aberration and others see it as a tendency inherent in the state, it is important to provide a more nuanced account of state failure and of the capacities of states to engage in state reform and meta-governance (for a good overview of the literature, see Taylor 2013). Fifth, more research is needed into the appropriate scales of state action, governance, and meta-governance in relation to the growing complexities of the world market, world politics, and the emerging world society. Particularly problematic here is the unresolved search for a new scale that can handle both the 'little' and the 'big' problems confronting contemporary societies – or the reassertion of the national scale. These processes have been discussed more in the 'North', but they are also influencing the 'South'. Finally, given that the state is no longer taken for granted as the primary locus of political action, social solidarity, or ethico-political authority, there are important issues about how to reground and relegitimate state actions, how to redesign them to suit the new functions, and how to facilitate the delivery of old and new tasks.

Whither the State?

Speculating on the long-term future of the state is a fool's game – even more so than attempting to encompass the 'motley diversity of present-day states' (see below) within a single theoretical framework. This is why the introduction to this book emphasized the heuristic necessity as well as the heuristic potential of approaching the state from at least six different theoretical perspectives and noted that each could be associated with several different standpoints. The analysis in subsequent chapters has adopted this general strategy; but, while doing so, it has tended to focus on the capitalist type of state and on states in capitalist society. The reason is that profit-oriented, market-mediated accumulation (as articulated with different forms of political capitalism) is the dominant principle of societal organization on a world scale and therefore the most relevant entry point for the analysis of the contemporary state. But this state of affairs should not – and does not – exclude taking different entry points when studying particular states or particular conjunctures. Indeed doing so is essential to enabling a full appreciation of the polymorphic character of states and state power.

The strategic–relational approach (SRA) set out in preceding chapters can also provide some guidelines for reflecting on the future of the state – albeit in the sense of *present futures* rather than *future futures* (on this distinction, see Adams and Groves 2007; Koselleck 1985; Luhmann 1982; Esposito 2011). At stake here is what exists *in potentia* in the present-day state system as currently organized, in the shadow of finance-dominated accumulation, and the logic of (national) security in an increasingly turbulent and crisis-prone world order. What types of state and what forms of regime might follow the gradual decomposition, sudden collapse, or overthrow of the present-day state and interstate system – that is, the question of future futures – is currently a matter of speculation, ripe for competing political imaginaries. On these, as Niklas Luhmann noted, 'the only thing we know about the future is that it will be different from the past (1998: 21). An important guideline for thinking about present futures was already noted 140 years ago by Karl Marx, in his critique of *The Gotha Programme* prepared by the German Workers Party led by Ferdinand Lassalle. The *Programme* was replete with references to present-day society and the present state. Marx commented:

> 'Present-day society' is capitalist society, which exists in all civilized countries, more or less free from medieval admixture, more or less modified by the particular historical development of each country, more or less developed. On the other hand, the 'present-day state' changes with a country's frontier. It is different in the Prusso-German Empire from what it is in Switzerland, and different in England from what it is in the United States. The 'present-day state' is therefore a fiction.
>
> Nevertheless, the different states of the different civilized countries, in spite of their motley diversity of form, all have this in common: that they are based on modern bourgeois society, only one more or less capitalistically developed. They have, therefore, also certain essential characteristics in common. In this sense, it is possible to speak of the

'present-day state' in contrast with the future, in which its present root, bourgeois society, will have died off. (Marx 1989: 94–5)

In this light we can reflect on the relation between present-day society (that is, an emerging world society that is currently organized under the dominance of the logic of profit-oriented, market-mediated accumulation, with all its contradictions, antagonisms, and crisis tendencies) and the 'present-day' state (that is, the forms of government + governance organized in the shadow of hierarchy, which together comprise the world of states) (see chapter 8). For the former, we need to consider major macrotrends; for the latter, we should focus on the four elements and six dimensions of the state that are constitutive of the *polity* rather than the more contingent and changing nature of *politics* or the fine details of policy – considering all the scope that exists in politics and policy for random events, the vagaries of party politics and of the social movements on the political scene, political and policy errors, trial-and-error experimentation, and so on.

Ernst Bloch argued that Marx was little concerned with romantic introspection into the inner recesses of the heart or with lengthy, time-consuming, and abstract private speculation about possible future utopias. On the contrary, his critique revealed

> all the more sharply the recesses, fissures, cracks, and contrasts incorporated in the objectively existing economy....The abstract utopias had devoted nine tenths of their space to a portrayal of the State of the future and only one tenth to the critical, often merely negative consideration of the present. This kept the goal colourful and vivid of course, but the path towards it, in so far as it could lie in given circumstances, remained hidden. Marx devoted more than nine tenths of his writings to the critical analysis of the present, and he granted relatively little space to descriptions of the future. (Bloch 1986b: 620)

In this spirit, there are four major macrotrends that will constrain the development of the leading capitalist states:

1   the intensification of global, regional, and local environmental crises due to the primacy of capital accumulation, rivalries between national states or fractions of capital over how to address it, and North–South conflicts with repercussions on environmental security, resource wars, failed states, civil unrest, climate refugees, and so forth (Hamilton, Gemmene, and Bonneuil 2015; Klare 2001, 2012; Le Billon 2005; Moore 2015a, 2015b; Smith 2013; Global Commission on the Economy and Climate 2014);

2 the intensification of the contradictions, crisis tendencies, and antagonisms in the world economy – including a growing polarization of wealth and incomes; surplus population; and increasing precarity for subordinate classes (Chase-Dunn and Lawrence 2011a, 2011b; Harvey 2005; Elsner 2012; Standing 2011);

3 a continuing relative decline, economic and political, of the United States as a global hegemon, which will lead to increasing efforts to secure 'full-spectrum dominance' through an expansion of the national security apparatus and homeland security apparatus, increasing interventions abroad and paramilitary policing at home, and all manner of blowback – especially as China pursues its own long war of geopolitical and geoeconomic positioning, both regionally and globally, and, through collaboration with Russia, consolidates its emerging strength in the Eurasian region (Boukalas 2014a; Engdahl 2009; Escobar 2015; Jessop 2011; Li 2008; McNally 2012; Patomäki 2008); and

4 the strengthening of international, transnational, and supranational governmental arrangements and governance regimes that serve the interests of transnational capital and marginalize civil society (Gill 1995, 2011; Overbeek and van Apeldoorn 2012; Stephen 2014).

On this basis, the present future of statehood does not entail the end of the state as a distinctive form of the territorialization of political power, but there will be more complicated forms of multispatial meta-governance organized in the shadow of national and regional states (see chapters 7 and 8). The growing tensions between the logic of differential accumulation, especially in the shadow of neoliberal finance-dominated institutions and strategies at a global scale, and the conflicting, multidimensional, and often zero-sum demands of 'security' will lead to a further erosion of formal democratic institutions and substantive democratic practices – an erosion accompanied by the intensification of tendencies towards authoritarian statism, with a much more decisive turn to militarization and paramilitarization and a greatly enhanced 'super-vision' state.

The various trends that Poulantzas identified in his analysis of authoritarian statism (see chapter 9) have become more marked in response to the growing political crisis in the power bloc, the representational crisis of the political system, the legitimacy and state crises associated with the twin failures of the postwar interventionist state and the neoliberal turn, and the growing challenge to the primacy of the national territorial state in the face of globalization. We should particularly note the continued decline of parliament and rule of law, the growing autonomy of the executive, the increased importance of presidential or prime ministerial powers, the consolidation of authoritarian, plebiscitary parties that largely represent the state to the popular masses, and – something neglected by Poulantzas – the mediatization of politics as the mass media play an increasing role in shaping political imaginaries, programmes, and debates. A stronger emphasis on issues of national security and pre-emptive policing associated with the so-called war on terror at home and abroad has reinforced the attack on human rights and civil liberties.

There will be a further move from national welfare states to more postnational workfare regimes in advanced capitalist states and a reinforcement of current tendencies towards enduring states of austerity (Jessop 2002, 2015c). Stable states at the semi-periphery may develop a tendency towards workfare regimes, in order to respond to the expansion of 'middle-class' consumption and compensate for growing precarity among subaltern classes, including the displaced rural population. There will also be further pressure from transnational capital to safeguard its interests at all levels or scales of government + governance, as the new constitutionalism is rolled out further and there is greater integration of military, police, and cybersecurity apparatuses. Here I must endorse the prescience of Poulantzas's analysis of authoritarian statism and corroborate it with reflections that go beyond the critique of political economy, to include a critique of political ecology. But this is not to concede ground to the TINA mantra of 'there is no alternative'; it is to highlight the fractures and frictions that create the space for alternatives.

Whither State Theory?

I conclude with seven general theses about the state; and then I make some proposals for a future research agenda. These proposals connect some arguments in preceding chapters and bring out the more general implications of an SRA to the state and state power.

First, the state must be analysed both as a complex institutional ensemble, with its own modes of calculation and operational procedures, and as a site of political practices, which seek to deploy its various institutions and capacities for specific purposes. Rather than trying to define the core of the state in a priori terms, we need to explore how its boundaries are established through specific practices within and outside the state. Moreover, in identifying this core, one is claiming neither that this identification exhausts the state nor that this core (let alone the extended state) is a unified, unitary, coherent ensemble or agency. The boundaries of the state and its relative unity as an ensemble or agency would instead be contingent. This indicates a need to examine the various projects and practices that imbue the state with relative institutional unity and facilitate its coherence with the wider society. We often find several rival emergent 'states', which reflect competing state projects that have no overall coherence with the operations of the state system.

Second, considered as an institutional ensemble rather than a real (or fictive) subject, the state does not (and cannot) exercise power. It comprises an ensemble of centres that offer unequal chances to different forces, internal and external, to act for different political purposes. Thus it is not the state that acts: it is always specific sets of politicians and state officials located in specific parts of the state system. Yet political forces do not exist independently of the state: they are shaped in part through its forms of representation, its internal structure, and its forms of intervention. It is the latter that activate specific powers and state capacities inscribed in particular institutions and agencies. We should also explore the various potential structural powers or state capacities (both in the plural) inscribed in the state as an institutional ensemble. Moreover, although the state system does have its own distinctive resources and powers, it also has distinctive liabilities – as well as needs for resources that are produced elsewhere in its environment. How far and in what ways such powers (and any associated liabilities) are realized will depend on the action, reaction, and interaction of specific social forces located both within and beyond this complex ensemble. The realization of state powers depends on structural ties between the state and its encompassing political system, the strategic links among state managers and other political forces, and the complex web of interdependencies and social networks linking the state and the political system to their broader environment. And, as in all cases of social action, there are unacknowledged conditions influencing the success or failure of the exercise of state powers as well as unanticipated consequences that follow from them. In short, state power is a complex social relation that reflects the changing balance of social forces in a determinate conjuncture.

Third, an adequate account of the state can only be developed as part of a theory of society. Its structural powers and capacities cannot be understood by focusing on the state alone – even assuming that one could define its institutional boundaries with precision. This does not mean that the state has no distinctive properties and can therefore be fully derived and explained from other factors and forces: for, once constituted historically and characterized by its own distinctive forms of organization and modes of calculation, the state does acquire a logic of its own. It means instead that, for all its institutional separation and operational autonomy, the state is embedded not only in the broader political system but also in its wider natural and societal environment. The powers of the state, and hence the exercise and impact of state power are always conditional and relational.

Fourth, if the fourth element of a state (in the approach proposed in this book) is the state idea – that is, its mystifying concern with the illusory general interest of a divided society – and if state power concentrates and condenses power relations within society as a whole, the state can only be understood by examining the emergence of projects to promote the general interest and by relating them to the changing balance of forces beyond as well as within the state. However, while the state is the key site of the construction of the 'illusory community' that provides the reference point for the formation of the general will, the political imaginary is always selective and inevitably marginalizes some wills and interests. This is the special field of the critique of ideology.

Fifth, modern societies are so complex and differentiated that no subsystem could be structurally 'determinant in the last instance'; nor could any organization form the apex of a singular hierarchy of command whose rule extends everywhere. There are instead many different subsystems, and even more centres of power. Many of them have developed to an extent that places them beyond direct control by outside forces, the state included. Each is nonetheless involved in complex relations of functional and resource interdependence with other subsystems and is also faced with the problem that it cannot directly control the actions of the other subsystems in its environment. This engenders a paradox in which modern societies reveal both a growing independence and a growing interdependence among their parts.

Sixth, the state is the supreme embodiment of this paradox. On the one hand, it is just one institutional ensemble among others within a social formation; on the other, it is distinctively charged with overall responsibility, in the last instance for managing the interdependence of these other institutional ensembles and for maintaining the cohesion of the formation of which it is a part. As both part and whole of society, it is continually asked by diverse social forces to resolve society's problems and no less continually doomed to generate 'state failure', since many problems lie well beyond its control and may even be aggravated by attempted intervention. However, as one institutional order among others, it can only act through its own institutions, organizations, and procedures. Thus, although the state is empowered to make and enforce collectively binding decisions, its actions in this respect are a specific, selective concentration and condensation of struggles within the overall political system and their success depends on conditions and forces beyond its immediate reach. In this sense, the success of the state depends on its integration into an historical bloc characterized by a non-necessary, socially constituted, and discursively reproduced relative unity. Such an historical bloc would emerge from the evolutionary structural coupling of different institutional orders and from the impact of various strategic projects intended to bring about some measure of correspondence. It could well reflect the primacy of one institutional order that has attained the greatest degree of operational autonomy within the decentred social formation.

Seventh, many differences among state theories are rooted in contrary approaches to various structural and strategic moments of this paradox. Trying to comprehend the overall logic (or, perhaps, 'illogic') of this paradox could yield a productive entry point for resolving some of these differences and for facilitating a more comprehensive analysis of the strategic–relational character of the state in a polycentric social formation. It follows that an adequate theory of the state can only be produced as part of a wider theory of society. This is precisely where we find many of the unresolved problems of state theory.

If we take these general theses seriously, then research on the state should proceed in tandem with more general theoretical and empirical work on the structuration of social relations. Thus, if state theorists continue to define their field of research as the state, this need not suggest that they adopt a reified, fetishistic concept of the state. Instead it could mean that, within the general context of research concerned with the dialectic of structure and strategy, their special field of interest is state power. This would involve research on two main issues. On the one hand, state theorists would focus on the distinctive ways in which the specific institutional and organizational ensemble identified as the state condenses and materializes relations of social power; on the other hand, they would examine how the political imaginary (in which ideas about the state play a crucial orienting role) is articulated, mobilizes social forces around specific projects, and finds expression on the terrain of the state.

Notes

Chapter 1 Introduction

1. Similar philosophical reflections have accompanied the formation of other kinds of state across time–space, not only in Europe but elsewhere.
2. Major studies include the classical accounts of Max Weber (1978), Otto Hintze (1975), and Otto Brunner (1992); and, more recently, Perry Anderson (1974a, 1974b), Ernest Barker (1966), Robert Bonney (1995), Samuel Finer (1997b, 1997c), Heidi Gerstenberger (2008), Michael Mann (1986, 1996), Gianfranco Poggi (1978), James Strayer (1970), and Charles Tilly (1992).
3. Green and Shapiro (1996) provide a useful critique of rational choice approaches.
4. Pluralism is also a distinctive normative tradition in political theory, which I do not discuss here; but see, for example, Connolly 1983, 2005; and Wissenburg 2009.

Chapter 2 The Concept of the State

1. This section derives its title from Abrams (1988), discussed below.
2. Here Abrams actually writes 'concept of the state'. I substituted 'account' for 'concept' to avoid confusion with the concept of the state, as used elsewhere in this text and as analysed in work in conceptual history and historical semantics.
3. Here *state system* refers to the more or less coherent assemblage of institutions and practices that comprises a single state (for Abrams, this

is implicitly a national territorial state) – and not to the *interstate system*.

4. Adjective of ancient Greek origin, derived from 'phantasmagoria' and meaning 'multiple', 'shifting', 'illusory', 'phantom-like'. Some commentaries on Marx's use of this word in connection with commodity fetishism and political illusionism say that 'phantasmagorical' was introduced in the context of an exhibition on optical illusions held in London in 1802 in which spectral technology was used to conjure up ghostly apparitions and make them disappear again.

5. Later in the same text, *Political Theology*, Schmitt writes that 'the sovereign decides whether there is an extreme emergency as well as what must be done to eliminate it' (1985: 7, cited in McCormick 2004: 203n).

6. In addition to references to a relevant translation, where it exists, it is conventional among Gramsci scholars to cite the original notebook (*quaderno* or Q) and section heading (§).

7. The early years of air travel saw analogous disputes over how far sovereignty stretched upwards and outwards above a given state's territory. Different commercial, political, and military interests are reflected in rival definitions of the boundary between air (or atmospheric) space and outer space (Bernhardt 1989). This is still contested, especially with current prospects of commercial travel into outer space (Listner 2012).

8. In contrast, Roma, gypsies, or other travelling communities seek freedom to move and settle temporarily within territory that is already controlled by another state.

9. McNicoll (2003: 731) dates the first use of the word in Great Britain to 1771; the first official population census was approved in 1800.

10. In a recent and provocative book, Jens Bartelson (2013) argues that recognition of sovereignty in interstate relations no longer depends on the ability to defend borders and exercise sovereign authority *inside* the state, but now hinges on whether that power is exercised responsibly, in line with the norms and values of an imagined international community.

11. In the former case, this may be due to a *coup d'état* or foreign invasion; in the latter, to denial of the incumbent government's legitimacy and/or a plan to overthrow it.

12. A consociational federation is 'a nonterritorial federation in which the polity is divided into "permanent" transgenerational religious, cultural, ethnic or ideological groupings known as "camps", "sectors", or "pillars" federated together and jointly governed by coalitions of the leaders of each' (Elazar 1991: xiv; cf. Lijphart 1969).

13. Finer proposed another typology, with a much broader historical sweep, based on the presence or absence of a centralized and standardized administration and of a homogenized culture, language, and law (1997a: 13).

14. In the latter case it gives rise to 'methodological nationalism'.

15. Normal and exceptional are relative to a given type of state: in the capitalist type of state, normality is equated with democratic republic forms (see chapter 7).

Chapter 3 The State as a Social Relation

1. The concepts of representational crisis, crisis of hegemony, and organic crisis derive from Gramsci (1971); 'rationality crisis' and 'legitimacy crisis' from Habermas (1976); and institutional crisis from Poulantzas (1974, 1979).
2. The common usage derives from Edmund Burke's alleged 1787 description, reported in Carlyle (1908), of the role of the press as a check on clergy, aristocracy, and House of Commons.
3. See, respectively, Taylor (1978), Dutton (2009), and Allegri and Ciccarelli (2014).
4. Max Weber drew this distinction in order to classify the motives and calculus guiding social action. The calculation of material interests was instrumental, oriented to relative costs and benefits, and concerned with outcomes; action oriented to ideal interests was unconditional and involved values 'determined by a conscious belief in the value for its own sake of some ethical, aesthetic, religious, or other form of behaviour, independently of its prospects of success' (Weber 1978: 24–25). Weber also discussed in this work traditional action (based on custom) and affectual action (motivated by feelings). Tradition can be a source of legitimate authority (*Herrschaft*); and affectual action can be related to charisma or feelings of, say, revenge (US foreign policy after 9/11 might fit in here).
5. *Raison d'état* as used here is starkly different from its usage in Cerny's conceptual couplet *raison d'état* vs *raison du monde*. For Cerny, the former refers to a more nation-state-centred government rationality, the latter to a more transnational, neopluralist governmentality oriented to a still emerging world-political superstructure (see Cerny 2010: passim and esp. 27, 157, 175, 244, 269, 297, 306).
6. The term comes from the Latin *camera*, 'vault', which has produced the German *Kammer*, 'treasury'.
7. The rise of a rational bureaucracy and territorial integration, modern communication systems, and mass education boost infrastructural power; and industrialized warfare may motivate efforts at social inclusion (or promises thereof) in order to compensate for wartime sacrifices.
8. The term comes from Gramsci (1971: 252 = Q14, §74: 1743) and parallels the idea of 'black markets'.
9. Republican parties in the United States have been busy using vote suppression techniques in recent years, exploiting the Supreme Court decision in Citizens United *v* Federal Election Commission (558 US 310)

(2010), establishing 'independent' political organizations to raise and spend funds, and hiding the extent of their coordination with the official campaigns of their candidates.

10. The *Parteienstaat*, as a state form in postwar advanced capitalism, was more common in postfascist and postauthoritarian democracies (Germany, Austria, Italy, and Greece) with a strong state tradition and politicized bureaucracies (Leibholz 1966; von Beyme 1993).

11. These 'imperatives' are discursively constructed (in part through parties), but also have material foundations. They are linked to accumulation strategies, state projects, and hegemonic visions and, if they prove organic, they help to consolidate a power bloc and to transform and consolidate a historical bloc (Gramsci 1971: 366–7 = Q 10 II, §6).

12. A recent counterexample was Obama's first presidential campaign; but this proved short-lived, as his administration reverted to type and money became even more important in shaping campaigns.

13. This is a neologism coined by Andrew Dunsire (1990: 4; see also Dunsire 1993 and 1996). Although Dunsire does not explain its etymology, this is clearly a compound derived from the Latin *libra* (balance) with the preposition *cum* (with) and it indicates, for him, manipulating the balance among a plurality of objects, processes, or relations. We might add that the difference between equilibrate and collibrate is that equilibration tends to involve two things being balanced (e.g., scales), whereas collibration is the judicious balancing of several forces. Dunsire explains it as follows: 'Collibration or co-libration is a neologism to describe divide and rule, loading the scales, rigging the market, fiddling the books, levelling the playing field, moving the goalposts, and so on. All signify disturbing a balance, or helping to establish a balance, or shifting a point of balance' (1996: 318–19). Thus collibration uses built-in checks and balances based on separate institutional or organizational expressions of binary oppositions to tip the balance (1996: 320–1). In an earlier article Dunsire wrote:

> The essence of collibration as a tool of governance is to identify, in any area of interest, what antagonistic forces already operate, judge whether the point at which isostasy [equilibrium produced by equal pressures, tensions, or suctions] is occurring is consonant with public policy, and then intervene if necessary not by 'calling in' the matter for central decision, or committing oneself to laying down a standard or prohibition, but by altering the balance in favour of the side or interest which needs a degree of support. (Dunsire 1990: 17)

In other words, it modifies the relations among different checks and balances in a system that expresses different sides of an opposition, antagonism, or contradiction (Dunsire 1996: 320–1; cf. Jessop 2013). A similar idea is proposed by Pierre Bourdieu when he suggests that the state, as 'the central bank of symbolic capital' as well as of other kinds of capital (in his sense of the term), is the centre of 'meta-capital' – that is, modifies the relations among different kinds of capital (e.g., economic, symbolic, cultural, informational, political) to maintain the public interest and/or to preserve its own interests (Bourdieu 2014: 197, 222–3, 345–6). Collibration is not a purely technical or technocratic process but, like other aspects of state power, involves efforts to secure or rework a wider 'unstable equilibrium of compromise' organized around specific objects, techniques, and subjects of government or governance. For further discussion, see chapters 3, 6, and 8.

14. See, notably, the novel *Sybil, a Tale of Two Nations* by Benjamin Disraeli, future British prime minister at the time. The novel was published in 1845, the same year as Engels's *The Condition of the Working Class in England*. Disraeli proposed a paternalistic integration of the working class into the social and political order.

15. Where state managers internalize this juridical convention and it becomes an essential part of their own identity and orientation, one might talk of the state as a collective subject.

Chapter 4   Power, Interests, Domination, State Effects

1. Aspects of lived experience include relationality (lived relation to others), corporeality (lived body), spatiality (lived space), and temporality (lived time). Some might add spirituality (lived relation to the spirit world through internal conversations with imagined others; see, e.g., Archer 2003).

Chapter 5   The State and Space–Time

1. Stasavage (2011) explores the coevolution of representative assemblies and public borrowing in Europe in the medieval and early modern eras. Active forms of political representation allowed certain European states to gain early and advantageous access to credit, but this depended on a compact geography and a strong mercantile presence. Active representative assemblies in small states – assemblies dominated by mercantile groups that made loans to governments – were more likely to preserve access to credit. Thus smaller European city-states such as Genoa and Cologne had an advantage over larger territorial states like France and Castile, because mercantile elites organized political institutions to effectively monitor public credit. However, while this state of affairs benefited city-states in need of finance, Stasavage argues that its long-run effects were more ambiguous. City-states with the best access to credit often had the most closed and oligarchic systems of representation; this discouraged economic innovations and eventually led to the transformation of these states into rentier republics.

2. Even cyberspace needs a terrestrial infrastructure, is increasingly subject to territorial parcellization or extraterritorial control, and operates more or less intensively and densely in place, scale, and networks.

3. Fordism, understood as mass production, has not disappeared: it has been 'offshored' or 'outsourced', initially to peripheral Fordist economies in North America and Southern Europe, later to Latin America, East Asia, and postsocialist Europe.

Chapter 6   State and Nation

1. For the sake of clarity and at the risk of repetition, the territory should comprise more than one city and its hinterland.
2. Martial rape is a weapon against ethnic and cultural nations, destroying families and cultures.

Chapter 7   Government + Governance in the Shadow of Hierarchy

1. On the concept of *Bund* (plural *Bünde*), see Herman Schmalenbach (1922).

Chapter 8   The World Market and the World of States

1. Hartmut Rosa distinguishes technological acceleration, social acceleration grounded in functional differentiation and specialization, and the increasing pace of life and perceived scarcity of time (Rosa 2013). This typology misses the influence of the spatiotemporal logic of differential accumulation, which shapes technological innovation and its wider social impact (e.g., Castree 2009).

Chapter 9   Liberal Democracy, Exceptional States, and the New Normal

1. Lenin used this phrase in his 1917 brochure *State and Revolution*. Thus 'the bourgeois democratic republic is the best possible political shell for capital and, once it has gained possession of this shell, capital establishes its power so securely that no change of persons, institutions, or parties can shake it' (Lenin 1972: 393).
2. This is how Swedberg (1998) translates Weber's description of one of his subtypes of political capitalism: the corresponding German is *außerordentliche Lieferungen politischer Verbände*.
3. For the moment I leave aside predatory capitalism associated with the conduct of 'wars', whether true wars of conquest or colonization or metaphorical but profitable 'wars' on drugs, terror, and so on.

4. Writing in 1942, in response to Schmitt, Walter Benjamin noted that the 'state of exception' has become the norm; Giorgio Agamben would later add that, in the new millennium, it has become permanent (Agamben 2005: 1–32).

5. In this sense, states retain their formal sovereignty to introduce legislation or modify regulations; but they risk large financial penalties that might well lead government to think twice before proceeding.

6. US authorities use 'enduring' to avoid the word 'permanent' when describing military occupations and bases in the Middle East and elsewhere. Likewise, while one cannot know whether the politics of austerity will be permanent, it is certainly intended to endure for an indefinite period and as long as deemed necessary by US authorities.

References

All urls have been last accessed on 22 May, 2015.

Abrams, P. (1988). Notes on the difficulty of studying the state. *Journal of Historical Sociology* 1(1): 58–89.

Adams, B. and Groves, C. (2007). *Future Matters: Action, Knowledge, Ethics*. Brill: Leiden.

Adler, P. S. (2001). Market, hierarchy, and trust: The knowledge economy and the future of capitalism. *Organization Studies* 12(2): 215–34.

Agamben, G. (2005). *State of Exception*. University of Chicago Press: Chicago.

Agnew, J. and Corbridge, S. (1995). *Mastering Space*. Routledge: London.

Albert, M. (2005). Politik der Weltgesellschaft und Politk der Globalisierung: Überlegungen zur Emergenz von Weltstaatlichkeit. In B. Heintz, R. Münch, and T. Hartmann (eds) *Weltgesellschaft: Theoretische Zugänge und empirische Problemlagen. Zeitschrift für Soziologie Sonderheft* 34: 223–39.

Albert, M. and Brock, L. (1996). De-bordering the state: New spaces in international relations. *New Political Science* 35: 69–107.

Albo, G. and Fanelli, C. (2014). Austerity against democracy: An authoritarian phase of neoliberalism? Socialist Project Canada. At www.socialistproject.ca/documents/AusterityAgainstDemocracy.pdf

Ali, T. (2002). *The Clash of Fundamentalisms: Crusades, Jihads, and Modernity*. Verso: London.

Allegri, G. and Ciccarelli, R. (2014). What is the fifth estate? *OpenDemocracy*, 24 February. At https://www.opendemocracy.net/can-europe-make-it/giuseppe-allegri-roberto-ciccarelli/what-is-fifth-estate

Almond, G. (1960). Introduction: A functional approach to political systems. In G. Almond and J. S. Coleman (eds), *The Politics of Developing Areas*. Princeton University Press: Princeton, pp. 3–64.

ALTER-EU [Alliance for Lobbying Transparency and Ethics Regulation in the EU] (2010). *Bursting the Brussels Bubble: The Battle to Expose Corporate Lobbying at the Heart of the EU*. ALTER-EU, Brussels. At http:// www.alter-eu.org/sites/default/files/documents/bursting-the-brussels -bubble.pdf

Althusser, L. (1971) [1969]. Ideology and ideological state apparatuses (notes towards an investigation). In idem, *Lenin and Philosophy and Other Essays*. New Left Books: London, pp. 127–86.

Althusser, L. (2006). *Philosophy of the Encounter: Later Writings 1978–87*. Verso: London.

Altvater, E. (1994). Operationsfeld Weltmarkt, oder Die Transformation des souveränen Nationalstaats in den nationalen Wettbewerbsstaat. *Prokla* 24(4): 517–47.

Amable, B. (2009). Structural reforms in Europe and the (in)coherence of institutions. *Oxford Review of Economic Policy* 25(1): 17–39.

Amin-Khan, T. (2012). *The Post-Colonial State in the Era of Capitalist Globalization: Historical, Political and Theoretical Approaches to State Formation*. Routledge: London.

Amitai-Preiss, R. and Morgan, D. O. (2000). *The Mongol Empire and Its Legacy*. Brill: Leiden.

Anderson, B. (1981). *The Imagined Community*. New Left Books: London.

Anderson, J. (1996). The shifting stage of politics: New mediaeval and postmodern territorialities. *Environment and Planning D: Society and Space*, 14: 133–53.

Anderson, P. (1974a). *Lineages of the Absolutist State*. New Left Books: London.

Anderson, P. (1974b). *Passages from Antiquity to Feudalism*. New Left Books: London.

Anderson, P. (1976). *Considerations on Western Marxism*. New Left Books: London.

Andreski, S. (1968). *Military Organization and Society*. Routledge and Kegan Paul: London.

Ansell, C. (2000). The networked polity: Regional development in Western Europe. *Governance* 13(2): 303–33.

Anter, A. and Breuer, S. (eds) (2007). *Max Webers Staatssoziologie: Positionen und Perspektiven*. Nomos: Baden-Baden.

Anthias, F. and Yuval-Davis, N. (eds) (1989). *Woman–Nation–State*. Macmillan: Basingstoke, UK.

Archer, M. S. (2003). *Structure, Agency and the Internal Conversation*. Cambridge University Press: Cambridge.

Arendt, H. (1956). Authority in the twentieth century. *Review of Politics* 18(4): 403–17.

Arrighi, G. (1994). *The Long Twentieth Century: Money, Power and the Origins of Our Times*. Verso: London.

Axtmann, R. (2004). The state of the state: The model of the modern state and its contemporary transformation. *International Political Science Review* 25(3): 259–79.

Badie, B. and Birnbaum, P. (1983). *The Sociology of the State*. University of Chicago Press: Chicago.

Badiou, A. (2005). A speculative disquisition on the concept of democracy. In idem, *Metapolitics*. Verso: London, pp. 78–95.

Bagehot, W. (1963) [1867]. *The English Constitution*. Fontana: London.

Balasopoulos, A. (2012). Introduction: Intellectuals and the state: Complicities, confrontations, ruptures. *Occasion: Interdisciplinary Studies in the Humanities* 3(1): 1–34.

Balibar, E. (1990). The nation form: History and ideology. *Review: Fernand Braudel Center* 13(2): 329–61.

Barak, G. (1991). *Crimes by the Capitalist State: An Introduction to State Criminality*. SUNY Press: New York.

Barber, B. (1995). *Jihad vs McWorld: Terrorism's Challenge to Democracy*. Random House: New York.

Barfield, T. J. (2001). The shadow empires: Imperial state formation along the Chinese–Nomad frontier. In C. M. Sinopoli and T. N. D'Altroy (eds), *Empires: Perspectives from Archaeology and History*. Cambridge University Press: Cambridge, pp. 8–41.

Barkan, J. (2011). Law and the geographic analysis of economic globalization. *Progress in Human Geography* 35(5): 589–607.

Barker, E. (1966). *The Development of Public Services in Western Europe 1660–1930*. Archon Books: Hamden, CT.

Barrow, C. W. (1993). *Critical Theories of the State: Marxist, neo-Marxist, post-Marxist*. University of Wisconsin Press: Madison.

Barry, A. (2002). The anti-political economy. *Economy and Society* 31(2): 268–84.

Barry, B. (1965). *Political Argument*. Routledge and Kegan Paul: London.

Bartelson, J. (1995). *A Genealogy of Sovereignty*. Cambridge University Press: Cambridge.

Bartelson, J. (2001). *Critique of the State*. Cambridge University Press: Cambridge.

Bartelson, J. (2013). *Sovereignty as Symbolic Form*. Routledge: London.

Bashford, A. (2006). Global biopolitics and the history of world health. *History of the Human Sciences* 19(1): 67–88.

Bayart, P., Ellis, S., and Hibou, B. (eds) (2009). *The Criminalization of the State in Africa*. Indiana University Press: Bloomington.

Beaulac, S. (2004). The Westphalian model in defining international law: Challenging the myth. *Australian Journal of Legal History* 8(2): 181–213.

Beck, U. (2005). *Power in the Global Age*. Polity: Cambridge.

Beck, U. and Grande, E. (2007). *Cosmopolitan Europe: Paths to Second Modernity*. Polity: Cambridge.

Beer, S. (1990). Recursion zero: Metamanagement. *Systems Practice* 3(3): 315–26.

Béland, D. and Cox, R. H. (eds) (2011). *Ideas and Politics in Social Science Research*. Oxford University Press: Oxford.

Bell, S. and Hindmoor, A. (2009). *Rethinking Governance: The Theory of the State in Modern Society*. Cambridge University Press: Cambridge.

Bentham, J. (1970). [1789]. *Introduction to the Principles of Morals and Legislation*. Clarendon: Oxford.

Bentley, A. F. (1908). *The Process of Government: A Study of Social Pressures*. University of Chicago Press: Chicago.

Bernhardt, R. (ed.) (1989). *Encyclopedia of Public International Law*, vol. 11: *Law of the Sea, Air and Space*. Elsevier: Amsterdam.

Bevir, M., (ed.) (2007). *Encyclopedia of Governance*. SAGE: London.

Bevir, M. (2010). *Democratic Governance*. Princeton University Press: Princeton, NJ.

Biggs, M. (1999). Putting the state on the map: Cartography, territory, and European state formation. *Comparative Studies in Society and History* 41(2): 374–405.

Biller, P. (2000). *The Measure of Multitude: Population in Medieval Thought*. Oxford University Press: Oxford.

Bloch, E. (1986a). *The Principle of Hope*, vol. 1. Blackwell: Oxford.

Bloch, E. (1986b). *The Principle of Hope*, vol. 2. Blackwell: Oxford.

Blockmans, W. P. (1978). A typology of representative institutions in late medieval Europe. *Journal of Medieval History* 4(2): 189–215.

Blockmans, W. P. (1996). The growth of nations and states in Europe before 1800. *European Review* 4(3): 241–51.

Blok, A. (1975). *The Mafia of a Sicilian Village 1860–1960: A Study of Violent Peasant Entrepreneurs*. Harper Torch: New York.

Blum, W. (2001). *Rogue State: A Guide to the World's Only Superpower*. Zed: London.

Blyth, M. and Katz, R. S. (2005). From catch-all politics to cartelisation: The political economy of the cartel party. *West European Politics* 28(1): 33–60.

Börzel, T. and Risse, T. (2010). Governance without a state: Can it work? *Regulation and Governance* 4(2): 113–34.

Boldt, H., Conze, W., Haverkate, G., Klippel, D., and Koselleck, R. (1992). Staat und *Souveränität*. In O. Brunner, W. Conze, and R. Koselleck (eds), *Geschichtliche Grundbegriffe Historisches Lexicon zur Politisch-Sozialen Sprache in Deutschland*, vol. 6. Klett-Colta: Stuttgart, pp. 1–154.

Bonney, R. (1995). *Economic Systems and State Finance: The Origins of the Modern State in Europe, 13th to 18th Centuries*. Oxford University Press: Oxford.

Boukalas, C. (2014a). *Homeland Security, Its Law and Its State: A Design of Power for the 21st Century*. Routledge: London.

Boukalas, C. (2014b). No exceptions: Authoritarian statism: Agamben, Poulantzas and homeland security. *Critical Studies on Terrorism* 7(1): 112–30.

Bourdieu, P. (1994). Rethinking the state: Genesis and structure of the bureaucratic field. *Sociological Theory* 12(1): 1–18.

Bourdieu, P. (2014). *On the State: Lectures at the Collège de France, 1989–1992*. Polity: Cambridge.

Bratsis, P. (2003). The construction of corruption, or rules of separation and illusions of purity. *Social Text* 21: 1–33.

Bratsis, P. (2006). *Everyday Life and the State*. Anthem: London.

Braudel, F. (1975). *Capitalism and Material Life: 1400–1800*. Harper Colophon: New York.

Brennan, J. (2007). Dominating nature. *Environmental Values* 16(4), 513–28.

Brenner, N. (2004). *New State Spaces: Urban Restructuring and State Rescaling in Western Europe*. Oxford University Press: Oxford.

Bretthauer, L., Gallas, A., Kannankulam, J., and Stolty, I. (eds) (2011). *Reading Poulantzas*. Merlin: London.

Breuer, S. (2014). *Der charismatische Staat: Ursprünge und Frühformen staatlicher Herrschaft*. WBG: Darmstadt.

Brown, W. (1992). Finding the man in the state. *Feminist Studies* 18: 7–34.

Brubaker, R. (1992). *Citizenship and Nationhood in France and Germany*. Harvard University Press: Cambridge, MA.

Bruff, I. (2013). The rise of authoritarian neoliberalism. *Rethinking Marxism* 26(1): 113–29.

Brunner, O. (1992). *Land and Lordship: Structures of Governance in Medieval Austria*. University of Pennsylvania Press: Philadelphia.

Bruyneel, K. (2007). *The Third Space of Sovereignty: The Postcolonial Politics of US–Indigenous Relations*. University of Minnesota Press: Minneapolis.

Burkett, P. (1999). *Marx and Nature: A Red and Green Perspective*. St Martin's Press: New York.

Bussolini, J. (2010). What is a dispositive? *Foucault Studies* 10: 85–107.

Calhoun, C. (1995). *Critical Social Theory: Culture, History, and the Challenge of Difference*. Blackwell: Oxford.

Callinicos, A. (2009). *Imperialism and Global Political Economy*. Polity: Cambridge.

Campbell, B. B. and Brenner, A. D. (eds) (2000). *Death Squads in Global Perspective*. Palgrave Macmillan: Basingstoke, UK.

Canak, W. L. (1984). The peripheral state debate: State capitalist and bureaucratic authoritarian regimes in Latin America. *Latin American Research Review* 19(1): 3–36.

Canovan, M. (2004). The leader and the masses: Hannah Arendt on totalitarianism and dictatorship. In P. Baehr and M. Richter (eds), *Dictatorship in History and Theory: Bonapartism, Caesarism, and Totalitarianism*. Cambridge University Press: Cambridge, pp. 241–60.

Canovan, M. (2005). *The People*. Polity: Cambridge.

Canovan, M. (2008). The people. In J. S. Dryzek, B. Honig, and A. Phillips (eds), *The Oxford Handbook of Political Theory*. Oxford University Press: New York, pp. 349–62.

Carlyle, T. (1908) [1840]. *On Heroes and Hero Worship*. James Fraser: London.

Carneiro, R. L. (1981). The chiefdom: Precursor of the state. In G. Jones and R. Kautz (eds), *The Transition to Statehood in the New World*. Cambridge University Press: Cambridge, pp. 33–79.

Carroll, W. K. (2010). *The Making of a Transnational Capitalist Class: Corporate Power in the 21st Century*. Zed: London.

Castells, M. (1992). Four Asian tigers with a dragon head. In J. Henderson and R. P. Appelbaum (eds), *States and Development in the Pacific Rim*. SAGE: London, pp. 33–70.

Castree, N. (2009). The spatio-temporality of capitalism. *Time & Society* 18(1): 26–61.

CEO [Corporate European Observatory] (2004). *Lobby Planet Brussels: The EU Quarter*. CEO: Brussels.

CEO [Corporate European Observatory] (2011). *Lobby Planet Brussels: The EU Quarter*, 2nd edn. CEO: Brussels.

Cerny, P. G. (1997). Paradoxes of the competition state: The dynamics of political globalization. *Government and Opposition* 32(2): 251–74.

Cerny, P. G. (2010). *Rethinking World Politics: A Theory of Transnational Neopluralism*. Oxford University Press: Oxford.

Chang, D. O. (2009). *Capitalist Development in Korea: Labour, Capital and the Myth of the Developmental State*. Routledge: London.

Chang, H. J. (2007). *The East Asian Development Experience: The Miracle, the Crisis and the Future*. Zed: London.

Chase-Dunn, C. and Lawrence, K. S. (2011a). The next three futures. Part I: Looming crises of global inequality, ecological degradation, and a failed system of global governance. *Global Society* 25(2): 137–53.

Chase-Dunn, C. and Lawrence, K. S. (2011b). The next three futures. Part II: Possibilities of another round of US hegemony, global collapse, or global democracy. *Global Society* 25(3): 269–85.

Chibber, V. (2003). *Locked in Place: State-Building and Late Industrialization in India*. Princeton University Press: Princeton, NJ.

Chilcote, R., Hadjiyannis, S., López, F. A. III, Nataf, D., and Sammis, E. (1990). *Transition from Democracy to Dictatorship: Comparative Studies of Spain, Portugal and Greece*. Taylor & Francis: New York.

Chomsky, N. (2001). *Rogue States: The Rule of Force in World Affairs*. Pluto: London.

Chomsky, N. (2012). *Occupy*. Penguin: Harmondsworth, UK.

Cioran, E. M. (1975) [1949]. *A Short History of Decay*. Arcade: New York.

Claessen, H. J. M. and Skalnik, P. (1978). The early state: Theories and hypotheses. In eidem (eds), *The Early State*. Mouton: The Hague, pp. 3–29.

Clark, C. and Lemco, J. (1988): The strong state and development: A growing list of caveats. *Journal of Developing Societies* 4(1): 1–8.

Clark, J. and Jones, A. (2012). After 'the collapse': Strategic selectivity, Icelandic state elites and the management of European Union accession. *Political Geography* 31: 64–72.

Clarke, S. (1977). Marxism, sociology, and Poulantzas's theory of the state. *Capital & Class* 2: 1–31.

Coleman, J. (1990). *Foundations of Social Theory*. Belknap Press: Cambridge, MA.

Collinge, C. (1999). Self-organization of society by scale: A spatial reworking of regulation theory. *Environment and Planning D: Society and Space* 17(5): 557–74.

Connolly, W. E. (ed.) (1969). *Pluralism in Political Analysis*. Atherton: New York.

Connolly, W. E. (1983). *The Terms of Political Discourse*, 2nd edn. Princeton University Press: Princeton.

Connolly, W. E. (2005). *Pluralism*. Duke University Press: Durham, NC.

Cook, T. E. (2005). *Governing with the News: The News Media as a Political Institution*, 2nd edn. University of Chicago Press: Chicago.

Costa, O. and Magnette, P. (2003). The European Union as a consociation? A methodological assessment. *West European Politics* 26(3): 1–18.

Coulson, A. (1997). Transaction cost economics and its implications for local governance. *Local Government Studies* 23(1): 107–13.

Cox, L. and Nilsen, A. G. (2014). *We Make Our Own History: Marxism and Social Movements in the Twilight of Neoliberalism*. Pluto: London.

Cronin, D. (2013). *Corporate Europe: How Big Business Sets Policies on Food, Climate and War*. Pluto: London.

Crouch, C. (2004). *Post-Democracy*. Polity: Cambridge.

Crouch, C. (2005). *Capitalist Diversity and Change: Recombinant Governance and Institutional Entrepreneurs*. Oxford University Press: Oxford.

Crozier, M. J., Huntington, S. P., and Watanuki, J. (1975). *The Crisis of Democracy: Report on the Governability of Democracies to the Trilateral Commission*. New York University Press: New York.

Crutzen, P. J. (2006). The 'Anthropocene'. In E. Ehlers and T. Krafft (eds), *Earth System Science in the Anthropocene*. Springer: Berlin and Heidelberg, pp. 13–18.

Curtis, B. (2002). Foucault on governmentality and population: The impossible discovery. *Canadian Journal of Sociology* 27(4): 505–33.

Dalton, R. J. and Kuechler, M. (1990). *Challenging the Political Order: New Social and Political Movements in Western Democracies*. Polity: Cambridge.

Davies, J. S. (2011). *Challenging Governance Theory: From Networks to Hegemony*. Policy: Bristol.

de Vattel, E. (1758). *Le Droit des gens, ou Principes de la loie naturelle, appliqués à la conduite et aux affaires des nations et des souverains*, 2 vols. London.

Dean, M. (1990). *The Constitution of Poverty: Towards a Genealogy of Liberal Governance*. Routledge: London.

Delaney, D. (2005). *Territory: A Short Introduction*. Blackwell: Oxford.

Delanty, G. and Krishan, K. (eds) (2005). *Handbook of Nations and Nationalism*. SAGE: London.

Deleuze, G. and Guattari, F. (1983) [1972]. *Anti-Oedipus: Capitalism and Schizophrenia*. University of Minnesota Press: Minneapolis.

Demirović, A. and Sablowski, T. (2013). *The Finance-Dominated Regime of Accumulation and the Crisis in Europe*. Rosa Luxemburg Stiftung: Berlin.

Dierkes, M., Antal, A. B., Child, J., and Nonaka, I., (eds) (2001). *Handbook of Organizational Learning and Knowledge*. Oxford University Press: Oxford.

Disraeli, B. (1845). *Sybil, or a Tale of Two Nations*. At http://www.gutenberg.org/files/3760/3760-h/3760-h.htm

Dobel, J. P. (1978). The corruption of a state. *American Political Science Review* 72(3): 958–73.

Dodgshon, R. A. (1987). *The European Past: Social Evolution and Spatial Order*. Macmillan: London.

Dodgshon, R. A. (1998). *Society in Time and Space: A Geographical Perspective on Change*. Cambridge University Press: Cambridge.

Doehring, K. (2004). *Allgemeine Staatslehre: Eine systematische Darstellung*, 3rd edn. C. F. Müller: Heidelberg.

Domhoff, G. W. (2013). *Who Rules America? The Triumph of the Corporate Rich*, 7th edn. New York: McGraw-Hill.

Drori, G. S., Meyer, J. W., and Hwang, H. (eds) (2006). *Globalization and Organization: World Society and Organizational Change*. Clarendon: Oxford.

Dubiel, H. and A. Söllner (eds) (1981). *Wirtschaft, Recht und Staat im Nationalsozialismus: Analysen des Instituts für Sozialforschung, 1939–1942*. Suhrkamp: Frankfurt.

Dunsire, A. (1990). Holistic governance. *Public Policy and Administration* 5(4): 4–19.

Dunsire, A. (1993). Manipulating social tensions: Collibration as an alternative mode of government intervention. MPFIfG Discussion Paper 93/7. Max Planck Institut für Gesellschaftsforschung, Köln.

Dunsire, A. (1996). Tipping the balance: Autopoiesis and governance. *Administration & Society* 28(3): 299–334.

Dutton, W. H. (2009). The fifth estate emerging through the network of networks. *Prometheus* 27(1): 1–15.

Duverger, M. (1954). *Political Parties: Their Organization and Activity in the Modern State*. Methuen: London.

Dyson, K. F. H. (1982). *The State Tradition in Western Europe*. Martin Robertson: Oxford.

Earle, T. K. (1997). *How Chiefs Come to Power*. Stanford University Press: Stanford.

Easton, D. (1965). *A Systems Analysis of Political Life*. Wiley: New York.

Ebenau, M. (2012). Varieties of capitalism or dependency? A critique of the VoC approach for Latin America. *Competition & Change* 16(3): 206–23.

Eder, K. (1999). Societies learn and yet the world is hard to change. *European Journal of Social Theory* 2(2): 195–215.

Eisenstadt, S. N. (1963). *The Political Systems of Empires: The Rise and Fall of Bureaucratic Societies*. Free Press: New York.

Elazar, D. J. (1991). Introduction: Federalist responses to current democratic revolutions. In idem (ed.), *Federal Systems of the World: A Handbook of Federal, Confederal and Autonomy Arrangements*. Longman: Harlow, UK, pp. i–xxi.

Elden, S. (2007). Governmentality, calculation, territory. *Environment and Planning D: Society and Space* 25(3): 562–80.

Elden, S. (2010). Land, terrain, territory. *Progress in Human Geography* 36(6): 799–817.

Elfferding, W. (1983). Klassenpartei und Hegemonie. Zur impliziten Parteientheorie des Marxismus. In W. Elfferding, M. Jäger, and T. Scheffler, *Marxismus und Theorie der Parteien*. Argument Verlag: Berlin, pp. 7–35.

Elfferding, W. (1985). Zur Perspektive materialistischer Parteitheorie. *Prokla* 59: 142–51.

Elias, N. (1982) [1939]. *The Civilizing Process: State Formation and Civilization*. Blackwell: Oxford.

Elias, N. (1983) [1939]. *The Court Society*. Blackwell: Oxford.

Elsner, W. (2012). Financial capitalism – at odds with democracy: The trap of an 'impossible' profit rate. *Real-World Economics Review* 62: 132–59. http://www.paecon.net/PAEReview/issue62/Elsner62.pdf

Elster, J. (1982). The case for methodological individualism. *Theory and Society* 11(4): 453–82.

Engdahl, F. W. (2009). *Full Spectrum Dominance: Totalitarian Democracy in the New World Order*. Edition Engdahl: Wiesbaden.

Engelhardt, T. (2014). *Shadow Government: Surveillance, Secret Wars, and a Global Security State in a Single Superpower World*. Haymarket Books: Chicago.

Engels, F. (1972) [1875]. *The Origins of the Family, Private Property, and the State*. Lawrence & Wishart: London.

Escobar, P. (2015). Westward Ho on China's Eurasia BRIC road: The new Chinese dream. *Counterpunch*, 24 March.

Escolar, M. (1997). Exploration, cartography and the modernization of state power. *International Social Science Journal* 151: 55–75.

Esposito, E. (2011). *The Future of Futures: The Time of Money in Financing and Society*. Edward Elgar: Cheltenham, UK.

Esser, F. and Strömback, J. (eds) (2014). *Mediatization of Politics: Understanding the Transformation of Western Democracies*. Palgrave Macmillan: Basingstoke, UK.

Estulin, D. (2007). *The True Story of the Bilderberg Group*. TrineDay: Walterville, OR.

Evans, P. B. (1989). Predatory, developmental, and other apparatuses: A comparative political economy perspective on the Third World State. *Sociological Forum* 4(4): 561–87.

Evans, P. B. (1995). *Embedded Autonomy: States and Industrial Transformation*. Princeton University Press: Princeton, NJ.

Evans, P. B. (1997). The eclipse of the state? Reflections on stateness in an era of globalization. *World Politics* 50(1): 62–87.

Evans, P. B. (2011). Constructing the 21st century developmental state. In O. Edigheji (ed.), *Constructing a Democratic Developmental State in South Africa: Potentials and Challenges*. Human Sciences Research Council: Cape Town, pp. 37–58.

Evans, P. B., Rueschemeyer, D., and Skocpol, T. (eds) (1985). *Bringing the State Back In*. Cambridge University Press: Cambridge.

Falkner, G. (2005). *Complying with Europe: EU Harmonisation and Soft Law in the Member States*. Cambridge University Press: Cambridge.

Ferejohn, J. and Pasquino, P. (2004). The law of exception: A typology of emergency powers. *International Journal of Constitutional Law* 210: 333–48.

Ferguson, N. (2004). *Colossus: The Price of America's Empire*. Penguin: New York.

Ferguson, T. (1995). *Golden Rule: The Investment Theory of Party Competition and the Logic of Money-Driven Political Systems*. University of Chicago Press: Chicago.

Ferguson, Y. H. and Mansbach, R. W. (1989). *The State, Conceptual Chaos, and the Future of International Relations Theory*. Lynne Rienner: London.

Ferrera, M. (2008). The European welfare state: Golden achievements, silver prospects. *West European Politics* 31(1–2): 82–107.

Fine, R. (2007). *Cosmopolitanism*. Routledge: London.

Finer, S. E. (1975). State and nation-building in Europe: The role of the military. In C. Tilly (ed.), *The Formation of National States in Western Europe*. Princeton University Press: Princeton, pp. 84–163.

Finer, S. E. (1997a). *The History of Government*, vol. 1: *Ancient Monarchies and Empires*. Oxford University Press: Oxford.

Finer, S. E. (1997b). *The History of Government*, vol. 2: *The Intermediate Ages*. Oxford University Press: Oxford.

Finer, S. E. (1997c). *The History of Government*, vol. 3: *Empires, Monarchies and the Modern State*. Oxford University Press: Oxford.

Fischer, F. (2009). *Democracy and Expertise: Reorienting Policy Inquiry*. Oxford University Press: Oxford.

Flannery, K. V. (1972). The cultural evolution of civilization. *Annual Review of Ecological Systems* 3: 399–426.

Flannery, K. V. (1999). Process and agency in early state formation. *Cambridge Archaeological Journal* 9(1): 3–21.

Foisneau, L. (2010). Governing a republic: Rousseau's general will and the problem of government. *Republics of Letters* 2(1), 93–104.

Foucault, M. (1977) [1975]. *Discipline and Punish*. Allen Lane: London.

Foucault, M. (1980). *Power/Knowledge: Selected Interviews and Other Writings 1972–1977*. Pantheon: New York.

Foucault, M. (1981) [1976]. *The History of Sexuality*, vol 1. Penguin: Harmondsworth, UK.

Foucault, M. (2007). *Security, Territory, Population: Lectures at the Collège de France, 1977–1978*. Palgrave: Basingstoke, UK.

Foucault, M. (2008). *The Birth of Biopolitics: Lectures at the Collège de France, 1978–1979*. Palgrave: Basingstoke, UK.

Fraenkel, E. (1941). *The Dual State: A Contribution to the Theory of Dictatorship*. Oxford University Press: Oxford.

Fried, M. H. (1967). *The Evolution of Political Society: An Essay in Political Anthropology*. Random House: New York.

Friedmann, T. (2005). *The World is Flat.* Farrar, Straus and Giroux: New York.

Friedmann, T. (2008). *Hot, Flat, and Crowded.* Farrar, Straus and Giroux: New York.

Friedmann, T. (2011). *That Used to be Us.* Farrar, Straus and Giroux: New York.

Friedrichs, J. (2001). The meaning of new medievalism. *European Journal of International Relations* 7(4): 475–502.

Fukuyama, F. (1992). *The End of History and the Last Man.* Free Press: New York.

Fukuyama, F. (1995). *Trust: The Social Virtues and the Creation of Prosperity.* Free Press: New York.

Fukuyama, F. (2003). *State-Building: Governance and World Order in the 21st Century.* Cornell University Press: Ithaca, NY.

Fukuyama, F. (2011). *The Origins of Political Order: From Prehuman Times to the French Revolution.* Farrar, Straus and Giroux: New York.

Gailey, C. W. (1985). The state of the state in anthropology. *Annual Review of Anthropology* 9(1–4): 65–91.

Gambetta, D. (ed.) (1988). *Trust: Making and Breaking Cooperative Relations.* Blackwell: Oxford.

Gamble, A. (1973). *The Conservative Nation.* Routledge: London.

Gause III, F. G. (2013). Kings for all seasons: How the Middle East's monarchies survived the Arab Spring. Brookings Institute: Washington, DC / Doha: Qatar.

Gellner, E. (1983). *Nations and Nationalism.* Blackwell: Oxford.

Georgi, F. and Kannankulam, J. (2012). *Das Staatsprojekt Europa in der Krise: Die EU zwischen autoritärer Verhärtung und linken Alternativen.* Rosa Luxemburg Stiftung: Berlin.

Gerschenkron, A. (1962). *Economic Backwardness in Historical Perspective.* Cambridge University Press: Cambridge.

Gerstenberger, H. (2008). *Impersonal Power: History and Theory of the Bourgeois State.* Brill: Leiden.

Giddens, A. (1981). *A Contemporary Critique of Historical Materialism: Power, Property and the State.* Macmillan: London.

Giddens, A. (1985). *The Nation-State and Violence.* Polity: Cambridge.

Gilens, M. and Page, B. (2014). Testing theories of American politics: Elites, interest groups, and average citizens. *Perspectives on Politics* 12(3): 564–81.

Gill, S. (1991). *American Hegemony and the Trilateral Commission.* Cambridge University Press: New York.

Gill, S. (1995). The global Panopticon? The neo-liberal state, economic life and democratic surveillance. *Alternatives* 20(1): 1–49.

Gill, S. (ed.) (2011). *Global Crises and the Crisis of Global Leadership.* Cambridge University Press: Cambridge.

Giraldo, J. (1996). *Colombia: The Genocidal Democracy.* Common Courage Press: Monroe, ME.

Gitlin, T. (2012). *Occupy Nation: The Roots, the Spirit, and the Promise of Occupy Wall Street.* HarperCollins: New York.

Giugni, M. G. (1998). Was it worth the effort? The outcomes and consequences of social movements. *Annual Review of Sociology* 24: 371–93.

Gledhill, J., Bender, B., and Larsen, M. T. (eds) (1988). *State and Society: The Emergence and Development of Social Hierarchy and Political Centralization*. Unwin Hyman: London.

Glennon, M. J. (2014). *National Security and Double Government*. Oxford University Press: New York.

Global Commission on the Economy and Climate (2014). *Better Growth, Better Climate: The New Climate Economy Report*. World Resources Institute: Washington, DC.

Goldberg, D. T. (2002). *The Racial State*. Blackwell: Oxford.

Goldscheid, R. (1976) [1917]. Finanzwissenschaft und Soziologie. In R. Hickel (ed.), *Rudolf Goldscheid/Joseph Schumpeter, Die Finanzkrise des Steuerstaates*. Suhrkamp: Frankfurt, pp. 317–28.

Goody, J. (1980). *Technology, Tradition and the State in Africa*. Cambridge University Press: Cambridge.

Gorski, P. S. (2001). Beyond Marx and Hintze? Third wave theories of early modern state formation. *Comparative Studies in History and Society* 43(4): 851–61.

Gowan, P. (2000). *The Global Gamble: America's Faustian Bid for World Domination*. Verso: London.

Gramsci, A. (1971). *Selections from the Prison Notebooks*. Lawrence & Wishart: London.

Gramsci, A. (1995). *Quaderni del Carcere, edizione critica dell'Istituto Gramsci*, 4 vols. Einaudi: Turin.

Grandin, G. (2007). *Empire's Workshop: Latin America, the United States, and the Rise of the New Imperialism*. Henry Holt: New York.

Green, D. and Shapiro, I. (eds) (1996). *Pathologies of Rational Choice Theory: A Critique of Applications in Political Science*. Yale University Press: New Haven, CT.

Green, P. and Ward, T. (2004). *State Crime: Governments, Violence and Corruption*. Pluto: London.

Greven, M. (2010). Sind Parteien in der Politik alternativlos oder ist ihre Rolle historisch begrenzt? In D. Gehne and T. Spier (eds), *Krise oder Wandel der Parteiendemokratie?* VS Verlag: Wiesbaden, pp. 225–35.

Grofman, B. and Lijphart, A. (eds) (2003). *Electoral Laws and their Political Consequences*. Agathon Press: New York.

Gross, O. (2000). The normless and exceptionless exception: Carl Schmitt's theory of emergency powers and the norm–exception dichotomy. *Cardozo Law Review* 21: 1824–67.

Grossman, C. (1986). A framework for the examination of states of emergency under the American Convention on Human Rights. *American University International Law Review* 1(1): 35–55.

Günther, G. (2004) [1973]. Life as polycontexturality. In H. Fahrenbach (ed.), *Wirklichkeit und Reflexion*. Neske: Pfüllingen, pp. 187–210. (Reprinted in *Vordenker*, February 2004. At www.vordenker.de)

Gunther, R. and Diamond, L. (2003). Species of political parties: A new typology. *Party Politics* 9(2): 167–99.

Gunther, R., Montero, J. R., and Linz, J. J. (eds) (2002). *Political Parties: Old Concepts and New Challenges*. Oxford University Press: Oxford.

Haanappel, P. P. C. (2003). *The Law and Policy of Air Space and Outer Space: A Comparative Approach*. Kluwer Law International: The Hague.

Haas, P. M. and Haas, E. B. (1995). Learning to learn: Improving international governance. *Global Governance* 1(4): 255–85.

Habermas, J. (1989) [1962]. *The Structural Transformation of the Public Sphere: An Inquiry Into a Category of Bourgeois Society*. MIT Press: Cambridge, MA.

Habermas, J. (1976). *Legitimation Crisis*. Hutchinson: London.

Habermas, J. (2002). *The Post-National Constellation*. Polity: Cambridge.

Hacker, J. and Pierson, P. (2011). *Winner-Take-All-Politics: How Washington Made the Rich Richer – and Turned Its Back on the Middle Class*. Simon & Schuster: New York.

Häusler, J. and Hirsch, J. (1987). Regulation und Parteien im Übergang zum 'post-Fordismus'. *Das Argument* 165: 651–71.

Hall, J. A. and Ikenberry, G. J. (1989). *The State*. Open University Press: Buckingham.

Hall, P. A. and Soskice, D. (eds) (2001). *Varieties of Capitalism: The Institutional Foundations of Comparative Advantage*. Oxford University Press: Oxford.

Hall, P. A. and Taylor, R. C. R. (1996). Political science and the three new institutionalisms. *Political Studies* 44(4): 936–57.

Hall, S. (1983). The great moving right show. In S. Hall and M. Jacques (eds), *The Politics of Thatcherism*. Lawrence & Wishart: London, pp. 19–39.

Hamilton, C., Gemenne, F., and Bonneuil, C. (eds) (2015). *The Anthropocene and the Global Environmental Crisis*. Routledge: London.

Handel, M. I. (1990). *Weak States in the International System*, 2nd edn. Frank Cass: London.

Hannah, M. (2000). *Governmentality and the Mastery of Territory in nineteenth–century America*. Cambridge University Press: Cambridge.

Harding, S. (1991). *Whose Science? Whose Knowledge? Thinking from Women's Lives*. Cornell University Press: Ithaca, NY.

Harding, S. (ed.) (2003). *The Feminist Standpoint Theory Reader: Intellectual and Political Controversies*. Routledge: London.

Hardt, M. and Negri, A. (2000). *Empire*. Harvard University Press: Cambridge, MA.

Hartman, H. (1979). The unhappy marriage of Marxism and feminism: Towards a more progressive union. *Capital and Class* 8(1): 1–33.

Harvey, D. (1996). *The Condition of Post-modernity*. Blackwell: Oxford.

Harvey, D. (2005). *A Brief History of Neoliberalism*. Oxford University Press: Oxford.

Harvey, D. (2008). The right to the city. *New Left Review* 54: 23–40.

Hay, C. (1995). *Re-stating Social and Political Change.* Open University Press: Buckingham.

Hay, C. (2002). *Political Analysis.* Palgrave Macmillan: Basingstoke, UK.

Hayes, B. (2009). *NeoConOpticon. The EU Security–Industrial Complex.* Transnational Institute/Statewatch: Amsterdam.

Hegel, G. W. F. (1977) [1807]. *Phenomenology of Spirit.* Clarendon: Oxford.

Heidenheimer, A. J. (1986). Politics, policy and policey as concepts in English and continental languages. *Review of Politics* 48: 1–26.

Heigl, M. (2011). Social conflict and competing state projects in the semi-periphery: A strategic–relational analysis of the transformation of the Mexican state into an internationalized competition state. *Antipode* 43(1): 129–48.

Held, D. (1992). Democracy: From city-states to a cosmopolitan order? *Political Studies* 40: 10–32.

Heller, H. (1983) [1934]. *Staatslehre,* 6th edn. Mohr Verlag: Tübingen.

Héritier, A. and Rhodes, M (eds) (2011). *New Modes of Governance in Europe: Governing in the Shadow of Hierarchy.* Palgrave Macmillan: Basingstoke, UK.

Hilferding, R. (2007) [1911]. *Finance Capital: A Study in the Latest Phase of Capitalist Development.* Routledge: London.

Hintze, O. (1975). *The Historical Essays of Otto Hintze.* Oxford University Press: New York.

Hirsch, J. (1980). *Der Sicherheitsstaat: Das 'Modell Deutschland', seine Krise und die neuen sozialen Bewegungen.* EVA: Hamburg.

Hirsch, J. (1995). *Der nationale Wettbewerbsstaat: Staat, Demokratie und Politik im globalen Kapitalismus.* ID Archiv: Berlin.

Hirsch, J. (2005). *Materialistische Staatstheorie. Transformationsprozesse des kapitalistischen Systems.* VSA: Hamburg.

Hodai, B. (2013). *Dissent or Terror: How the Nation's Counter Terrorism Apparatus, in Partnership with Corporate America, Turned on Occupy Wall Street.* Center for Media and Democracy: Washington, DC.

Hood, C. (1998). *The Art of the State: Culture, Rhetoric and Public Management.* Oxford University Press: Oxford.

Hudson, M. (2011). Europe's deadly transition from social democracy to oligarchy. *Counterpunch,* 9–11 December. At http://michael-hudson.com/2011/12/europes-transition-from-social-democracy-to-oligarchy/

Hudson, M. (2012). *The Bubble and Beyond: Fictitious Capital, Debt Deflation and the Global Crisis.* Islet: Dresden.

Huntington, S. P. (1998). *The Clash of Civilizations and the Remaking of World Order.* Simon & Schuster: New York.

Ingham, G. K. (1984). *Capitalism Divided? The City and Industry in British Social Development.* Macmillan: Basingstoke, UK.

Innis, H. (1951). *The Bias of Communication.* University of Toronto Press: Toronto.

Isaac, J. C. (1987). *Power and Marxist Theory: A Realist Approach.* Cornell University Press: Ithaca, NY.

Ivanes, C. D. (2002). Romania: A kidnapped revolution and the history of a pseudo-transition. *Eras Journal* 2. At http://artsonline.monash.edu.au/eras/romania-a-kidnapped-revolution-and-the-history-of-a-pseudo-transition/

Jäger, M. (1979). Von der Staatsableitung zur Theorie der Parteien: Ein Terrainwechsel im Geister Antonio Gramscis. In Arbeitskreis westeuropäische Arbeiterbewegung (ed.), *Eurokommunismus und Theorie der Politik*. Argument Verlag: Berlin, pp. 45–64.

Jameson, F. (2002). *A Singular Modernity: Essay on the Ontology of the Present*. Verso: London.

Jellinek, G. (1905). *Allgemeine Staatslehre*, 2nd edn. Verlag O. Häring: Berlin.

Jenson, J. (1986). Gender and reproduction: Or, babies and state. *Studies in Political Economy* 20: 9–46.

Jenson, J. (2007). The European Union's citizenship regime: Creating norms and building practices. *Comparative European Politics* 5(1): 53–69.

Jessop, B. (1982). *The Capitalist State: Marxist Theories and Methods*. Martin Robertson: Oxford.

Jessop, B. (1985). *Nicos Poulantzas: Marxist Theory and Political Strategy*. Macmillan: Basingstoke, UK.

Jessop, B. (1990). *State Theory: Putting the Capitalist State in its Place*. Polity: Cambridge.

Jessop, B. (2002). *The Future of the Capitalist State*. Polity: Cambridge.

Jessop, B. (2004). Multi-level governance and multi-level meta-governance. In I. Bache and M. Flinders (eds.), *Multi-level Governance*. Oxford University Press: Oxford, pp. 49–74.

Jessop, B. (2007a). Dialogue of the deaf: Reflections on the Poulantzas–Miliband debate. In P. Wetherly, C. W. Barrow, and P. Burnham (eds), *Class, Power and the State in Capitalist Society*. Palgrave: Basingstoke, UK, pp. 132–57.

Jessop, B. (2007b). *State Power: A Strategic–Relational Approach*. Polity: Cambridge.

Jessop, B. (2009). Cultural political economy and critical policy studies. *Critical Policy Studies* 3(3–4): 336–56.

Jessop, B. (2011). Rethinking the diversity of capitalism: Varieties of capitalism, variegated capitalism, and the world market. In G. Wood and C. Lane (eds), *Capitalist Diversity and Diversity within Capitalism*. Routledge: London, pp. 209–37.

Jessop, B. (2013). Revisiting the regulation approach: Critical reflections on the contradictions, dilemmas, fixes, and crisis dynamics of growth regimes. *Capital & Class* 37(1): 5–24.

Jessop, B. (2014a). Capitalist diversity and variety: Variegation, the world market, compossibility and ecological dominance. *Capital & Class* 38(1): 43–56.

Jessop, B. (2014b). Repoliticizing depoliticization: Theoretical preliminaries on some responses to the American and Eurozone debt crises. *Policy & Politics* 42(2): 207–23.

Jessop, B. (2014c). Variegated capitalism, *Modell Deutschland*, and the Eurozone crisis. *Journal of Contemporary European Studies* 22(3): 248–60.

Jessop, B. (2015a). Comparative capitalisms and/or variegated capitalism. In I. Bruff, M. Ebenau, and C. May (eds), *New Directions in Critical Comparative Capitalisms Research*. Palgrave Macmillan: Basingstoke, UK, pp. 65–82.

Jessop, B. (2015b). The symptomatology of crises: Reading crises and learning from them: Some critical realist reflections. *Journal of Critical Realism* 14(3): 1–37.

Jessop, B. (2015c) Neo-liberalism, finance-dominated accumulation, and the cultural political economy of austerity. In K. Featherstone and Z. M. Irving (eds), *Politics of Austerity*. Palgrave Macmillan: London, 85–108.

Jessop, B., Brenner, N., and Jones, M. R. (2008). Theorizing sociospatiality. *Environment and Planning D: Society and Space* 26(3): 389–401.

Johnson, C. A. (1982). *MITI and the Japanese Miracle: The Growth of Industrial Policy, 1925–1975*. Stanford University Press: Stanford.

Johnson, C. A. (1987). Political institutions and economic performance: The government–business relationship in Japan, South Korea, and Taiwan. In F. C. Deyo (ed.), *The Political Economy of the New Asian Industrialism*. Cornell University Press: Ithaca, NY, pp. 136–64.

Johnson, C. A. (2002). *Blowback: The Costs and Consequences of American Empire*. Sphere: New York.

Jones, M. R. and Jessop, B. (2010). Thinking state/space incompossibly. *Antipode* 42(5): 1119–49.

Jones, R. (2007). *People/State/Territories: The Political Geographies of British State Transformation*. Wiley Blackwell: Oxford.

Joseph, J. (2012). *The Social in the Global: Social Theory, Governmentality and Global Politics*. Cambridge University Press: Cambridge.

Joseph, J. (2014). Combining hegemony and governmentality to explain global governance. *Spectrum: Journal of Global Studies* 6(1): 1–15.

Kaasch, A. and Martens, K. (eds) (2015). *Actors and Agency in Global Social Governance*. Oxford University Press: Oxford.

Kaczyinski, R. (2014). Transnational internal security, democracy and the role of the state. At http://www.inter-disciplinary.net/at-the-interface/wp-content/uploads/2012/06/Kaczynski_web_12_06_03.pdf

Kalpagam, U. (2000). The colonial state and statistical knowledge. *History of the Human Sciences* 13: 37–55.

Kang, D. C. (2002). *Crony Capitalism: Corruption and Development in South Korea and the Philippines*. Cambridge University Press: Cambridge.

Kannankulam, J. and Georgi, F. (2012). Die Europäische Integration als materielle Verdichtung von Kräfteverhältnissen: Hegemonieprojekte im Kampf um das 'Staatsprojekt Europa'. Phillips-Universität Marburg, Marburg. At http://www.uni-marburg.de/fb03/politikwissenschaft/eipoe/publikationen/publikationen/a30.pdf

Katz, R. S. and Mair, P. (1994). Party organizations: From civil society to the state. In eidem (eds), *How Parties Organize: Change and Adaptation in Party Organization in Western Democracies.* SAGE: London, pp. 1–22.

Katz, R. S. and Mair, P. (1995). Party organization, party democracy and the emergence of the cartel party. In P. Mair (1997). *Party System Change: Approaches, and Interpretations.* Clarendon: Oxford, pp. 93–119.

Katz, R. S. and Mair, P. (2002). The ascendancy of the party in public office. In R. Gunther, J. M. Montero, and J. J. Linz (eds), *Political Parties: Old Concepts and New Challenges.* Oxford University Press: Oxford, pp. 113–34.

Kautsky, K. (1914). Der Imperialismus. *Die Neue Zeit* 2(32), 11 September.

Kayaoğlu T. (2010). *Legal Imperialism: Sovereignty and Extraterritoriality in Japan, the Ottoman Empire, and China.* Cambridge University Press: Cambridge.

Keating, M. (2001). *Plurinational Democracy: Stateless Nations in a Post-sovereign Era.* Oxford University Press: Oxford.

Kellner, D. (2005). Western Marxism. In A. Harrington (ed.), *Modern Social Theory: An Introduction.* Oxford University Press: Oxford, pp. 154–74.

Kelly, D. (2003). *The State of the Political: Conceptions of Politics and the State in the Thought of Max Weber, Carl Schmitt and Franz Neumann.* Oxford University Press: Oxford.

Kelly, M. G. E. (2009). *The Political Philosophy of Michel Foucault.* Routledge: London.

Kelsen, H. (1945). *General Theory of Law and the State.* Harvard University Press: Cambridge, MA.

Kenway, P. (1980). Keynes, Marx and the possibility of crisis. *Cambridge Journal of Economics* 4(1): 23–36.

Kirchheimer, O. (1966). The transformation of Western European party systems. In J. La Palombara and M. Weiner (eds), *Political Parties and Political Development.* Princeton University Press: Princeton, NJ, pp. 177–200.

Kirchheimer, O. (1969). Party structure and mass democracy in Europe. In idem, *Politics, Law and Social Change: Selected Essays of Otto Kirchheimer.* Columbia University Press: New York, pp. 245–68.

Kitschelt, H. (1991). Industrial governance structures, innovation strategies, and the case of Japan: Sectoral or cross-national comparative analysis? *International Organization* 45(4): 453–93.

Kjaer, P. F. (2010). *Between Governing and Governance: On the Emergence, Function and Form of Europe's Post-National Constellation.* Hart: Oxford.

Klare, M. (2001). *Resource Wars: The New Landscape of Global Conflict.* Metropolitan Books: New York.

Klare, M. (2012). *The Race for What's Left: The Global Scramble for the World's Last Resources.* Metropolitan Books: New York.

Kofele-Kala, N. (2006). *The International Law of Responsibility for Economic Crimes: Holding State Officials Individually Liable for Fraudulent Enrichment.* Ashgate: Aldershot, UK.

Kohli, A. (2004). *State-Directed Development: Political Power and Industrialization in the Global Periphery*. Princeton University Press: Princeton, NJ.

Kooiman, J. (ed.) (1993). *Modern Governance: New Government–Society Interactions*. SAGE: London.

Kooiman, J. (2003). *Governing as Governance*. SAGE: London.

Kooiman, J. and Jentoft, S. (2009). Meta-governance: Values, norms and principles, and the making of hard choices. *Public Administration* 87(4): 818–36.

Koole, R. (1994). The vulnerability of the modern cadre party in the Netherlands. In R. Katz & P. Mair (eds), *How Parties Organize: Change and Adaptation in Party Organizations in Western Democracies*. SAGE: London, pp. 278–304.

Kornhauser, W. (1959). *The Politics of Mass Society*. Routledge & Kegan Paul: London.

Koselleck, R. (1985). *Futures Past: On the Semantics of Historical Time*. MIT Press: Cambridge, MA.

Kostiner, J. (ed.) (2000). *Middle East Monarchies: The Challenge of Modernity*. Lynne Rienner: Boulder, CO.

Krätke, M. (1984). *Die Kritik der Staatsfinanzen: Zur politischen Ökonomie des Steuerstaats*. VSA: Hamburg.

Kratochwil, F. (1986). Of systems, boundaries, and territoriality: An inquiry into the formation of the state system. *World Politics* 34(1): 27–52.

Kriesi, H., Lavenex, S., Esser, F., Matthes, J., Bühlmann, M., and Bochsler, D. (2013). *Democracy in the Age of Globalization and Mediatization*. Palgrave Macmillan: Basingstoke, UK.

Krouwel, A. (2003). Otto Kirchheimer and the catch-all party. *West European Politics* 26(2): 23–40.

Lachmann, R. (2010). *States and Power*. Polity: Cambridge.

Laclau, E. and Mouffe, C. (1985). *Hegemony and Socialist Stategy*. New Left Books: London.

Lange, S. (2003). *Niklas Luhmanns Theorie der Politik: Eine Abklärung der Staatsgesellschaft*. Westdeutscher Verlag: Opladen.

Lapavitsas, C. (2013). *Profiting without Producing: How Finance Exploits Us All*. Verso: London.

Larrain, J. (1986). *Theories of Development: Capitalism, Colonialism and Dependency*. Polity: Cambridge.

Larsson, B. (2013). Sovereign power beyond the state: A critical reappraisal of governance by networks. *Critical Policy Studies* 7(2): 99–114.

Lasswell, H. D. (1950). *National Security and Individual Freedom*. McGraw Hill: New York.

Latour, B. (2005). *Reassembling the Social: An Introduction to Actor–Network Theory*. Oxford University Press: New York.

Latour, B. (2010). *The Making of Law: An Ethnography of the Conseil d'état*. Polity: Cambridge.

Law, J. (2009). Actor network theory and material semiotics. In B. S. Turner (ed.), *The Blackwell Encyclopedia of Social Theory*. Wiley Blackwell: Oxford, pp. 142–58.

Le Billon, P. (2005). Diamond wars? Conflict diamonds and geographies of resource wars. *Annals of the American Association of Geographers* 98(2): 345–72.

Lefebvre, H. (1968). *Le Droit à la ville*. Anthropos: Paris.

Lefebvre, H. (1971). *Everyday Life in the Modern World*. Penguin: Harmondsworth, UK.

Lefebvre, H. (1991) [1978]. *The Production of Space*. Blackwell: Oxford.

Lefebvre, H. (2004) [1992]. *Rhythmanalysis: Space, Time and Everyday Life*. Continuum: London.

Leibholz, G. (1966). *Das Wesen der Repräsentation und der Gestaltwandel der Demokratie im 20. Jahrhundert*. Walter de Gruyter: Berlin.

Lemke, T. (1997). *Eine Kritik der politischen Vernunft: Foucaults Analyse der modernen Gouvernementalität*. Argument Verlag: Hamburg.

Lenin, V. I. (1972) [1917]. *State and Revolution*. In idem, *Collected Works*, vol. 35. Progress Publishers: Moscow, pp. 381–492.

Lepsius, M. R. (1993). *Demokratie in Deutschland: Soziologisch–historische Konstellationsanalysen, ausgewählte Aufsätze*. Vandenhoeck & Ruprecht: Göttingen.

Levene, M. (2005a). *Genocide in the Age of the Nation-State*, vol. 1: *The Meaning of Genocide*. I. B. Tauris: London.

Levene, M. (2005b). *Genocide in the Age of the Nation State*, vol. 2: *The Rise of the West and the Coming of Genocide*. I. B. Tauris: London.

Li, M. (2008). *The Rise of China and the Demise of the Capitalist World-Economy*. Pluto: London.

Lijphart, A. (1969). Consociational democracy. *World Politics* 21(2): 207–25.

Lijphart, A. (1999). *Patterns of Democracy: Government Forms and Performance in Thirty-Six Countries*. Yale University Press: New Haven, CT.

Lijphart, A. (2008). *Thinking about Democracy: Power Sharing and Majority Rule in Theory and Practice*. Routledge: London.

Lindblom, C. E. (1977). *Politics and Markets: The World's Political Economic Systems*. Basic Books: New York.

Lindsey, J. R. (2013). *The Concealment of the State*. Bloomsbury: London.

Ling, L. (1996). Feminist international relations: From critique to reconstruction. *Journal of International Communication* 3(1): 27–41.

Linz, J. J. (1990a). The perils of presidentialism. *Journal of Democracy* 1(1): 51–69.

Linz, J. J. (1990b). The virtues of parliamentarism. *Journal of Democracy* 1(3): 84–91.

Linz, J. J. (1993). State building and nation building. *European Review* 1(4): 355–69.

Linz, J. J. (1994). Presidential or parliamentary democracy: Does it make a difference? In J. J. Linz and A. Valenzuela (eds), *The Crisis of Presidential Democracy: Comparative Perspective*. Johns Hopkins University Press: Baltimore, MD, pp. 3–89.

Linz, J. J. (1998). Democracy's time constraints. *International Political Science Review* 19(1): 19–39.

Linz, J. J. (2000). *Totalitarian and Authoritarian and Regimes*. Lynne Rienner: Boulder, CO.

Linz, J. J. (2002). Parties in contemporary democracies: Problems and paradoxes. In R. Gunther, J. R. Montero, and J. J. Linz (eds), *Political Parties: Old Concepts and New Challenges*. Oxford University Press: Oxford, pp. 291–317.

Linz, J. J. and Stepan, A. (eds) (1996). *Problems of Democratic Transitions and Consolidation: Southern Europe, South America, and Post-Communist Europe*. John Hopkins University Press: Baltimore, MD.

Lipschutz, R. (2005). Global civil society and global governmentality. In G. Baker and D. Chandler (eds), *Global Civil Society*. Routledge: London.

Lipset, S. M. and Rokkan, S. (1967). Cleavage structures, party systems, and voter alignments: An introduction. In eidem (eds), *Party Systems and Voter Alignments: Cross-National Perspectives*. Free Press: New York, pp. 1–64.

Listner, M. (2012). Could commercial space help define and delimitate the boundaries of outer space? *Space Review: Essays and Commentary about the Final Frontier*, 29 October. At http://www.thespacereview.com/article/2180/1

Lloyd, G. (1983). *The Man of Reason: 'Male' and 'Female' in Western Philosophy*. University of Minnesota Press: Minneapolis.

Lofgren, M. (2014). Anatomy of the deep state. 21 February. At http://billmoyers.com/2014/02/21/anatomy-of-the-deep-state/#1

Loughlin, M. (2009). In defence of *Staatslehre*. *Der Staat* 48(1): 1–28.

Loughlin, M. (2014). *Foundations of Public Law*. Oxford University Press: Oxford.

Luhmann, N. (1979). *Trust and Power*. Wiley: Chichester.

Luhmann, N. (1982). The future cannot begin: Temporal structures in modern society. In idem, *The Differentiation of Society*. Columbia University Press: New York, pp. 271–88.

Luhmann, N. (1989). Staat und Staatsräson im Übergang von traditionaler Herrschaft zu moderner Politik. In idem, *Gesellschaftstruktur und Semantik 3*. Suhrkamp: Frankfurt, pp. 74–103.

Luhmann, N. (1998). *Observations on Modernity*. Polity: Cambridge.

Luhmann, N. (2000). *The Reality of the Mass Media*. Polity: Cambridge.

Lukács, G. (1971) [1923]. *History and Class Consciousness: Studies in Marxist Dialectics*. Merlin: London.

MacKay, J. (2006). State failure, actor–network theory, and the theorisation of sovereignty. *Brussels Journal of International Studies* 3: 61–98.

MacKinnon, C. (1989). *Towards a Feminist Theory of the State*. Harvard University Press: Cambridge, MA.

MacLaughlin, J. (2001). *Re-Imagining the State. The Contested Terrain of Nation-Building*. Pluto: London.

Mazzucato, M. (2013). *The Entrepreneurial State: Debunking Public vs Private Sector Myths*. Anthem: London.

McCormick, J. P. (2004). From constitutional technique to Caesarist ploy: Carl Schmitt on dictatorship, liberalism, and emergency powers. In

P. Baehr and M. Richter (eds), *Dictatorship in History and Theory: Bonapartism, Caesarism, and Totalitarianism*. Cambridge University Press: Cambridge, pp. 197–200.

McCoy, A. W. (2009). *Policing America's Empire: The United States, the Philippines, and the Rise of the Surveillance State*. University of Wisconsin Press: Madison.

McFarland, A. S. (2004). *Neopluralism: The Evolution of Political Process Theory*. University of Kansas Press: Lawrence.

McIntosh, D. (1977). The objective bases of Max Weber's ideal types. *History and Theory* 16(3): 265–79.

McMichael, P. (1996). *Development and Social Change: A Global Perspective*. Pine Forge Press: Thousand Oaks, CA.

McNally, C. A. (2012). Sino-capitalism: China's reemergence and the international political economy. *World Politics* 64(4): 741–76.

McNicoll, G. (2003). Population. In P. Demeny and G. McNicoll (eds), *Encyclopedia of Population*. Macmillan: New York, pp. 226–34.

Mainwaring, S. and Shugart, M. S. (1997). Juan Linz, presidentialism, and democracy: A critical appraisal. *Comparative Politics* 29(4): 449–71.

Mann, M. (1984). The autonomous power of the state. *European Journal of Sociology* 25(2): 187–213.

Mann, M. (1986). *The Sources of Social Power*, vol. 1: *A History of Power from the Beginning to AD 1760*. Cambridge University Press: Cambridge.

Mann, M. (1996). *The Sources of Social Power*, vol. 2: *The Rise of Classes and Nation-States*. Cambridge University Press: Cambridge.

Mann, M. (2008). The infrastructural power of the state. *Studies in Comparative International Development* 43: 355–65.

Mann, M. (2012a). *The Sources of Social Power*, vol. 3: *Global Empires and Revolution*. Cambridge University Press: Cambridge.

Mann, M. (2012b). *The Sources of Social Power*, vol. 4: *Globalizations, 1945–2011*. Cambridge University Press: Cambridge.

Maran, R. (1989). *Torture: The Role of Ideology in the French–Algerian War*. Praeger: New York.

Marshall, A. G. (2015). World Economic Forum: A history and analysis. Transnational Institute, Amsterdam. At www.tni.org/article/world-economic-forum-history-and-analysis (accessed 21 March 2015).

Marx, K. (1967) [1896]. *Capital*, vol. 3. Lawrence & Wishart: London.

Marx, K. (1975) [1843]. *Contribution to the Critique of Hegel's Philosophy of Law*. In MECW, vol. 3, pp. 3–129.

Marx, K. (1978a) [1850]. *The Class Struggles in France*. In MECW, vol. 10, pp. 47–145.

Marx, K. (1978b) [1852]. *The Eighteenth Brumaire of Louis Bonaparte*. In MECW, vol. 11, pp. 99–197.

Marx, K. (1986) [1858]. The rule of the pretorians. In MECW, vol. 15, pp. 464–7.

Marx, K. (1989) [1875]. Critique of the Gotha Programme. In MECW, vol. 28, pp. 75–99.

Marx, K. and Engels, F. (1976a) [1845–6]. *The German Ideology*. In *MECW*, vol. 5, pp. 19–539.

Marx, K. and Engels, F. (1976b) [1848]. *Manifesto of the Communist Party*. In *MECW*, vol. 6, pp. 477–519.

Mayntz, R. (2003). New challenges to governance theory. In H. Bang (ed.), *Governance as Social and Political Communication*. Manchester University Press: Manchester, pp. 27–40.

Medalye, J. (2010). Neoclassical, institutional, and Marxist approaches to the environment–economic relationship. At http://www.eoearth.org/view/article/154812

Messner, D. (1998). *The Network Society*. Cass: London.

Meuleman, L. (2008). *Public Management and the Metagovernance of Hierarchies, Networks and Markets*. Springer: Heidelberg.

Meyer, J. W., Boli, J., Thomas, G. M., and Ramirez, F. O. (1997). World society and the nation-state. *American Journal of Sociology* 103(1): 144–81.

Meyer, T. (2002). *Media Democracy: How the Media Colonize Politics*. Polity: Cambridge.

Michels, R. (1962) [1911]. *Political Parties*. Collier: New York.

Migdal, J. (1988). *Strong States and Weak Societies*. University of California Press: Berkeley.

Migliaro, L. R. and Misuraca, P. (1982). The theory of modern bureaucracy. In A. S. Sassoon (ed.), *Approaches to Gramsci*. Writers & Readers: London, pp. 70–91.

Miliband, R. (1969). *The State in Capitalist Society*. Weidenfeld & Nicolson: London.

Miliband, R. (1977). *Marxism and the State*. Oxford University Press: London.

Miller, P. and Rose, N. (2008). *Governing the Present. Administering Economic, Social and Personal Life*. Polity: Cambridge.

Misztal, B. (1996). *Trust in Modern Societies: The Search for the Bases of Social Order*. Cambridge University Press: Cambridge.

Mitchell, T. J. (1991). The limits of the state: Beyond statist approaches and their critics. *American Political Science Review* 85(1): 77–96.

Mitchell, T. J. (1999). Society, economy and the state effect. In G. Steinmetz (ed.), *State/Culture: State Formation after the Cultural Turn*. Cornell University Press: Ithaca, NY, pp. 76–97.

Montero, J. R. and Gunther, R. (2002). Introduction: Reviewing and Reassessing Parties. In R. Gunther, J. R. Montero, and J. J. Linz (eds), *Political Parties: Old Concepts and New Challenges*, pp. 1–38.

Moore, J. W. (2015a). The capitalocene. Part I: On the nature & origins of our ecological crisis. *Journal of Peasant Studies*.

Moore, J. W. (2015b). The capitalocene. Part II: Abstract social nature and the limits to capital. *Journal of Peasant Studies*.

Moore, S. W. (1957). *The Critique of Capitalist Democracy*. Paine Whitman: New York.

Morgan, E. S. (1988). *Inventing the People: The Rise of Popular Sovereignty in England and America*. W. W. Norton: New York.

Morgenthau, H. J. (1954). *Politics among Nations: The Struggle for Power and Peace*, 2nd edn. Alfred A. Knopf: New York.

Morgenthau, H. J. (1962). *Politics in the Twentieth Century*, vol. 1: *The Decline of Democratic Politics*. University of Chicago Press: Chicago.

Müller, J. C., Reinfeldt, S., Schwarz, R., and Tuckfield, M. (1994). *Der Staat in den Köpfen: Anschlüsse an Louis Althusser und Nicos Poulantzas*. Decaton: Mainz.

Müller, W. and Strøm, K. (1999). Party behavior and representative democracy. In eidem (eds), *Policy, Office, or Votes? How Political Parties in Western Europe Make Hard Decisions*. Cambridge University Press: Cambridge, pp. 279–309.

Mulvad, A. C. M. (2015). Competing hegemonic projects within China's variegated capitalism: 'Liberal' Guangdong vs. 'statist' Chongqing. *New Political Economy* 20(2): 199–227.

Nelson, B. R. (2006). *The Making of the Modern State: A Theoretical Evolution*. Palgrave: Basingstoke, UK.

Neocleous, M. (2000). *The Fabrication of Social Order: A Critical Theory of State Power*. Pluto: London.

Neocleous, M. (2003). *Imagining the State*. Open University Press: Maidenhead.

Neocleous, M. (2006). The problem with normality, or Taking exception to 'permanent emergency'. *Alternatives* 31(2): 191–213.

Nettl, J. P. (1968). The state as a conceptual variable. *World Politics* 20(4): 559–92.

Neumann, S. (1956). Toward a comparative study of political parties. In idem (ed.), *Modern Political Parties: Approaches to Comparative Politics*. University of Chicago Press: Chicago, pp. 395–421.

Newman, D. and Paasi, A. (1998). Fences and neighbours in the postmodern world: Boundary narratives in political geography. *Progress in Human Geography* 22: 186–207.

Nietzsche, F. W. (1994) [1887]. *On the Genealogy of Morals: A Polemic*. Cambridge University Press: Cambridge.

Nooteboom, B. (2002). *Trust: Forms, Foundations, Functions, Failures and Figures*. Edward Elgar: Cheltenham, UK.

Nordhaug, C. (2002). Globalisation and the state: Theoretical paradigms. *European Journal of Development Research* 14(10): 5–27.

Nordlinger, E. A. (1981). *The Autonomy of the Democratic State*. Harvard University Press: Cambridge, MA.

Nye, J. (2004). *Smart Power: The Means to Success in World Politics*. PublicAffairs: New York.

O'Connor, J. (1973). *The Fiscal Crisis of the State*. St Martins: New York.

Oberndorfer, L. (2015). From new constitutionalism to authoritarian constitutionalism: New economic governance and the state of European democracy. In J. Jäger and E. Springler (eds), *Asymmetric Crisis in Europe and Possible Futures*. Routledge: London, pp. 185–205.

Önis, Z. (1991). The logic of the developmental state. *Comparative Politics* 24(1): 109–26.

Offe, C. (1972). *Strukturprobleme des kapitalistischen Staates*. Suhrkamp: Frankfurt.

Offe, C. (1975). The theory of the capitalist state and the problem of policy formation. In L. N. Lindberg, R. Alford, C. Crouch, and C. Offe (eds), *Stress and Contradiction in Modern Capitalism*. D. C. Heath: Lexington, KT, pp. 125–44.

Offe, C. (1983). *Contradictions of the Welfare State*. Hutchinson: London.

Offe, C. (2000). Governance. An 'empty signifier'? *Constellations* 16(4): 550–63.

Ohmae, K. (1995). *The End of the Nation State: The Rise of Regional Economies*. Free Press: New York.

Ojakangas, M. (2012). Michel Foucault and the enigmatic origins of bio-politics and governmentality. *History of the Human Sciences* 25(1): 1–14.

Ong, A. (2000). *Flexible Citizenship: The Cultural Logics of Transnationality*. Duke University Press: Durham, NC.

Ortner, S. (1978). The virgin and the state. *Feminist Studies* 45(3): 9–35.

Osiander, A. (2001). Sovereignty, international relations, and the Westphalian myth. *International Organization* 55: 251–87.

Overbeek, H. and van Apeldoorn, B. (eds) (2012). *Neoliberalism in Crisis*. Palgrave Macmillan: Basingstoke, UK.

Palonen, K. (2006). Two concepts of politics, two histories of a concept? Conceptual history and present controversies. *Distinktion: Scandinavian Journal of Social Theory* 7(1): 11–25.

Panebianco, A. (1988). *Political Parties: Organization and Power*. Cambridge University Press: Cambridge.

Panitch, L. (2000). The new imperial state. *New Left Review* 2: 5–20.

Panitch, L. and Gindin, S. (2012). *The Making of Global Capitalism: The Political Economy of American Empire*. Verso: London.

Park, B. (2008). Turkey's deep state: Ergenekon and the threat to democratisation in the Republic. *The RUSI Journal* 153(5): 54–9.

Parker, G. (1996). *The Military Revolution*. Cambridge University Press: Cambridge.

Parsons, T. (1969). *Politics and Social Structure*. Free Press: New York.

Pashukanis, E. B. (1978) [1924]. *Law and Marxism: A General Theory*. Ink Links: London.

Pateman, C. (1989). *The Disorder of Women*. Polity: Cambridge.

Patomäki, H. (2008). *The Political Economy of Global Security*. Routledge: London.

Pauketat, T. R. (2007). *Chiefdoms and Other Archaeological Delusions*. AltaMira: Lanham, MD.

Paul, D. E. (2003). *Re-scaling IPE: Subnational States and the Regulation of Global Political Economy*. Routledge: London.

Peck, J. and Theodore, N. (2015). *Fast Policy: Experimental Statecraft at the Thresholds of Neoliberalism*. University of Minnesota Press: Minneapolis.

Peet, R. (2011). Inequality, crisis and austerity in finance capitalism. *Cambridge Journal of Regions, Economy and Society*, 4: 383–99.

Peters, B. G. and Pierre, J. (eds) (2004). *The Politicization of the Civil Service in Comparative Perspective*. Routledge: London.

Petit, V. (2013). *Counting Populations, Understanding Societies: Towards an Interpretative Approach*. Springer: Dordrecht.

Pierre, J. (ed.) (1999). *Debating Governance: Authority, Steering, and Democracy*. Oxford University Press: Oxford.

Pierson, P. (2002). Coping with permanent austerity: Welfare state restructuring in affluent democracies. *Revue française de sociologie* 43(2): 369–406.

Poggi, G. (1978). *The Development of the Modern State: A Sociological Introduction*. Polity: Cambridge.

Poguntke, T. and Webb, P. (eds) (2007). *The Presidentialisation of Politics*. Oxford University Press: Oxford.

Polanyi, K. (1957). *Trade and Market in the Early Empires: Economies in History and Theory*. Free Press: New York.

Pomper, P. (2005). The history and theory of empires. *History and Theory* 44 (Theme issue), 1–27.

Portelli, H. (1972). *Gramsci et le bloc historique*. Maspero: Paris.

Porter, B. D. (1994). *War and the Rise of the State: The Military Foundations of Modern Politics*. Free Press: New York.

Postone, M. (1993). *Time, Labor and Social Domination: A Reinterpretation of Marx's Theory*. Cambridge University Press: New York.

Poulantzas, N. (1973) [1968]. *Political Power and Social Classes*. New Left Books: London.

Poulantzas, N. (1974) [1972]. *Fascism and Dictatorship*. New Left Books: London.

Poulantzas, N. (1975). *Classes in Contemporary Capitalism*. New Left Books: London.

Poulantzas, N. (1976). *Crisis of the Dictatorships*. Verso: London.

Poulantzas, N. (1978). *State, Power, Socialism*. Verso: London.

Poulantzas, N. (1979) [1976]. The political crisis and the crisis of the state. In J. W. Freiburg (ed.), *Critical Sociology*. Halstead Press: New York, pp. 373–93.

Prescott, J. (1987). *Political Frontiers and Boundaries*. Allen & Unwin: London.

Price, R. M. (1991). *The Apartheid State in Crisis: Political Transformation of South Africa, 1975–1990*. Clarendon: Oxford.

Provan, K. G. and Kenis, P. (2008). Modes of network governance, structure, management, and effectiveness. *Journal of Public Administration Research and Theory* 18(2): 229–52.

Przeworski, A. (1977). Proletariat into a class: The process of class formation from Karl Kautsky's *The Class Struggle* to recent controversies. *Politics & Society* 7(4): 343–401.

Przeworski, A. (1993). *Democracy and the Market: Political and Economic Reforms in Eastern Europe and Latin America*. Cambridge University Press: New York.

Pufendorf, S. (1672) [1759]. *De iure naturae et gentium libri octo* [*Of the Law of Nature and Nations, Eight Books*]. Lund.

Puhle, H.-J. (2002). Still the age of catch-allism? *Volksparteien* and *Parteien-staat* in Crisis and Re-equilibration. In R. Gunther, J. R. Montero, and J. J. Linz (eds), *Political Parties: Old Concepts and New Challenges*. Oxford University Press: Oxford, pp. 58–83.

Purvis, T. (1998). Aboriginal peoples and the limits of the state–sovereignty–nation triplet: Historical and contemporary reflections on the nationalities principle. PhD Thesis, Lancaster University, United Kingdom.

Putnam, R. D. (2000). *Bowling Alone: The Collapse and Revival of American Community*. Simon & Schuster: New York.

Radice, H. (2000). Globalization and national capitalisms: Theorizing convergence and differentiation. *Review of International Political Economy* 7(4): 719–42.

Rapp, R. (1977). Gender and class: An archaeology of knowledge concerning the origin of the state. *Dialectical Anthropology* 2(4): 309–16.

Rasmus, J. (2010). *Epic Recession. Prelude to Global Depression*. Pluto: London.

Redmond, E. M. and Spencer, C. S. (2012). Chiefdoms at the threshold: The competitive origins of the primary state. *Journal of Anthropological Archaeology* 31: 22–37.

Rehmann, J. (2013). *Theories of Ideology: The Powers of Alienation and Subjection*. Brill: Leiden.

Reinhard, W. (ed.) (1999). *Die Verstaatlichung der Welt. Europäische Staatsmodelle undaußereuropäische Machtprozesse*. Oldenbourg Verlag: Munich.

Renan, E. (1882). Qu'est-ce qu'une nation? Lecture at the Sorbonne, Paris. At http://www.nationalismproject.org/what/renan.htm

Reno, Q. (1998). *Warlord Politics and African States*. Lynne Rienner: Boulder, CO.

Roberts, J. (2006). *Philosophizing the Everyday: Revolutionary Praxis and the Fate of Cultural Theory*. Pluto: London.

Roberts, J. T. (2011). Multipolarity and the new world (dis)order: US hegemonic decline and the fragmentation of the global climate regime. *Global Environmental Change* 21(3): 776–84.

Robinson, W. I. (2004). *A Theory of Global Capitalism: Transnational Production, Transnational Capitalists, and the Transnational State*. Johns Hopkins University Press: Baltimore, MD.

Robinson, W. I. (2012). Global capitalism theory and the emergence of transnational elites. *Critical Sociology* 38(3): 349–63.

Rogers, C. (ed.) (1955). *The Military Revolution Debate*. Westview Press: Boulder, CO.

Rohrschneider, R. and Whitefield, S. (2012). *The Strain of Representation*. Oxford University Press: Oxford.

Rokkan, S. (1999). *State Formation, Nation-Building and Mass Politics in Europe: The Theory of Stein Rokkan*. Oxford University Press: Oxford.

Rosa, H. (2013). *Social Acceleration: A New Theory of Modernity*. Columbia University Press: New York.

Rossiter, C. L. (1948). *Constitutional Dictatorship: Crisis Government in the Modern Democracies*.

Rothe, D. L. (2009). *State Criminality: The Crime of All Crimes*. Lexington: Lanham, MD.

Rousseau, J.-J. (1758). *Discours sur l'économie politique*. At http://www.ac-grenoble.fr/PhiloSophie/file/rousseau_economie_politique.pdf

Rousseau, J.-J. (1792). *Du contrat social, ou Principes du droit politique*. Rey: Amsterdam.

Routley, L. (2014). Developmental states in Africa? A review of ongoing debates and buzzwords. *Development Policy Review* 32(2): 159–77.

Rüb, F. (2005). Sind die Parteien noch zu retten? Zum Stand der gegenwärtigen Parteien und Parteiensystemforschung. *Neue Politische Literatur* 50(3): 397–421.

Ruggie, J. (1993). Territoriality and beyond. *International Organization* 47(1): 139–74.

Rupert, M. and Solomon, M. S. (2006). *Globalization and International Political Economy: The Politics of Alternative Futures*. Rowman and Littlefield: Lanham, MD.

Sassatelli, M. (2002). Imagined Europe: The shaping of a European cultural identity through EU cultural policy. *European Journal of Social Theory* 5(4): 435–51.

Sassoon, A. S. (1980). *Gramsci's Politics*. Croom Helm: London.

Satter, D. (2003). *Darkness at Dawn: The Rise of the Russian Criminal State*. Yale University Press: New Haven, CT.

Sauer, B. (1997). 'Die Magd der Industriegesellschaft': Anmerkungen zur Geschlechtsblindheit von Staats – und Institutionstheorien. In B. Kerchner and G. Wilder (eds), *Staat und Privatheit*. Westdeutscher Verlag: Opladen, pp. 29–53.

Schäfer, A. and Streeck, W. (eds) (2013). *Politics in the Age of Austerity*. Polity: Cambridge.

Scharpf, F. W. (1993). *Games in Hierarchies and Networks: Analytical and Empirical Approaches to the Study of Governance Institutions*. Campus: Frankfurt.

Scharpf, F. W. (1999). *Governing in Europe: Effective and Democratic?* Oxford University Press: Oxford.

Scheppele, K. L. (2004). Law in a time of emergency: States of exception and the temptations of 9/11. *Journal of Constitutional Law* 6(5): 1001–83.

Scheuerman, W. E. (1994). *Between the Norm and the Exception*. MIT Press: Cambridge, MA.

Scheuerman, W. E. (1996). *The Rule of Law Under Siege: Selected Essays of Franz L. Neumann and Otto Kirchheimer*. University of California Press: Berkeley.

Scheuerman, W. E. (2000). The economic state of emergency. *Cardozo Law Review* 21(5–6): 1869–94.

Scheuerman, W. E. (2003). *Liberal Democracy and the Social Acceleration of Time*. Johns Hopkins University Press: Baltimore, MD.

Scheuerman, W. E. (2006). Emergency powers. *Annual Review of Law and Society* 2: 257–77.

Scheuerman, W. E. (2008). *Frankfurt School Perspectives on Globalization. Democracy, and the Law*. Routledge: London.

Schmalenbach, H. (1922). Die soziologische Kategorie des Bundes. In W. Strich (ed.), *Die Dioskuren: Jahrbuch für Geisteswissenschaften*, Meyer & Jessen: Munich, pp. 35–105.

Schmitt, C. (1985) [1922]. *Political Theology: Four Chapters on the Concept of Sovereignty*. MIT Press: Cambridge, MA.

Schmitt, C. (1988) [1923]. *The Crisis of Parliamentary Democracy*. MIT Press: Cambridge, MA.

Schmitt, C. (2003) [1950]. *The Nomos of the Earth in the International Law of the Jus Publicum Europaeum*. Telos Press: New York.

Schmitt, C. (2013) [1921]. *Dictatorship: From the Origin of the Modern Concept of Sovereignty to Proletarian Class Struggle*. Polity: Cambridge.

Schmitter, P. C. (1996). Imagining the future of the Euro-polity with the help of new concepts. In G. Marks, F. W. Scharpf, and P. C. Schmitter (eds), *Governance in the European Union*. SAGE: London, pp. 121–50.

Schumpeter, J. A. (1954) [1918]. Crisis of the tax state. *International Economic Papers*, 4: 5–38.

Schuppert, G. F. (2010). *Der Staat als Prozess: Eine staatstheoretische Skizze in sieben Aufsätzen*. Campus: Frankfurt.

Scott, J. (1998). *Seeing like a State: How Certain Schemes to Improve the Human Condition Have Failed*. Yale University Press: New Haven, CT.

Scott, J. (2009). *The Art of Not Being Governed: An Anarchist History of Upland Southeast Asia*. Yale University Press: New Haven.

Scott, P. D. (2014a). *The American Deep State: Wall Street, Big Oil, and the Attack on US Democracy*. Rowman & Littlefield: Lanham, MD.

Scott, P. D. (2014b). The state, the deep state, and the Wall Street overworld. *Asia–Pacific Journal: Japan Focus* 12(5). At http://japanfocus.org/-Peter _Dale-Scott/4090/article.pdf

Segesvary, V. (2004). *World State, Nation States, or Non-Centralized Institutions? A Vision of the Future in Politics*. University Press of America: Lanham, MD.

Service, E. R. (1962). *Primitive Social Organization*. Harcourt Brace: New York.

Service, E. R. (1975). *Origins of the State and Civilization: The Process of Cultural Evolution*. Norton: New York.

Seymour, R. (2014). *Against Austerity*. Pluto: London.

Shaw, M. (2000). *Theory of the Global State*. Cambridge University Press: Cambridge.

Shefter, M. (1994). *Political Parties and the State: The American Historical Experience*. Princeton University Press: Princeton, NJ.

Sinclair, T. J. (2005). *The New Masters of Capital: American Bond Rating Agencies and the Politics of Creditworthiness*. Cornell University Press: Ithaca, NY.

Skinner, Q. (1989). State. In T. Ball, J. Farr, and R. L. Hanson (eds), *Political Innovation and Conceptual Change*. Cambridge University Press: Cambridge, pp. 90–131.

Skinner, Q. (2009). A genealogy of the modern state. *Proceedings of the British Academy* 162: 325–70.

Skocpol, T. (1979). *States and Social Revolutions: A Comparative Analysis of France, Russia, and China.* Cambridge University Press: Cambridge.

Smith, A. D. (1986). *The Ethnic Origins of Nations.* Blackwell: Oxford.

Smith, A. D. (1995). *Nations and Nationalism in a Global Era.* Polity: Cambridge.

Smith, D. E. (1990). *Texts, Facts and Femininity: Exploring the Relations of Ruling.* Routledge: London.

Smith, M. J. (1990). Pluralism, reformed pluralism and neopluralism: The role of pressure groups in policy-making. *Political Studies* 38(2): 302–22.

Smith, R. (2013). Capitalism and the destruction of life on Earth: Six theses on saving the humans. *Real-world economics review* 64. At http://www. paecon.net/PAEReview/issue64/Smith64.pdf

Söyler, M. (2013). Informal institutions, forms of state and democracy: The Turkish deep state. *Democratization* 20(2): 310–34.

Solty, I. (2013). The future of the left and world-wide socialism in the context of the fourth organic crisis of global(-izing) capitalism after the austerity turn: A Transatlantic perspective. In Chinese Academy of Social Sciences (ed.), *Socialism and the World Today.* Chinese Academy of Social Sciences: Beijing, pp. 67–94.

Spencer, C. S. (2003). War and early state formation in Oaxaca, Mexico. *Proceedings of the National Academy of Sciences* 100(20): 1185–7.

Spencer, C. S. (2010). Territorial expansion and primary state formation. *Proceedings of the National Academy of Sciences* 107(16): 7119–26.

Spruyt, H. (1993). *The Sovereign State and its Competitors: An Analysis of Systems Change.* Princeton University Press: Princeton, NJ.

Standing, G. (2011). *The Precariat: The New Dangerous Class.* Bloomsbury: London.

Stasavage, D. (2011). *States of Credit: Size, Power, and the Development of European Polities.* Princeton University Press: Princeton, NJ.

Steffen, W., Grinevald, J., Crutzen, P., and McNeill, J. (2011). The Anthropocene: Conceptual and historical perspectives. *Philosophical Transactions of the Royal Society* A369: 842–67.

Steinmetz, G. (2003). The state of emergency and the revival of American imperialism: Toward an authoritarian post-Fordism. *Public Culture* 15(2): 323–45.

Stepan, A., Linz, J. J., and Yadav, Y. (2010). *Crafting State-Nations. India and Other Multinational Democracies.* Johns Hopkins University Press: Baltimore, MD.

Stephen, M. D. (2014). Rising powers, global capitalism and liberal global governance: A historical materialist account of the BRICs challenge. *European Journal of International Relations* 20(4): 912–38.

Stockman, D. (2013). *The Great Deformation: The Corruption of Capitalism in America.* PublicAffairs: New York.

Strayer, J. R. (1970). *On the Medieval Origins of the Modern State*. Princeton University Press: Princeton, NJ.

Streeck, W. (2009). *Re-forming Capitalism: Institutional Change in the German Political Economy*. Oxford University Press: Oxford.

Streeck, W. (2014). *Buying Time: The Delayed Crisis of Democratic Capitalism*. Verso: London.

Streeck, W. and Schmitter, P. C. (eds) (1985). *Private Interest Government: Beyond Market and State*. SAGE: London.

Strether, L. (2015). A typology of corruption for Campaign 2016 and beyond. 18 May. At http://www.nakedcapitalism.com/2015/05/a-typology -of-corruption-for-campaign-2016-and-beyond.html

Stuart, D. T. (2008). *Creating the National Security State: A History of the Law That Transformed America*. Princeton University Press: Princeton, NJ.

Stützle, I. (2013). *Austerität als politisches Projekt: Von der monetären Integration Europas zur Eurokrise*. Westfälisches Dampfboot: Münster.

Sum, N.-L. and Jessop, B. (2013). *Towards a Cultural Political Economy: Putting Culture in its Place in Political Economy*. Edward Elgar: Cheltenham, UK.

Swedberg, R. (1998). *Max Weber and the Idea of Economic Sociology*. Princeton University Press: Princeton, NJ.

Swedberg, R. (2003). The changing picture of Max Weber's sociology. *Annual Review of Sociology*, 283–306.

Talmon, S. (1998). *Recognition of Governments in International Law: With Particular Reference to Governments in Exile*. Clarendon: Oxford.

Tarrow, S. (2011). Occupy Wall Street is not the Tea Party of the Left: The United States' long history of protest. *Foreign Affairs*, 10 October.

Taylor, A. (2013). *State Failure*. Palgrave Macmillan: Basingstoke, UK.

Taylor, C. (2001). *Modern Social Imaginaries*. Duke University Press: Durham, NC.

Taylor, P. J. (1994). The state as container: Territoriality in the modern world system. *Progress in Human Geography* 18(3): 151–62.

Taylor, P. J. (1995). Beyond containers: Internationality, interstateness, interterritoriality. *Progress in Human Geography* 18(2): 151–62.

Taylor, P. J. (2000). World cities and territorial states under conditions of contemporary globalization. *Political Geography* 19(1): 5–32.

Taylor, P. J. (2003). *World City Network. A Global Urban Analysis*. Routledge: London.

Taylor, P. J. (2004). From heartland to hegemony: Changing the world in political geography.*Geoforum* 15(4): 403–11.

Taylor, R. (1978). *The Fifth Estate: Trade Unions in the Modern World*. Routledge and Kegan Paul: London.

Teschke, B. (2003). *The Myth of 1648: Class, Geopolitics and the Making of Modern International Relations*. Verso: London.

Therborn, G. (2010). *From Marxism to Post-Marxism?* Verso: London.

Théret, B (1992). *Régimes économiques de l'ordre politique*. Presses Universitaires de France: Paris.

Thompson, M. (2012). Foucault, fields of governability, and the population–family–economy–nexus in China. *History and Theory* 51(1): 42–62.

Tilly, C. (ed.) (1975). *The Formation of National States in Western Europe*. Princeton University Press: Princeton, NJ.

Tilly, C. (1992). *Coercion, Capital and European States, AD 990–1990*. Blackwell: Oxford.

Tölölyan, K. (1991). Rethinking diaspora(s): Stateless power in the transnational moment. *Diaspora* 5: 3–36.

Tsoukalas, K. (2003). Globalisation and the 'executive committee': Reflections on the contemporary capitalist state. *Socialist Register 2003*: 56–75.

Tunander, O. (2009). Democratic state vs. deep state: Approaching the dual state of the West. In E. Wilson (ed.), *Government of the Shadows: Parapolitics and Criminal Sovereignty*. Pluto: London, pp. 56–72.

Valler, D., Tait, M., and Marshall, T. (2013). Business and planning: A strategic–relational approach. *International Planning* 18(2): 143–67.

van Apeldoorn, B. (2002). *Transnational Capitalism and the Struggle over European Integration*. Routledge: London.

van Creveld, M. (1999). *The Rise and Decline of the State*. Cambridge University Press: Cambridge.

van der Pijl, K. (2007). *Nomads, Empires and States: Modes of Foreign Relations and Political Economy*, vol. 1. Pluto: London.

van der Muhll, G. E. (2003). Ancient empires, modern states, and the study of government. *American Review of Political Science* 6: 345–76.

Viroli, M. (1992). *From Politics to Reason of State: The Acquisition and Transformation of the Language of Politics, 1250–1600*, Cambridge University Press: Cambridge.

Voigt, R. (ed.) (2000). *Abschied vom Staat: Rückkehr zum Staat?* 3rd digital edn. At www.staatswissenschaft.com/pdf/IfS-Werkstatt1.pdf

Volkov, V. (2000). The political economy of protection rackets in the past and the present. *Social Research* 67(3): 709–44.

von Beyme, K (1993). *Die politische Klasse im Parteienstaat*. Suhrkamp: Frankfurt.

Walby, S. (2003). The myth of the nation-state: Theorizing society and politics in a global era. *Sociology* 38(3): 529–46.

Waldner, D. (1999). *State Building and Late Development*. Cornell University Press: Ithaca, NY.

Walker, B. (1997). Social movements as nationalisms, or The very idea of a Queer Nation. *Canadian Journal of Philosophy*, 26(suppl. 1): 505–47.

Wallerstein, I. (2000). *The Essential Wallerstein*. New Press: New York.

Waltz, K. (1979). *Theory of International Politics*. McGraw-Hill: Boston, MA.

Weber, M. (1961). *General Economic History*. Collier: New York.

Weber, M. (1978). *Economy and Society*. Bedminster Press: New York.

Weber, M. (1994). *Weber: Political Writings*. Cambridge University Press: Cambridge.

Wedel, J. (2009). *Shadow Elite*. Basic Books: New York.

Weiss, L. (1998). *The Myth of the Powerless State: Governing the Economy in a Global Era*. Polity: Cambridge.

Weiss, L. (2013). *America Inc.? Innovation and Enterprise in the National Security State*. Cornell University Press: Ithaca, NY.

Weiss, L. and Hobson, J. (1995). *States and Economic Development: A Comparative Historical Analysis*. Polity: Cambridge.

Wendt, A. (2003). Why a world state is inevitable. *European Journal of International Relations* 9: 491–542.

Wikipedia (2013). The king is dead, long live the king! At http://en.wikipedia.org/wiki/The_king_is_dead,_long_live_the_king!

Williams, C. (2010). *Ecology and Socialism: Solutions to Capitalist Ecological Crisis*. Haymarket: Chicago, IL.

Willke, H. (1986). The tragedy of the state: Prolegomena to a theory of the state in polycentric society. *Archiv für Sozial- und Rechtsphilosophie* 72(4): 455–67.

Willke, H. (1992). *Die Ironie des Staates*. Suhrkamp: Frankfurt.

Willke, H. (1997). *Supervision des Staates*. Suhrkamp: Frankfurt.

Willke, H. (2014). *Demokratie in Zeiten der Konfusion*. Suhrkamp: Frankfurt.

Wilson, E. (ed.) (2009). *Government of the Shadows: Parapolitics and Criminal Sovereignty*. Pluto: London.

Wissel, J. (2007). *Die Transnationalisierung von Herrschaftsverhältnissen: Zur Aktualität von Nicos Poulantzas' Staatstheorie*. Nomos: Baden-Baden.

Wissenburg, M. (2009). *Political Pluralism and the State: Beyond Sovereignty*. Routledge: London.

Wittfogel, K. A. (1957). *Oriental Despotism: A Comparative Study of Total Power*. Yale University Press: New Haven, CT.

Wolf, F. O. (2011). *The European Command Method*. Rosa Luxemburg Stiftung: Berlin.

Woo, J. E. (1991). *Race to the Swift: State and Finance in Korean Industrialization*. Columbia University Press: New York.

Woo-Cumings, M. (1999). Introduction: Chalmers Johnson and the politics of nationalism and development. In eadem (ed.), *The Developmental State*. Cornell University Press: Ithaca, NY, pp. 1–31.

Woolf, S. J. (1989). Statistics and the modern state. *Comparative Studies in Society and History* 31(3): 588–604.

World Bank (1993). *The East Asian Miracle: Economic Growth and Public Policy*. Oxford University Press: New York.

Wright, H. T. (1977). Recent research on the origins of the state. *Annual Review of Anthropology* 6: 379–97.

Wright, H. T. (2006). Early state dynamics as political experiment. *Journal of Anthropological Research* 62(3): 305–19.

Yergin, D. (1977). *Shattered Peace: The Origins of the Cold War and the National Security State.* Houghton Mifflin: Boston, MA.

Yuval-Davis, N. (1997). *Gender and Nation.* SAGE: London.

Zeitlin, J. and Trubek, D. M. (eds) (2003). *Governing Work and Welfare in a New Economy.* Oxford University Press: Oxford.

Zeitlin, J. and Pochet, P., with Magnusson, L. (eds) (2005). *The Open Method of Coordination in Action.* P. I. E.-Peter Lang: Berlin.

Zielonka, J. (2001). How new enlarged borders will reshape the European Union. *Journal of Common Market Studies* 39(3): 507–36.

Zielonka, J. (2006). *Europe as Empire: The Nature of the Enlarged European Union.* Oxford University Press: Oxford.

Ziltener, P. (2001). *Strukturwandel der europäischen Integration: Die Europäische Union und die Veränderung von Staatlichkeit.* Westfälisches Dampfboot: Münster.

Index of Names

Subject Index

This is in part a thematic index, which identifies where concepts are discussed even when a specific (indexed) word or phrase related to them does not occur in the text. A single page reference (e.g., 10) shows that a term (or concept) is mentioned on that page; a single page reference followed by 'f' or 'ff' (e.g., 10ff) indicates that the term occurs or is discussed on that page and on the next (10f) or next few (10ff) pages; a range of pages (e.g., 10–13) shows that these pages are especially relevant for that term; page numbers in **bold** indicate where the most significant occurrences or group of occurrences of that term occurs. A page reference ending in 'n' (e.g., 254n) indicates a footnote at that page.